Professionalism in Early Childhood Education and Care WITHDRAWN

The professionalism of the early childhood sector has gained prominence on the policy agendas of many countries. National pedagogical frameworks or curricula and an upsurge of pathways to gaining or upgrading qualifications have led to a pervasive terminology of professionalism. Yet, despite the pervasiveness of this terminology, the question of what professionalism means in early years contexts remains open to debate.

This book draws together the work of an international group of scholars who have engaged with this question. They ask: How can professionalism be conceptualised in early childhood settings? How might one act professionally in increasingly diverse and changing social and cultural contexts? Do we have a common ground of understanding about these terms? Are there key concepts that can be agreed upon? Drawing on research and experience across a wide range of national contexts, this book seeks an understanding of early childhood professionalism in local contexts that might throw light on the global implications of this term.

This book was published as a special issue in the *European Early Childhood Education Research Journal*.

Carmen Dalli is an Associate Professor (Reader) in the School of Educational Psychology and Pedagogy, and Director of the Institute for Early Childhood Studies, at Victoria University of Wellington in New Zealand. She was a founding member of the national working group that developed the Early Childhood Code of Ethics for Aotearoa New Zealand in the mid-1990s and retains an interest in issues of professionalism and ethical practice in early childhood practice. With Mathias Urban, University of East London, she convenes an international special interest group on professionalism in early childhood within the European Early Childhood Research Association. She combines a research focus on professional practice with policy scholarship, and with research on the lived experience of childcare, particularly for under-three year olds in group-based early childhood services, their parents and their teachers.

Mathias Urban is a Reader in Education (Associate Professor) at the Cass School of Education, University of East London. He works and publishes internationally on dialogic approaches to quality, evaluation and professionalism in working with young children, families and communities. Together with Carmen Dalli, Victoria University of Wellington, NZ, he convenes an international special interest group on professionalism in early childhood. Mathias' recent publications include a special edition of Contemporary Issues in Early Childhood (CIEC): *Rethinking Professionalism in Early Childhood: untested feasibilities and critical ecologies* and *Early Childhood Education in Europe: Achievements, challenges and possibilities*, a study conducted for Education International. He is currently coordinating a pan-European research project on *Competence requirements of staff in Early Childhood Education and Care*, funded by the EU Commission. Mathias is a member of the Board of Trustees of the European Early Childhood Education Research Association (EECERA).

Professionalism in Early Childhood Education and Care

International perspectives

Edited by Carmen Dalli and Mathias Urban

Routledge
Taylor & Francis Group
LONDON AND NEW YORK

First published 2010 by Routledge
2 Park Square, Milton Park, Abingdon, Oxon, OX14 4RN

Simultaneously published in the USA and Canada
by Routledge
711 Third Avenue, New York, NY 10017

Routledge is an imprint of the Taylor & Francis Group, an informa business

First issued in paperback 2011

This book is a reproduction of the *European Early Childhood Education Research Journal*, volume 16, issue 2. The Publisher requests to those authors who may be citing this book to state, also, the bibliographical details of the special issue on which the book was based

Typeset in Times New Roman PS by Value Chain, India

British Library Cataloguing in Publication Data
A catalogue record for this book is available from the British Library

ISBN13: 978-0-415-50892-6 (pbk)
ISBN13: 978-0-415-57405-1 (hbk)

Contents

EECERA

European Early Childhood Educational Research Association

What are the aims of EECERA?

- to provide an interdisciplinary, academic and rigorous forum on the international stage for the development and dissemination of high quality research on early childhood education and care (ECEC);

- to explore topical, theoretical and empirical research and encourage new methodologies;

- to facilitate collaboration and cooperation between researchers working in this field;

- to encourage a clear articulation of the links between research, policy and practice in ECEC;

- to give mutual support and offer peer group interaction to researchers in early childhood education;

- to raise the visibility and status of ECEC research worldwide

Benefits of Joining EECERA:

- Free subscription to the *European Early Childhood Education Research Journal* (*EECERJ*) now published by Routledge, three times per year;

- Free online access to *EECERJ* (including full, historical archive) via the new EECERA website which is currently in development;

- Opportunity to join and establish Special Interest Groups on a range of topics;

- Access to support for writing and publication of scholarly articles and books;

- Research networking and collaboration opportunities;

- Access to a writing and research meeting retreat in Greece at preferential rates;

- Regular discounts on Routledge books;

- Representation on EECERA Board of Trustees;

- Opportunity to shape EECERA policy and activity through members' annual meeting;

- Opportunity to host the conference at your own institution.

**To become an EECERA member, please visit
www.informaworld.com/EECERJ and complete the membership form**

ABSTRACTS

Dealing with uncertainty: challenges and possibilities for the early childhood profession

Mathias Urban

In many countries, strategies to further develop services and institutions for the education and care of young children are linked to a discourse on professionalism. Ambitious policy goals, it is argued, can only be achieved by a skilled and qualified workforce whose practice is guided by a professional body of knowledge. This article argues that the prevailing conceptualisation of the early childhood professional is constructed out of a particular, hierarchical mode of producing and applying expert knowledge that is not necessarily appropriate to professional practice in the field of early childhood education. However, it is highly effective and contributes to forming a professional habitus that contradicts the relational core of early childhood practice. Drawing on the conceptual framework of hermeneutics, the article explores an alternative paradigm of a relational, systemic professionalism that embraces openness and uncertainty, and encourages co-construction of professional knowledges and practices. Research, in this frame of thinking, is understood as a dialogic activity of asking critical questions and creating understandings across differences, rather than producing evidence to direct practice.

Towards professionalism in early childhood practicum supervision – a personal journey

Yael Dayan

The role of a practicum supervisor of early childhood students has received limited research attention in discussions of professional practice in this field. This article discusses four phases in the author's personal journey towards professionalism in this role. The phases reflect an ongoing research-practice cycle: Phase 1 involved a research study on the role perception of the early childhood practicum supervisor; the second phase corresponded to the implementation of findings from Phase 1 and involved a transition from a behaviourist approach to a humanistic-democratic approach in supervising, and the emergence of further research questions. The third phase comprised a research study on children's perspectives on early childhood teacher education and training; and the fourth phase included an attempt to facilitate the participation of children in the supervising process. The article shows how each of these phases has contributed to a framework for examining and enhancing the practicum supervisory process on the basis of humanistic-democratic values.

Pedagogy, knowledge and collaboration: towards a ground-up perspective on professionalism

Carmen Dalli

Drawing on a national survey of New Zealand early childhood teachers' views on ethics and professionalism in their practice, this article discusses three key themes that emerged as core conceptual elements in how teachers in education and care settings defined professionalism. The three themes were: a distinct pedagogical style; specialist knowledge and practices; and collaborative relationships. Elements that were perceived as unprofessional or undesirable in an early childhood professional were also identified. It is argued that as the early childhood field debates the meaning of professionalism, teachers' views can contribute a 'ground-up' perspective that can enable the concept of professionalism to be reconceptualised in ways that reflect the reality of teachers' work experiences.

Preschool teachers' and student preschool teachers' thoughts about professionalism in Sweden

Marja Kuisma and Anette Sandberg

This article discusses the different ways in which students and preschool teachers at two Swedish universities interpret the concept of professionalism. Data for this article are drawn from a study conducted in two different urban areas of Sweden which explored the following four questions: (1) What does the concept of professionalism imply for preschool teachers and students? (2) What does a professional teacher do in a preschool/school/after-school recreation centre? (3) How is professionalism developed? (4) What does preschool teachers' professionalism mean in comparison with professionalism in other closely related professions such as day-care attendants or recreational pedagogues? The survey was conducted using a questionnaire that students completed during a lesson at the university and by their supervisors at preschools. Data from the study are interpreted against a theoretical background that problematises the concept of 'professionalism' within the societal context of preschools in Sweden.

What's in a name? Seeking professional status through degree studies within the Scottish early years context

Kate Adams

This article draws on two small-scale pieces of research that investigated the views of twenty-five final year students in the BA Early Childhood Studies programme at a Scottish university, and the views of ten recent graduates about early years job titles and perceptions of professionalism. Pen-and-paper questionnaires were used in both studies, with one study also including an analysis of texts from a final-year reflective assignment on professionalism. The article also discusses the impact of recent changes in the Scottish context, including: the introduction of a regulatory body, Scottish Social Services Council (SSSC); the National Review of the Early Years and Childcare Workforce; and changes in required qualifications for the future of an early years profession on early years workers' aspirations for professional status. It argues that the 'new' early years profession is in danger of being stillborn or dissipated across such a wide age range that the 'early' focus is lost.

A Finnish viewpoint on professionalism in early childhood education

Kirsti Karila

This article discusses professionalism in early childhood education through the analytical tool of a research-based multi-level perspective that sees this as a cultural, communal, organisational, and individual phenomenon. Starting from an understanding of professionalism derived from a model of professional expertise, the article discusses the Finnish day-care context at the social and cultural level, followed by a discussion of field-specific knowledge as a tool for building professionalism. Professionalism is further examined as it plays out in the employees' working environment, the day-care centre and its working culture and from the perspective of the professionals themselves. Key characteristics of professionalism in the Finnish early childhood education sector are also summarised.

Professionalism – a breeding ground for struggle. The example of the Finnish day-care centre

Jarmo Kinos

This article examines the Finnish day-care centre out of a neo-Weberian–Bourdieuan frame of reference. The leading idea is that the day-care centre field is continuously shaping as a result of both inner struggles and struggles with other fields. The state, the education system, and trade unions act as the dealers of professional playing cards. Struggles are fought with strategies of social closure over capitals and positions. The study aims at not only describing the object but at understanding the dynamics involved.

The concept of professionalism refers to the ideology of a professional group, according to which the group acts purposefully and in an organised manner to pursue their own interests within the rules of the game of the society. The aim of the professional group is, on the one hand, to maintain the advantages obtained and, on the other, to strengthen their position by allying themselves with the élite of the society. This project of professionalisation entails that professional groups are aiming at a professional status, distinctive from the 'ordinary work' and/or semi-professional status, in order to increase their influence in society and their expertise, and to gain better working conditions. During the process, professional groups easily enter into conflicts with various others, such as professional groups in the field, especially with the professions closest to them (e.g. day care and early childhood education). Professional status is backed up by the state and the educational system in particular. The special features of the process are: (1) the project of professionalisation takes a long time; (2) in each country the project of professionalisation has features specific to that country; and (3) the professional groups meet both supporters and opponents on the way.

Nannies, nursery nurses and early years professionals: constructions of professional identity in the early years workforce in England

Gill McGillivray

Recent policy in England has created a new status of 'Early Years Professional', thus imposing professionalisation of the early years workforce. There has been an increase in policy focus on those working with young children, and such a focus raises questions about practitioners' own responses to the debate about their training, education, qualifications and work. How early years practitioners see themselves, their collective or individual identity, or both, may be unsettled by being the centre of discussion and reform.

This research aimed to investigate historical and recent texts using discourse analysis to expose discourse that may have shaped and contributed to the workforce's construction of their professional identity. A theoretical framework of professional identity, proposed by Tucker, is useful in its recognition of how prevailing and contemporary discourses contribute to the construction of professional identity.

Findings suggest that constructs may exacerbate uncertainty, change and struggle for the workforce, and that there are complex and enduring aspects of professional identity that may influence perceptions. Imposed changes in training, assessment and qualifications, long-held beliefs evident in discourse, ideology and day-to-day practices also contribute to constructs of professional identity.

The implications for practice are a need to recognise the complexity of professional identity and therefore the needs of some members of workforce as they move towards professionalisation. It is also argued that the voice of the workforce has been absent historically, and that current reform provides an opportunity for listening and responding.

Developing professionalism within a regulatory framework in England: challenges and possibilities

Linda Miller

Early Childhood Education and Care (ECEC) is now firmly on government agendas in many countries, including England, and the need to develop a professional workforce is generally agreed. The reform of the children's workforce in England acknowledges that increasing the skills and competence of this workforce is critical to its success. Two new professional roles, as routes to creating a more professional workforce, are discussed in this article: the Senior Practitioner and the more recent Early Years Professional role. The article provides a critical review of policy developments leading to the creation of these roles and discusses the tensions and challenges of developing new professional roles within the context of meeting externally prescribed requirements and standards. The article questions whether such standards and requirements help to create this new professionalism or whether, as some critics have argued, they inhibit professional autonomy and promote a model of technical practice. The article draws on a broader international study of professionalism in ECEC and uses data from the English part of this project to illustrate that practitioners working in this English context can and do develop a sense of professional identity and engage in practices which can be described as 'professional'.

Discourses of professional identity in early childhood: movements in Australia

Christine Woodrow

The provision of early childhood education and care for children and families has received unprecedented community attention in recent times. In the resulting policy flows, competing and contradictory discourses of professional identity have emerged. In part, these are also shaped by dominant political and economic discourses, and interact with existing and emerging discourses of professionalism within the early childhood sector to both constrain and expand possible professional identities. This article explores some dimensions of these policy trajectories, in particular the increasingly dominant presence of corporatised childcare, and recent strategies to regulate early childhood teachers and courses. The potential impact of these on conceptualisations of professional identity in the Australian context is discussed, and frameworks of caring, reconceptualised leadership and the concept of 'robust hope' are signposted as possible conceptual resources for building robust early childhood professional identities.

Introduction

Carmen Dalli[a] and Mathias Urban[b]

[a]*Victoria University of Wellington, New Zealand;* [b]*Martin-Luther-University Halle-Wittenburg, Germany*

This book is a collection of work by members of the Special Interest Group on Professionalism in Early Childhood Education and Care who met for the first time in a hotel lobby at the annual European Early Childhood Education Research Association (EECERA) conference in Malta in 2004. It was first published as a special edition of the European Early Childhood Education Research Journal in 2008.

Gathered from all corners of the globe, a group of early childhood researchers, scholars and tertiary lecturers, discussed a simple question: What does it mean to be 'professional' in early childhood education and care? An easy afternoon exercise, one might suppose, given the expertise gathered in the circle. It quickly became apparent that the simple question did not have a simple answer. Instead, it spawned a multitude of questions and an engaged discussion that has continued at each subsequent conference. The discussions stretched out between conferences as members organised pre-conference meetings around the annual EECERA conference, held symposia within the conference, and initiated the cross-national project *A day in the life of an early years practitioner* which involved researchers from six countries (e.g., see Miller, chapter 10).

In retrospect, setting up this international working group was a very timely move given the unprecedented attention that early childhood education and care is gaining in many countries. Over the last years, many countries have set ambitious policy goals to increase both the quantity and quality of services for young children and their families. In most cases, the strategies to develop the early years' systems are hooked to a strategy to further develop the workforce, which is increasingly seen as central to achieving policy intentions. As a consequence, the *professionalism*, and the *professionalising*, of the early childhood workforce have become key issues not only in multitudinous policy documents but also in scholarly discourses in academic journals and at conferences. Curricula, or national pedagogical frameworks, have been introduced as a means to foster professional practice. Qualifications, in-service training/education and an increasing number of university degrees are contributing to the notion that there is a profession in early childhood and an associated need for 'professional' development.

Yet, while the terminology of early childhood professionalism is increasingly pervasive, from our perspective there remains a slight unease. Do we really understand what being professional means in the early childhood work context? How can *profession* be conceptualised in early childhood settings? How might one *act professionally* in increasingly diverse and rapidly changing social and cultural contexts? And: Do we have a common ground of understanding about these terms? Do we have key concepts that we can agree on?

The idea of a publication based on the work of the special interest group arose out of discussions that highlighted a common interest in engaging with these questions and seeking an understanding of professionalism in local contexts that might throw light on its global implications. This book addresses these issues.

Approaching the subject from different theoretical and practical perspectives, the various chapters explore *professionalism* as a conceptual issue, as a policy issue in diverse local contexts, and as a matter that impacts on all aspects of practice, including the practicum component of early childhood teacher preparation courses. From these diverse analytical perspectives, *professionalism* can be understood as a *discourse* as much as a *phenomenon*: as something that is constantly under re-construction.

Aiming to understand *professionalism* as a process (with many contradictions) rather than a finite construct, then, inevitably draws attention to the actors and to the relationships that link them. Within the special interest group, some key questions that have stood out have included: To what extent should professional *autonomy* lie at the core of early childhood occupations – and how can this autonomy be achieved? How can *critical thinking* be introduced and encouraged in professional preparation, practice and reflection? And how can early childhood professionals be encouraged not only to operate from a value-based and ethical perspective, but to contribute to the co-creation of professional ethics and knowledge?

As convenors of the *professionalism* special interest group, we undertook the editing of this work as the first step in opening up our discussions to a wider audience. The collection in this volume throws light on the range of topics discussed within the group: it does not exhaust them. Most chapters are grounded in a specific local context – but they are by no means exemplars, representing *the* Finnish or *the* Australian or any other case. We prefer to see them as individual lenses that focus on the issue of professionalism from their particular vantage point.

Chapters 2, 3 and 4 traverse a range of ideas about the construction of professionalism, professional knowledge, and professional practice. Mathias Urban explores the ways knowledge is produced in hierarchical professional systems and argues for an alternative paradigm where research and practice are linked reciprocally through the hermeneutical concept of creating understandings. Yael Dayan describes her personal journey as an experienced practicum supervisor seeking a democratic and humanistic professionalism that is not merely notional but inherently practical. Carmen Dalli, drawing on practitioners' voices, adds a ground-up perspective to definitions of professionalism.

The next two chapters introduce students' perspectives into the picture: In a joint paper, Marja Kuisma and Anette Sandberg trace the different perceptions and interpretations of professionalism of a group of student teachers and their supervising teachers. Kate Adams, reporting on a study carried out with students and recent graduates, investigates the importance of occupational titles and degree-level studies for professional identity; by embedding her discussion in an account of recent policy changes in the Scottish context, Adams highlights the impact of structural changes on individuals' sense of professional identity, including the potential for newly-emerging identities to be prematurely disrupted.

Situated in the same socio-cultural context, Finland, chapters 7 and 8 address professionalism from two distinct angles and arrive at different but complementary positions. Starting from a model of professionalism as professional expertise, Kirsti Karila discusses professionalism as a multi-level phenomenon impacted by national policies as well as municipal implementation, structural arrangements within work settings, and personal life story. By analysing different definers of professionalism at the different levels against practitioners' perspectives of their role, Karila highlights some current contradictions. Jarmo Kinos applies a Neo-Weberian-Bourdieuan perspective to the professionalisation of the day care workforce. This enables him to unravel some of the contradictory and conflictual processes that emerge when professional groups struggle for resources and social capital.

Gill McGillivray and Linda Miller both explore the impact of an imposed professionalisation. In chapter 9 McGillivray analyses the changes over time in discourses on professionalism and how they contribute to shaping the professional identities of those who are seldom talked with, but are often talked about. In chapter 10 Linda Miller elaborates on the tensions and challenges that have arisen in the UK with the introduction of the role of the early years professional. While acknowledging the limitations of externally imposed standards, Miller argues that the new role is crucial to raising standards and to the establishment of a new multi-professional role. She suggests that it is possible for training providers and practitioners to challenge regulatory frameworks and to become active in developing a sense of identity even in the face of complex workforce reform.

Chapter 11 raises sobering concerns about the future of professional identity in contexts where the corporatisation of childcare provision is fast taking hold producing an enterprise culture that most early childhood practitioners would not recognise as part of their professional identity. Woodrow argues that the issue is a troubling one especially in the Australian context where early childhood professional identity is also under threat from accountability procedures in teacher education institutions that are privileging school learning and eroding early childhood expertise.

This book provides a collection of starting points of an ongoing discussion in the Special Interest Group on Professionalism in Early Childhood Education and Care. Building on what has become a tradition in this group, we end this compilation with some preliminary insights drawn from themes that emerge across the various perspectives included in this book. This leaves us with yet more questions than answers – it is intentionally so.

On behalf of the Special Interest Group on Professionalism in Early Childhood Education and Care, we wish to thank EECERA for its support and encouragement and for providing a hospitable and inspiring environment at the annual conferences. We thank the contributors for sharing their thoughts and the members of the Special Interest Group for the discussions that made this publication possible.

Wellington NZ, and London UK, January 2010

Dealing with uncertainty: challenges and possibilities for the early childhood profession

Mathias Urban

Martin-Luther-University Halle-Wittenberg, Germany

ABSTRACT: In many countries, strategies to further develop services and institutions for the education and care of young children are linked to a discourse on professionalism. Ambitious policy goals, it is argued, can only be achieved by a skilled and qualified workforce whose practice is guided by a professional body of knowledge. This article argues that the prevailing conceptualisation of the early childhood professional is constructed out of a particular, hierarchical mode of producing and applying expert knowledge that is not necessarily appropriate to professional practice in the field of early childhood education. However, it is highly effective and contributes to forming a professional habitus that contradicts the relational core of early childhood practice. Drawing on the conceptual framework of hermeneutics, the article explores an alternative paradigm of a relational, systemic professionalism that embraces openness and uncertainty, and encourages co-construction of professional knowledges and practices. Research, in this frame of thinking, is understood as a dialogic activity of asking critical questions and creating understandings across differences, rather than producing evidence to direct practice.

RÉSUMÉ: Dans de nombreux pays, les stratégies pour développer plus avant les services et institutions d'accueil et d'éducation de la petite enfance sont liées à un débat sur le professionnalisme. Une politique ambitieuse, dit-on, ne peut réussir que grâce à une force de travail compétente et qualifiée dont les pratiques sont guidées par un corps de connaissances professionnelles. Cet article défend l'idée que la conception dominante du professionnel de la petite enfance est construite à partir d'un mode de production et d'application de connaissances expertes, particulier et hiérarchique, qui n'est pas obligatoirement approprié à la pratique professionnelle dans le champ de l'éducation préscolaire. Elle est toutefois effective et contribue à former l'habitus professionnel, entrant en contradiction avec la dimension relationnelle centrale de la pratique auprès des jeunes enfants.

ZUSAMMENFASSUNG: In vielen Ländern werden derzeit Strategien zu Ausbau und Weiterentwicklung der Institutionen und Angebote für die Bildung, Betreuung und Erziehung junger Kinder mit einem Diskurs zur Professionalität in diesem Feld verknüpft. Die anspruchsvollen politischen Ziele können nur verwirklicht werden, so die Argumentation, mithilfe gut ausgebildeter und qualifizierter Fachkräfte, deren Praxis von einer professionellen Wissensbasis geleitet wird. In diesem Beitrag wird argumentiert, dass vorherrschende Konzeptualisierungen des professionellen Frühpädagogen aus einem besonderen, hierarchischen Modus der Erzeugung und Anwendung von Expertenwissen heraus konstruiert sind; einem Modus der dem professionellen Handeln im Feld nicht notwendigerweise angemessen ist. Ungeachtet dessen ist er höchst wirksam und trägt zur Herausbildung eines professionellen Habitus bei, der im Widerspruch zu dem auf wechselseitigen Beziehungen aufgebauten Kern frühpädagogischer Praxis steht. Ausgehend von einem hermeneutischen Denkansatz erörtert der Beitrag ein alternatives Paradigma einer systemischen Professionalität, die Offenheit und Unsicherheit begrüßt, ernst nimmt und zur Ko-Konstruktion von professionellem Wissen und Praktiken ermutigt. Forschung wird in diesem Denkansatz als dialogische Praxis und als zentrales Merkmal einer systemischen Professionalität verstanden. Sie ermöglicht, kritische Fragen zu bearbeiten und trägt dazu bei, Verstehen über Differenz zu erzeugen, statt Faktenwissen für die Anwendung in der Praxis.

RESUMEN: En muchos países, las estrategias para continuar desarrollando los servicios e instituciones para la educación y el cuidado de los niños menores, están enlazadas con un discurso sobre profesionalismo. Metas políticas ambiciosas, se argumenta, pueden ser logradas solamente por una fuerza de trabajo hábil y calificada, cuya práctica es guiada por un cuerpo de conocimiento profesional. Este articulo argumenta que la conceptualizacion prevaleciente de la profesionalización pre-escolar esta construida por un modo particular y jerárquico de producir y aplicar conocimientos de expertos, que no es necesariamente apropiada a las practicas profesionales del campo de la educación pre-escolar. En todo caso, esta es altamente efectiva y contribuye a formar hábitos que contradicen el corazón relacional de la práctica pre-escolar. Basado en un marco de referencia de hermenéutico, el artículo explora un paradigma alternativo, de un profesionalismo relacional y sistémico que abarca la actitud abierta y la incertidumbre, y que fomenta la co-construcción del conocimiento y de las prácticas profesionales. La investigación, en este marco de pensamiento, es entendida como una actividad dialogica de hacer preguntas criticas y crear comprensiones entre diferencias, más que de producir evidencias directas para la práctica.

Introduction: professionalism: a new paradigm in early childhood?

> To begin with, you will be relieved to know that I am not going to tell you what to do. (Winnicott 1987, 15)

The famous introduction to D.W. Winnicott's classic *The Child, the Family and the Outside World* appears to be perfect for any attempt to approach the contradictory debates on the early years profession that have gained new prominence in many countries in recent years. Albeit explicitly addressed at non-professionals – Winnicott writes about a young mother's experience of giving birth to a child – it covers the whole dilemma of adults working in the societal institution set up to educate and care for young children. The dilemma unfolds between the day-to-day experience of having to act concretely, spontaneously and autonomously in ever-changing, uncertain situations which, to a large extent, are determined by factors beyond the practitioners' control, and the pressure that arises from increasing socio-cultural and socio-economic expectations to produce predetermined outcomes in this complex work context.

Along with an increasing division of labour, modern societies, over the past two centuries, tend to successively extend the responsibility for the upbringing of young children from the family domain to public institutions. Care and early education, which once used to be common social practice, have become specialised tasks for those who are specifically identified as early years practitioners: pre-school teachers, childcare workers, pedagogues, to name only a few. Roles, work contexts, levels of formal qualification, remuneration, and so on, of the early years practitioners always varied widely in different institutions or 'services', and in different periods of time. In this article I want to explore a phenomenon that, in recent years, appears to have become inseparable from the numerous attempts to further develop the provision of early childhood education and care, nationally as well as in an increasingly globalised discourse: it is the unprecedented way in which both scholarly discourse and policy documents are referring to the early years workforce as something that has to be *professionalised* that provides the starting point for my argument.

Over the past decade, many countries have set ambitious policy goals to increase both quantity and quality of provision. The political agendas are driven by common concerns about employment, competitiveness and gender equality. As the Organisation for Economic Co-operation and Development (OECD) points out in the recent report on early childhood education and care (ECEC) policies in twenty participating countries, factors for turning governments' attention to institutions and services for young children are obvious. They include:

> The wish to increase women's labour market participation; to reconcile work and family responsibilities on a basis more equitable for women; to confront the demographic challenges faced by OECD countries (in particular falling fertility rates and the general ageing of populations), and the need to address issues of child poverty and educational disadvantage. (OECD 2006, 12)

It is in this economical and political climate, that, for instance, the European Union expresses the need to increase the *numbers* of childcare places and, at the Barcelona summit in 2002, agreed on providing fully subsidised childcare places for 33% of children aged 0–3 and for 90% of children from 3 to mandatory school age by 2010. According to OECD figures (OECD 2006, 78), only five countries[1] had reached these goals by 2006, but 'several' others are described as being on the way to achieving similar coverage.

The main concern, at least from the perspective of governments of countries we regularly refer to as being 'developed', is that 'economic prosperity depends on mainstreaming a high employment/population ratio' (OECD 2006, 78), and policies to bring more women into the workforce have been put in place in most OECD countries. It is questionable, however, whether it is legitimate to speak about services *for children* when the driving factors for investing in them are so clearly economic in the first place.

From a pragmatic point of view, one could argue, anything that helps place early childhood high on governments' agendas should be welcome. But there is another side to the coin of the economic rationale that gets out of sight too often: policies to increase female labour market participation, introduced in times of economic growth, are at risk of being abolished as soon as the economy faces a deceleration or decline. Not only are they unsustainable – they are also a highly effective means of governing, that is, of controlling women's, men's and children's participation in the society on the whole: fundamental rights to participation in a democratic society are in effect, then, granted or denied according to the rationales of an increasingly globalised economy that lack any democratic legitimacy.

But there are other rationales, too, that have moved early childhood institutions onto policy agendas, as well as onto electoral agendas, as the OECD report points out. Besides being a condition for gender equality in an economy-dominated society, the expansion of early childhood institutions is seen as crucial for educational attainment, as the fundament for lifelong learning and social inclusion and equity. Concurrently, the policy context includes new international and national attention to children's rights and participation framed by the United Nations Convention on the Rights of the Child and recognised explicitly in the Charter of Fundamental Rights of the European Union.

The policy commitment to ECEC provision at European level is also combined with a recognition that the provision has to be of good quality. There have been important European and national discussions on what quality entails, including the publication in 1996 of *Quality Targets in Services for Young Children* by the European Commission Network on Childcare and Other Measures to Reconcile Employment and Family Responsibilities (1996). The title of the network notwithstanding – it fits seamlessly into the general socio-economic argumentative framework predominant in the late 1990s – *Quality Targets* is an important document as it offers a multi-dimensional framework for quality, including, among others, targets for policy, investment, participation and professionalisation. Furthermore, the acknowledgement of a socio-economic necessity for early childhood provision may have paved the way for the general acknowledgement, today, that more and better services require substantial investment.

National policy developments reflect the European and international debate. Many European countries have introduced national policies on 'quality' in early childhood education and care in the past decade. In 2004, through a 'Quality Decree' for example, Flanders introduced a participative evaluation system in which 'quality' is seen as an ongoing construction, jointly determined by parents, staff, children and management (Peeters 2005; Urban 2006). The 'National Quality Initiative' in Germany also pursued a systemic approach to 'quality', developing, for the first time after the reunification, quality standards and evaluation procedures for an early childhood sector that is characterised mainly by the principles of *federalism* (with the political and administrative responsibility for childcare and education lying at state (*Länder*) level and detached from the national government) and *subsidiarity* (which means that even though there is a public responsibility to ensure and plan for provision, the services are mainly provided by voluntary organisations) (Preissing 2003; Urban 2003, 2005b). Ireland, to give a third example, has been struggling to develop 'quality' in a highly fragmented, diverse and under-financed childcare sector (OECD 2004; 2006, 353; Murray 2006). Following intensive consultations with various stakeholders, *Síolta*, the National Framework for Quality, was launched in 2006. The document aims at supporting 'individual professional practice and development'; it provides a 'tool for management, strategic planning and policy development' as well as 'a common base for the interactions of a varied team of professionals' (Centre for Early Childhood Development and Education 2006).

It is necessary to keep in mind that the concept of 'quality' itself is highly problematic. It has been widely challenged by authors for its implicit relatedness to notions of universality, technocratic manageability and measurability (Pence and Moss 1994; Dahlberg, Moss, and Pence 1999, 2007; Urban 2003, 2005b). Too often, the language of 'quality' is employed to legitimise the proliferating maze of regulations in early childhood education and care, and to undermine instead of support professional autonomy. We should, therefore, be cautious not to lose the 'shared unease' with the terminology and the implications of this technical and managerial concept, as Dahlberg, Moss, and Pence remind us (2007, 3). Quality remains a questionable concept, a problem that needs to be explored rather than to be taken for granted or to be presented as the solution. While we need to be critical about 'quality' and its implications for practice, in a broader policy context, arguing for 'better quality' can be an effective driving force.

What interests me in the context of this article is the way the discourses on 'quality' and 'professionalism' seem to merge without difficulty at first sight. It seems to be generally recognised, today, that the workforce is central for achieving the ambitious policy goals of increasing both quantity and quality of provision. Recent research supports this notion (Siraj-Blatchford, Sylva, and Muttock 2002; Dalli 2003, 2005; MacNaughton 2005; Oberhuemer 2005) and along with policies to increase 'quality', many countries have been introducing policies that aim at 'professionalising' the workforce in recent years. In

England, for example, the extensive *Every Child Matters* strategy (Department for Education and Skills [DfES] 2004) links explicitly to a *Children's Workforce Strategy* (DfES 2005) that aims at building a 'world-class workforce for children and young people' (DfES 2005). The message is clear: early childhood practitioners need to be 'qualified', 'trained' and 'skilled' in order to achieve the highly ambitious 'outcomes' of *Every Child Matters*. Moreover, the strategy aimed at, and resulted in, redefining the workforce on the whole. The new formal status of 'Early Years Professional' has been established, thus introducing to – and, as some authors write – imposing the notion of professionalism on the early years workforce (cf. the contributions of Gill McGillivray and Linda Miller in this volume).

Like England, other countries, today, are facing major workforce challenges. In many countries the workforce is split between early childhood *teachers* and *childcare workers*, reflecting a deep institutional divide between early childhood education and care that – at the same time – is increasingly questioned by practitioners, researchers and policy makers alike. The work itself is also recognised to be changing and increasingly demanding, because of increasing diversity among children and families and the complexity of the work in the institutions set up to serve them (Woodhead 1996; OECD 2001, 2006). Early childhood practitioners have to address not only the need to provide care, but also broader requirements – educational, social and cultural – for example, collaborating with parents from diverse backgrounds and with diverse local communities.

While the work contexts are challenging and changing, and practitioners are increasingly expected to 'act professionally' within these contexts, the terminology itself remains obscure. Carmen Dalli (2003), analysing the wording of job advertisements in New Zealand, reports that employers are either expecting applicants to join an existing team of professionals or are looking for people with a professional attitude. Kate Adams, in her contribution to this volume, explores understandings of professionalism in one European country (Scotland), only to find as many as eleven job titles for practitioners working with young children. Admittedly, the two studies reflect the situation in New Zealand and Scotland, respectively. From an outside perspective, however, both findings contribute to a broad picture that is identifiable in individual countries as well as in the international discourse: increasingly high expectations (to *act professionally!*) have to be met by individual practitioners, while the structures wherein this professional practice takes place remain fragmented. Oberhuemer and Ulich (1997) have pointed out that there is no consensus on the role of practitioners working with young children. Ten years on, despite an unprecedented attention for early childhood education and care in the public debate, the picture has not changed significantly. Or has it?

D.W. Winnicott talks about the young mother's relief of *not being told what to do*. Even though she may prefer to 'avoid thinking things out' (1987, 17), as long as there is love, the baby will probably get a good start. Early childhood practitioners, in their contradictory professional context, cannot feel this relief. In work contexts where they are expected not only to give children 'a good start' but to achieve predetermined, assessable outcomes, practitioners are increasingly being told *what to do*, what works and what counts. And they are subject to a powerful strategy to bring forward a particular view of professional practice – which needs to be questioned, as I want to argue in the following sections.

Talking the talk: dominant discourses and regimes of truths?

Traditionally, conceptualisations of 'profession' have always been linked to 'knowledge'. Whatever the actual practice in a given profession, it is embedded in a system of knowledge production and application that distinguishes professional practice from other forms of production of goods or services in any society. Most influential for developing this notion of 'profession' as a particular organisational form in modern societies – that are structurally differentiated to a large extent – was the American sociologist Talcott Parsons (1902– 1979). Parsons' work aimed at developing a generalised, abstract concept for describing what he called 'the Social System' (1951). Parsons elaborated his general theoretical framework of 'structural-functionalism' by exploring its relevance to various sub-systems of modern society, including the professions (Parsons 1968). Even though Parsons' theoretical work has been criticised widely by sociologists for its implicit social determinism and conservatism, his explanation of a profession as a societal sub-system is still effective to date. Key features of the professional system – the ones you find in dictionaries of sociology, for instance – include a *central regulatory body* (to ensure the quality of performance of the individual professional), a professional *code of conduct* and an effective means of *producing and managing the professional body of knowledge*. Another central characteristic of the professional system, according to this perspective, is the existence of an effective control of entrance, regulating, for instance, numbers, selection and training of future professionals.

Sociological literature on professionalism abounds, and from the 1970s, a stark critique of the roles and agendas of professions – in general – emerges. Referring to Marx and Gramsci, for example, professionalism is seen as an effective means of a particular 'intellectual class' to gain influence and power, and to secure social status and economic advantage in a structurally unequal society:

> Professionalization is thus an attempt to translate one order of scarce resources – special knowledge and skills – into another – social and economic rewards. To maintain scarcity implies a tendency to monopoly: monopoly of expertise in the market, monopoly of status in a system of stratification. (Larson 1977, vxii)

Again, *knowledge*, and the modes of its production, distribution and application, plays a central role in this game of power. But as sociologists tend to take more general approaches to the phenomenon of professionalism, one could also question to what extent this generalisation provides an adequate ground for exploring the characteristics of professionalism in early childhood – which is the intention of this analysis. I want to argue that what is presented to us as being *general* about professionalism in early childhood policy documents, regulatory frameworks, curricula, and so on, can also be seen as manifestation of a particular discourse: a very specific way of talking about professionalism that is neither neutral nor necessarily appropriate for the field of early childhood education and care (see also Dalli in this volume). It is, on the contrary, an effective means of control and regulation of diverse individual practice through dominant knowledge – something that has been described by Michel Foucault as a 'regime of truths'. The way we talk about practice (or the way it is talked and written about by those whose voices are heard and considered as relevant) does not merely give an explanation of what is going on. It is an active agent instead. Discourses, writes Foucault, are 'practices that systematically form the objects [and subjects] of which they speak' (Foucault 1972, 49).

Going back to the starting point of this argument – the unprecedented attention to early childhood, its institutions and, in consequence, its workforce in national and international politics – what stands out through the influential documents is the clear distinction between those who talk and those who are talked about.[2] Early childhood education and care, as societal sub-system as well as a professional system, is highly stratified. The gap between the Education Committee of the OECD and a childcare worker or early childhood teacher is considerable. Consultations, held at national level by government departments who are introducing new policies, hardly ever reach the individual practitioner who is supposed to be working towards realising the policies. But stratification and distinction is not limited to relationships with 'external' agencies, like international organisations and government departments. It is clearly visible within the professional system itself. Scholarly discussions about what it means and entails to be 'professional' in early childhood often express expectations towards the individual practitioner, but seldom acknowledge the inequities of the knowledge producing and processing structures within the system that are highly effective as tools of regulation and self-regulation.

The epistemological hierarchy in our field consists of distinct layers, where the professional body of knowledge is *produced* (academic research, scholarly debate), *transferred* (professional preparation, pre- and in-service training) and *applied* (practice). There is a powerful top-down stream of knowledge presented as relevant for practice, and a similar downstream of expectations and advice about what needs to done at the practice levels of the hierarchy. Not only does this layout of the early childhood professional system constantly increase the pressure on practitioners, who, finding themselves at the bottom of the epistemological hierarchy, have to meet these expectations imposed on them. It also contributes to constructing and reinforcing a particular dichotomy in the field: There is, this perspective suggests, a clear distinction between theory and practice. And this theory/practice dichotomy links well with a structural-functionalist framework, where a social 'problem' – and the way it is defined – is distinct from its 'solution'. The role of the 'professionals', in this framework, is to contribute to 'solving' a given problem by applying their specific knowledge, which they have acquired through formalised training.

A good example of the prevalence of the structural-functionalist conceptualisation of professionalism is the *Every Child Matters* programme in England, and the way it links to the *Children's Workforce Strategy* (DfES 2004, 2006). The programme clearly defines the social problem (structural inequality and disadvantage that is putting increasing numbers of children and families 'at risk', drastically illustrated by the neglect, abuse and eventual killing of Victoria Climbié). It provides a clear set of goals that are presented as assessable outcomes (every child to be healthy, safe, enjoying and achieving, making positive contributions, achieving economic well-being). The related *Workforce Strategy* is explicit about how the outcomes can be achieved:

> To ensure that children and young people achieve the five Every Child Matters outcomes, it is vital to have a children's workforce that is skilled, well-led and supported by effective, shared systems and processes. (Department for Children, Schools and Families 2007)

The strategy then goes on defining the mode in which a body of knowledge is produced and managed, applied and, finally, used as means of entry-control for those wishing to join the profession as it 'sets out action to be taken nationally and locally to ensure that there are the skills, ways of working and capacity to deliver change for children' (Department for Children, Schools and Families 2007).

The 'skills' necessary to 'deliver' are drawn from a 'Common Core of Skills and Knowledge' that are 'needed' to work 'effectively' (Department for Children, Schools and Families 2007). Everyone working with children, then, is expected by an anonymous 'we' to demonstrate their competences in the areas defined by the Common Core, which is also presented as the future foundation for qualification, training and development of the workforce (Department for Children, Schools and Families 2007).

My intention here is certainly not to point a priggish finger at the English example. There is a multitude of similar examples to be found in policies and strategic documents in many countries, including my own.[3] Far from being unique, with respect to this analysis of professional systems, the *Workforce Strategy* represents a highly effective discourse, 'that systematically form[s] the objects [and subjects] of which [it] speak[s]' (Foucault 1972, 49).

The mechanisms of 'professional' knowledge production, distribution and application that are implicit in these examples link to a wider predominant discourse on children and childhood in modern society, which, increasingly, is concerned about gaining certainties through regulation and achieving predetermined goals. It contributes to constructing a particular understanding of early childhood institutions as 'sites for technical practice, seeking the best methods and procedures to delivering predetermined outcomes' (Dahlberg and Moss 2005, 2). This science-led search for problem-solving methods is built on two basic (and taken-for-granted) assumptions:

> a stable, defined and transmittable body of knowledge, but also implicitly a particular subject, today the autonomous and flexible child. The defining question for this possibility is 'What works?': which technical practices will most effectively ensure the desired outcomes? (Dahlberg and Moss 2005, 2)[4]

There are, in consequence, obvious professional tasks arising from this Parsonian problem-setting/problem-solving mindset, in which scientific knowledge, as Dahlberg and Moss argue, provides the main means for achieving order:

> We know the adult we want the child to become, we know the world in which the adult must live and work. The challenge is to produce the adult to fit into that world, in the most cost-effective way – and with the help of scientific knowledge-as-regulation the challenge can be met. (Dahlberg and Moss 2005, 6)

Dominant discourses that furtively turn into means of regulation, or regimes of truths, hide under different veils. Discussing conceptualisations of professionalism in early childhood, 'evidence-based practice' is one of them. It is nurtured by an increasingly influential critique of educational practices in general, which are accused of 'failing' largely because they are not informed by educational 'research knowledge'.[5] Considerable efforts are being taken in many countries and internationally (and considerable amounts of money spent) to promote the idea of education as an evidence-based practice and of teaching as an evidence-based profession (Biesta 2007). Supposedly aiming at narrowing the gap between research, policy and practice, Biesta argues, the prevalence of the concept of 'evidence-based practice' leads, on the contrary, to an increasing tension between scientific and democratic control over research as well as practice:

> On the research side, evidence-based education seems to favour a technocratic model in which it is assumed that the only relevant research questions are questions about the effectiveness of educational means and techniques, forgetting, among other things, that what counts as 'effective' crucially depends on judgements about what is educationally desirable. (Biesta 2007, 5)

For educational practitioners, working in an environment where 'effectiveness' is defined externally, and where the decisions about what desirable outcomes should be have already been made, then, it is almost impossible to make these judgements themselves in a way that is relevant for their actual working context (i.e. the particular children, families and communities they are working with). Evidence-based practice, as something derived from educational science as means of knowledge production, and to be implemented, disqualifies practitioners and deprives them of their professional autonomy. Moreover, it actively hinders a practice that is constantly developed by asking critical questions:

> The focus on 'what works' makes it difficult, if not impossible to ask the questions of what it should work *for* and who should have a say in determining the latter. (Biesta 2007, 5)

'Evidence-based practice', and the framework of professional epistemology it implies, is by no means as *neutral* as it may appear. Judgements and values lie at the very core of the concept, but, in a powerful shift, the processes of judging, valuing and contextual meaning-making are steered away from practitioners. But it is another implication of this concept that brings it even closer to the questions I am pursuing in this inquiry. Evidence-based practice is embedded in a very specific paradigm that Oliver and Conole (2003) summarise as follows:

> At the heart of evidence-based practice lies a concern for the effectiveness and the best way of researching this, it has been argued, is by means of experimentation … The form of experimentation that has found particular favour within evidence-based practice is the randomised control trial. This is privileged on the basis of a search for causality … Indeed, this method has become all but synonymous with evidence-based practice, having been used to define in American law what counts as 'rigorous' research and how evidence-based practice should be implemented. (388)

This, as Biesta argues, produces a notion of professional practice as intervention, which, in fact, is a causal model of professional practice. The basic assumption of this model is that professionals act – or intervene – in a particular situation in order to bring about certain effects that can be determined beforehand. There is, it is suggested, a secure relation between the intervention and its outcomes (Biesta 2007, 7). But what if, for some reason, the desired effect does not show?

Even if it is reasonable to say that substantial investment in early childhood services and programmes does make a difference, it is unlikely that *each* individual child will be of *better health*, *achieving* better at compulsory school and enjoying *economic well-being* as a result of these programmes. My argument here is that the powerful conceptualisation of the early childhood professional in a paradigm of clearly defined problems, predetermined outcomes and evidence-based, hence 'right', practices implies failure – without acknowledging that 'failure', or the uncertainty about what the outcomes of the interaction with a child in a complex situation will be, lie at the very core of the early childhood profession.

This, in consequence, leaves early childhood practitioners with a fundamental dilemma: in order to achieve recognition, in public and in the domain they are working in, they have to construct and communicate their professional identity *against* the key characteristics of their practice. Reporting and commenting on their practice, and the difficulties they are facing in day-to-day interactions with children and families, practitioners clearly express this dilemma. Data from recent and ongoing research suggest that practitioners are increasingly moving from a simplistic and technical to a relational and therefore uncertain perception of their practice. At the same time they seek, sometimes desperately, to avoid uncertainty, mistakes and 'failure' – constructing themselves, in their responses to studies, in conversations with parents or in the public sphere, as 'experts' who know what to do and who are being told what to do by a knowledge-producing system that guides their practice.[6]

Discourses form the subjects of which they speak and, in early childhood, contribute to constructions of professional identity (cf. McGillivray in this volume). They do so to the extent that the factors that shape perceptions and behaviour are too often not perceived as being external at all. They become internalised and form what could be called, following Pierre Bourdieu (1977), a particular 'professional habitus'.[7]

Walking the walk: professionalism in early childhood as a relational concept

> The reason life is so strange is that we have simply no idea what is around the next corner,
> something most of us have learned to forget. (Colum McCann: Zoli)

The problem with this professional habitus, shaped by a particular way of *knowing how we know what we know* (professional epistemology), is that, quite often, it contradicts day-to-day experiences of early childhood practitioners. First of all: early childhood education is a messy business. Its 'practice' unfolds in interactions between children and adults, individuals and groups, families and communities, laypersons and 'professionals' – all pursuing their own and often contradictory interests. These relationships are all but static. Even though we pretend to be in control, and we invent all sorts of implements to formalise the interactions (e.g. settings, classes, morning sessions, circle time, parent–teacher meetings, distinct 'free play' sessions, and so on), they constantly shift and rearrange in unpredictable patterns.[8] Moreover, they are by no means made of one-way communications but are always reciprocal. Situations and 'problems' that early childhood practitioners are dealing with on a day-to-day basis are highly complex. Think of the young mother who, smelling of alcohol (again!), is handing over her child, who apparently has a temperature, on a Monday morning – a situation that is not unusual to early childhood practitioners. But what are the factors that 'determine' this situation? What is 'the problem'? Is it the mother's addiction, the family's living conditions in a 'disadvantaged' neighbourhood, the child's illness and the centre's health and safety policy, the child's need for positive experiences given the irresponsibility of the mother? Most likely, it is a tangle of all of them, and of a hundred other things that would come to mind if we would dwell on this example.

What is characteristic of these complex situations, that are so common in early childhood practice, is that they elude any simplistic *problem-solving-through-application-of-knowledge* mechanism. Even the most common situations in early childhood practice do not present themselves as clearly distinguishable problems, or simple tasks that imply one particular action towards their 'solution'. Instead, practitioners find themselves challenged by the problem of 'setting the problem', which, according to Donald Schön (1983), is an activity of meaning making that involves value-based decisions and experience, and which cannot be dealt with by 'applying' standard theories and techniques:

> In real-world practice, problems do not present themselves to the practitioner as givens. They must be constructed from the materials of problem situations which are puzzling, troubling, and uncertain. In order to convert a problematic situation to a problem, a practitioner must do a certain kind of work. *He must make sense of an uncertain situation that initially makes no sense.* (Schön 1983, 40, emphasis added)

This activity of *making sense* of uncertain situations, then, takes place with the practitioner being part of the situation herself. The challenge is to get into a 'reflective conversation' with the situation, thus re-framing it in order to both understand and change it. Practice itself, from this perspective, is a sphere where professional 'knowledge' is produced – by practitioners who are in relationships with others (children!), and from questions arising from the situations they are involved in.

Whatever the results or 'outcomes' of early childhood practice, they are clearly not due to the practitioner acting *on* a particular individual, or group. That is not to say there are no outcomes. But they inevitably emerge from *interactions* between the practitioner and the child, both embedded in complex socio-ecologic contexts. Early childhood practice is a constant co-construction – and therefore necessarily open and undeterminable.[9]

There are other reasons, beyond the immediate interaction between practitioner and child, that contribute to the inevitable and necessary openness of early childhood practice. The social and cultural contexts of the relationships between children and adults – that we usually refer to as *education* – have changed dramatically in modern societies. Exploring the changes in 'western' societies after World War II, and the 'New Relationships between the Generations' that arose from these changes, Margaret Mead (1978) introduced the concept of a cultural shift from what she called *postfigurative* to *prefigurative* ways of teaching and learning. While in postfigurative cultures, that are more or less static, adults' knowledge and experience can be 'passed down' from the older generation, providing the younger with adequate equipment to master their lives, this is no longer the case in modern societies under conditions of change. We only need to look at the changes that occurred during our own lifetime (e.g. the rise of information technology, unprecedented global migration, the shaping of local living conditions through the effects of a globalised economy, and so on) to understand that today we don't know *what* to teach our children in order to enable them to cope with future challenges. In our prefigurative culture, adults' experiences and knowledge can no longer be projected linearly, to serve as a blueprint for our children's future. This has radically reversed educational relationships as in prefigurative cultures it is no longer the parent or the grandparent that represents what is to come – but the child, Mead explains (1978, 83). Adults, instead of leading children into a future that is by and large already known, now 'are equally immigrants into the new era' (70).[10]

The implicit conceptual shift from acquisition of knowledge to an active, co-constructivist *making of experiences* appears to be uncontested today – at least in our understandings of children's learning. We talk about children as 'active learners', promote a 'pedagogy of listening' and dialogue (Rinaldi 2005, 57), and recent research emphasises that children's exploring and meaning-making activities unfold their full potential only when they take place in meaningful, child-led interactions between children and adults – in activities Siraj-Blatchford and Sylva (2004, 720) refer to as 'sustained shared thinking'. When it comes to the implications for conceptualisations of the early childhood profession, the situation is contradictory, thus contributing to the practitioners' dilemma. As individuals (or team members), practitioners are living and acting a relational, reciprocal, open and inevitably uncertain professionalism, and they are increasingly expected to do so by those who dominate the discourse that subsequently manifests in qualification and workforce strategies. They are, at the same time, part of a professional system that, instead of being co-constructive, and all but embracing uncertainty, still largely operates within a paradigm of hierarchical knowledge production and application. Acting professionally under conditions of change, following Margaret Mead, would require new models instead:

> Now, with our greater understanding of the process, we must cultivate the most flexible and complex part of the system – the behaviour of adults. We must, in fact, teach ourselves how to alter adult behaviour so that we can give up postfigurative upbringing, with its tolerated cofigurative components, and discover prefigurative ways of teaching and learning that will keep the future open. We must create new models for adults who can teach their children not what to learn, but how to learn, not what they should be committed to but the value of commitment. (Mead 1978, 87)

The paradigmatic shift, however, remains yet to be achieved. The question is whether or not we can move on from questioning individual practices of practitioners to questioning practices at every layer of the early childhood professional system – and the system as a whole. The professional system, and its practices, comprises individual and collective practices in any early childhood setting, as well as in training[11] and professional development, in academia, in the administrative and political sphere, and in research in these contexts itself.

Since all of these elements are embedded in – and contribute to – the wider social, historical, economic and political context of a society, with its local, national and increasingly global dimensions, they can be referred to as ecological. The challenge, then, is to promote a *critical ecology of the profession*, in early childhood and beyond, that is informed by the political and social realities that produce knowledges and practices, 'together with the use of this knowledge to *strategically transform* education in socially progressive directions' (MacNaughton 2003, 3).

A different paradigm: professionalism in early childhood as an activity of creating understandings

We have already seen that there are inherent tensions and contradictions between the way professional habitus is unwittingly shaped by a dominant discourse of knowledge, expertise, technology, etc., and the key characteristics of professional practice in the field of early childhood. Explored from this perspective, the fundamental dilemma of the early childhood profession, today, is that practitioners are left in an impossible situation: they are expected to act professionally – within a professional system that is largely *unprofessional*, considering the key requirements of the field. It is hard to see, therefore, how a sustainable change in professional practice can be achieved without a radical change of the conceptualisation of the entire professional system. A key feature of this professional system, as we have seen, is the way knowledges and understandings of the subjects and objects of its practice are constructed.

But from a relational (i.e. *critically ecological*) understanding of the early childhood profession, the prevailing concept of 'research', conducted to produce 'evidence' to direct the professional practice, is no longer tenable.

Critical authors in the human and social sciences have been suggesting an alternative model of creating understanding that appears to be more suitable for complex interactions between 'self-interpreting, meaning-making human beings' (Taylor 1995). Rooted in the thinking of German philosopher Hans-Georg Gadamer (1960; Gadamer, Weinsheimer, and Marshall 2004) and known as *Hermeneutics*, it places *the way we are in the world* (ontology) before the constitution of warranted knowledge (epistemology). *Hermeneutics* entails a different conception of the notions of research and knowledge, although its preference of *being* does not mean knowledge does not matter. But, as Schwandt (2004, 35) argues, 'asking and answering questions about the nature of knowledge is not the way to begin modelling what is entailed in understanding human reality'. My argument, here, is that the key to modelling an alternative paradigm for early childhood professionalism lies in the hermeneutic concept of *understanding* because it radically questions the hierarchy between those who produce *knowledge-through-research* and those who apply and deliver. In hermeneutic inquiry, knowledge is not brought forth by the intellectual or methodological activity of the researcher. *Coming to an understanding*, in contexts of human realities, is a dialogic process 'in which one participates, not an activity over which one exercises methodological control' (Schwandt 2004, 38). The way participants engage in the mutual activity of coming to an understanding of a situation resembles Donald Schön's description of practitioners who are constantly engaged in 'reflective conversations with the situation'. However, it adds a new dimension to it as it allows for the individual practitioner to become an actor in the system that generates professional knowledge.

Seeking to get involved in such a dialogue is a risky business for all participants – but mostly for researchers. Linked into a mutual (as opposed to an individual) process of meaning-making, researchers can no longer treat their informants as a generalised other, 'seeking only to understand typical behaviour so that one can predict the other's behaviour in order to achieve one's own purposes. Nor can one simply claim a kind of special mystical union or empathy with others through which one presumes to understand others better than they understand themselves' (Schwandt 2004, 38). In a hermeneutic frame of thinking, the 'other' in this dialogic encounter has to be acknowledged in his or her autonomy and for his or her genuine contribution to the emergence of an understanding. This, then, is no longer a question of choosing appropriate methodologies for research with (as opposed to *on)* practice but an ethical one as it requires making a choice and taking a stand: to being open to others and to respecting their autonomy, presuming, as Warnke (2002, 93, as cited in Schwandt 2004) explains, 'they possess an independence and voice we must address and by which we ourselves are addressed'.

The counterpart of this respect for the autonomous other is the recognition of the researcher's own ways of understanding and knowing (one's own hermeneutical situation, according to Gadamer) – and the historically and culturally conditioned biases that have shaped them. Gadamer (Gadamer, Weinsheimer, and Marshall 2004) argues that it is impossible to gain understanding of any subject without first studying one's own tradition, and the prejudices which our position within that tradition has nurtured in us. An exercise that, once begun, will not only increase our awareness, but will enable us to gain new insights from our inquiries. Here lies, of course, another risk for the researcher's identity which has been nurtured in the safe haven of the knowledge production part of the system:

> To listen to others different from ourselves we must remain open and that means parts of our interpretative forestructure is rendered at risk. Said differently, active listening requires personal vulnerability. Risking self-identity is dangerous. (Garrison 1996, 449)

The necessarily participatory project of *creating understandings* through systematically organising dialogues in which all participants equally talk and listen challenges the hegemony of expertise and dominant knowledge – but it also bridges the gap between the *ways of being* and the *ways of knowing* in a professional system. 'Dialogue across differences' is possible – and it opens a perspective to overcome the inherent dilemma of the early childhood profession as it 'embraces difference, diversity, and the messiness of human life rather than seeking, in the first instance, to resolve it' (Schwandt 2004, 40).

Creating understandings through *dialogue across differences*, then, offers a real possibility to reconceptualise the mode knowledge and practice are developed in the professional system. In order to create change, in early childhood, the dialogic interactions between 'researcher' and 'practitioner' (a dichotomy that becomes obsolete) need to be contextualised. In other words, instead of being a purposeless bilateral conversation between the partners, they become systematic inquiries *into*, and explorations of, possibilities for acting *in* complex, uncertain situations with children, families and communities in order to change them. Research, from this perspective, is a practice itself – as much as 'practice' is constant inquiry. A similar notion of 'practice' as a purposeful dialogic relationship which can be organised systematically to create understandings as well as to create change has guided the educational and political work of Paolo Freire throughout his life. He introduced the concept of dialogue in his early writings as a core activity to overcome hierarchical relationships in education:

> Through dialogue, the teacher-of-the-students and the student-of-the-teacher cease to exist and a new term emerges: teacher-student with students-teachers. The teacher is no longer merely the-one-who-teaches, but one who is himself taught in dialogue with the students, who in turn while being taught also teach. They become jointly responsible for a process in which all grow. (Freire 2000, 80, first published in 1970)

Re-visiting his beginnings in later writings, Freire (Freire and Freire 1997) emphasises the radical nature of the dialogic project in education and society. Far from being 'a tool' for teaching, he explains, 'dialogism' is a requirement of human nature and a sign of the educator's democratic stand (93). Dialogic relationships also link *acting* and *knowing* reciprocally: they are, Freire writes, 'a fundamental practice to human nature and to democracy on the one hand' but also 'an epistemological requirement' (93). Systematic dialogue, as understood and practiced by Paolo Freire, could be seen as a *way of knowing*, inseparable from a *way of being* of the educational practitioner-researcher, grounded in the openness of education that Freire describes as its very nature:

> One of the roots of education, which makes it specifically human, lies in the radicalness of an inconclusion that is perceived as such. The permanence of education lies in the constant character of search, perceived as necessary. Likewise, here lie also roots of the metaphysical foundation of hope. How would it be possible for a consciously inconclusive being to become immersed in a permanent search without hope? My hope starts from my nature as a project. For this reason I am hopeful, and not for pure stubbornness. (Freire and Freire 1997, 93)

Towards systemic professionalism in early childhood: hopeful examples and an open framework instead of a conclusion

In Ireland, the '*éist*' diversity and equality in early childhood initiative is successfully involving early childhood practitioners in questioning their practices regarding the diversity of children and families in an increasingly unequal society. The project has created a space for practitioners' inquiries into their day-to-day practice; it encourages them to experiment and to reflect on their experiences (Murray and O'Doherty 2001). Raising awareness of one's own cultural prejudices and biases has been a starting point of the project's ongoing journey. Practitioners' voices and their experiences from this project are informing national and regional policies on diversity and equality (e.g. Office of the Minister for Children 2006) and the project now engages in systematic professional development through a national network of 'trainers'. '*éist*' has been and is a key member of a European network on 'Diversity in Early Childhood Education and Training' (DECET), which offers a forum for practitioners, researchers and policy makers at international level.

In Germany, in 2003, practitioners together with a research team at the University of Halle-Wittenberg set out on a project to develop an early years curriculum, funded by the Department for Social Affairs of the state of Saxony-Anhalt. Designed as a participatory action research project, Bildung: *elementar* (Urban, Huhn, and Schaaf 2004) systematically offered a space for practitioners to develop and pursue their own research questions regarding children's learning and how to best support it. Starting from practitioners' experiences and 'tacit knowledge', the questions that emerged in the process then framed a systemic critical reflection, involving practitioners, members of the academic research team and a wide range of actors in the field, including parents. The curriculum document that was developed in this joint process consequently focuses on professional attitudes towards co-constructive pedagogy. Instead of listing early learning goals, it offers a framework of questions that support practitioners in observing and inspiring children's learning. The curriculum explicitly names the responsibilities of actors at all layers of the professional system, including those involved in research, continuous professional development and policy making. Bildung: *elementar* demonstrates how the knowledge-production-and-application model can be reversed and that professional knowledge can be successfully co-constructed. The curriculum has been made mandatory for all services for children from birth to compulsory school age in 2004; the Bildung: *elementar* project has since built a professional learning network involving practitioners in an increasing number of early childhood settings across the state (Bildung: elementar 2007).

Funded by the Department of Education, the New Zealand *Centres of Innovation* initiative (Ministry of Education 2007) provides resources and a secure framework for developing local responses to local requirements – which are then employed to inform changes of the EC system as a whole. Early childhood settings across the country are encouraged to apply for this initiative by illustrating practices they consider to be innovative and which they want to explore and further develop in a three-year action research process. The participatory action research is facilitated by a 'research associate', typically a researcher from the university, who has to be identified by the centre. The initiative draws on the diversity of local experiences, and the capability of practice to bring about innovation and to contribute actively to building a professional body of knowledge. While policy provides a stable and well-resourced framework for the local research and its dissemination, academic researchers take on the role of 'critical friends' (Urban 2007), working at eye level with practitioners and communities to pursue questions of relevance for the entire professional system.

Some cornerstones emerge from these vignettes – and from the multitude of other possible examples – for a professional system in early childhood that operates differently from prevailing mechanisms of knowledge production, distribution and application. First of all, there is shift of perspectives, as the focus moves from the individual practitioner (who has to be professionalised in order to apply and deliver) towards the reciprocal relationships between the various actors and their roles at different layers of the system: a complex *ecology of the profession* rather than a trivial machinery. *Professionalism*, then, can be understood as an attribute of the entire system, to be developed in its reciprocal relationships.

Second, a key feature of a professional system would be its ability to encourage and systematically create spaces for dialogue and for asking critical questions at every layer of the system – and to value the multitude and diversity of answers as key to creating new understandings. The challenge is to create a professional environment for constant inquiry – not only into individual practice, but for critical inquiry into the context and the preconditions for this practice, including the life situations of children and the cultural, historical, economic and political realities and inequalities that shape them. A professional system that unfolds around critical questions about the taken-for-granted preconditions and assumptions builds on Donald Schön's concept of the reflective practitioner – but it expands it to *critical* reflectiveness,[12] which, as a feature of the system rather than of the individuals within it, is a transformative practice in the tradition of Freire's concept of *conscientisation*.

A third cornerstone of a professional system in early childhood education arises from Paolo Freire's notion of *hope* (as an ontological need, as he explains it). Educational practice is there for a purpose and it implies change. A professional system grounded on a Freirean concept of *hope* offers a perspective to address the direction of this change. The *hoped-for* has to be debated – and this directs the attention from the restricting question of *what works* towards questions of meaning, value and purpose. Encouraging and empowering actors at all layers of the system to engage in these processes of meaning-making and exploration of possible futures is necessary, as Freire (2004, 2) explains: 'As an ontological need, hope needs practice in order to become historical concreteness. That is why there is no hope in sheer hopefulness. The hoped-for is not attained by dint of raw hoping. Just to hope is to hope in vain.'

Notes

1. Belgium (Flanders), Denmark, France, Norway and Sweden.
2. This distinction clearly shows in historical as well as in recent debates on early childhood, as Gill McGillivray demonstrates in her contribution to this issue.

3. In Germany, for example, early childhood curricula have been introduced at state level in recent years only. Some of them represent clear examples of the phenomenon discussed above: educational underachievement of groups of children growing up under precarious conditions is identified as a 'problem' which is to be 'solved' through application of effective methodology provided by 'science', and applied by 'skilled' practitioners.

4. For a detailed analysis of how even supposedly holistic and open frameworks can contribute to producing this particular neo-liberal version of the universal child, see Iris Duhn's excellent critique of Te Whāriki, the New Zealand early childhood curriculum (Duhn 2006).

5. For an extended critique of this particular paradigm, in which research knowledge is comprised of a scientific 'grasp of the object', see Schwandt (2004) and Taylor (2002).

6. I am referring to recent and ongoing studies, carried out in various contexts: Carmen Dalli's work on professional ethics and identities in New Zealand (Dalli 2003); first findings of the international 'Day in the Life of an Early Years Practitioner' project, presented at the 2007 annual conference of EECERA; 'Bildung: elementar', a participatory curriculum development project in Germany (Urban 2005a; Urban and Murray 2005); and an international study on 'Strategies for Change' in ECEC systems (Urban 2007).

7. Bourdieu explains 'habitus' as 'lex insita'(immanent law) (1977, 81), a system of dispositions through which certain behaviour is considered 'natural' among a community. These dispositions are constantly but unwittingly produced and reproduced by the members of the community: 'actions and works are the product of a *modus operandi* of which he [the member; M.U.] is not the producer and has no conscious mastery, they contain an 'objective intention' … which always outruns his conscious intentions' (Bourdieu 1977, 79).

8. Besides early childhood education, there are other examples of systems whose dynamics are highly sensitive to their initial conditions but seem to develop in unpredictable ways. The so-called butterfly effect is one of them. In mathematics, the behaviour of these systems is referred to as *deterministic chaos*.

9. Obviously, this can be said of any professional practice that constitutes interactions with fellow human beings. There is a clear distinction, though, from technical practice, where a distinct action (e.g. pushing the 'right' button) produces a predictable result.

10. A notion that has been adopted, twenty years later, by Michel Vandenbroeck (1999, 30) as he writes about fostering children's identities in rapidly changing societies.

11. I am using the term *training* reluctantly, and only because it is how education, preparation and continuous learning of early childhood practitioners are usually referred to. *Training*, as a particular concept of learning through instruction, repetitive practice, etc., is about acquiring skills to apply and deliver technologies. *Training* is about being taught how to do things right. Its connotations contradict the very essence of professional and educational practice as a transformative practice of mutual dependence and respect, co-construction and shared meaning making between human beings.

12. Glenda MacNaughton, in her 2005 book titled *Doing Foucault in Early Childhood Studies*, explains that connecting the 'critical' to reflection is about directing the attention away from the individual and towards 'the operation and effects of power relationships *between* people'. She describes *critical reflection* as 'the process of questioning how power operates in the process of teaching and learning and then using that knowledge to transform oppressive or inequitable teaching and learning processes' (7). MacNaughton provides excellent examples of *critical questions* for early childhood practitioners (MacNaughton 2003). My concern is, though, that this concept of critical reflection can unintentionally carry a risk of individualising the responsibility for developing critically reflective practice, thus imposing an enormous pressure on the individual practitioner.

References

Biesta, G. 2007. Why "what works" won't work: Evidence-based practice and the democratic deficit in educational research. *Educational Theory* 57, no. 1: 1–22.

Bildung: elementar. 2007. Bildung: elementar. http://www.bildung-elementar.de/.

Bourdieu, P. 1977. *Outline of a theory of practice.* Cambridge: Cambridge University Press.

Centre for Early Childhood Development and Education. 2006. *Síolta.* http://www.siolta.ie/about.php.

Dahlberg, G., and P. Moss. 2005. *Ethics and politics in early childhood education.* London and New York: RoutledgeFalmer.

Dahlberg, G., P. Moss, and A. Pence. 1999. *Beyond quality in early childhood education and care. Postmodern perspectives.* London: Falmer.

————. 2007. *Beyond quality in early childhood education and care: Languages of evaluation,* 2nd ed. New York: Routledge.

Dalli, C. 2003. Professionalism in early childhood practice: Thinking through the debates. Paper presented at the 13th annual conference of EECERA at the University of Strathclyde, September 3–6, in Glasgow.

————. 2005. The New Zealand story of EC professionalisation. Paper presented at the International Conference on Change Agents in Early Childhood Education and Care, EC+P, Early Childhood and Profession at the International Centre for Research, Studies and Development, Martin-Luther-University, in Halle-Wittenberg, Germany, 19–20 April 2005.

Department for Children, Schools and Families. 2007. Workforce Reform. http://www.everychildmatters.gov.uk/deliveringservices/workforcereform/.

Department for Education and Skills (DfES). 2004. *Every child matters: Change for children.* London: DfES.

————. 2005. *Children's workforce strategy. A strategy to build a world-class workforce for children and young people.* London: DfES.

————. 2006. *Children's workforce strategy: The government's response to the consultation.* London: DfES.

Duhn, I. 2006. The making of global citizens: Traces of cosmopolitanism in the New Zealand early childhood curriculum, Te Whāriki. *Contemporary Issues in Early Childhood* 7, no. 3: 191–202.

European Commission Network on Childcare and Other Measures to Reconcile Employment and Family Responsibilities. 1996. *Quality targets in services for young children.* Brussels: European Commission.

Foucault, M. 1972. *The archeology of knowledge.* New York: Pantheon.

Freire, P. 2000. *Pedagogy of the oppressed,* 30th anniversary ed. New York: Continuum.

————. 2004. *Pedagogy of hope. Reliving pedagogy of the oppressed.* London: Continuum.

Freire, P., and A.M.A. Freire. 1997. *Pedagogy of the heart.* New York: Continuum.

Gadamer, H.G. 1960. *Wahrheit und Methode: Grundzüge einer philosophischen Hermeneutik.* Tübingen: Mohr.

Gadamer, H.G., J. Weinsheimer, and D.G. Marshall. 2004. *Truth and method,* 2nd, rev. ed., translation revised by Joel Weinsheimer and Donald G. Marshall. London and New York: Continuum.

Garrison, J. 1996. A Deweyean theory of democratic listening. *Educational Theory* 46, no. 4: 429–51.

Larson, M.S. 1977. *The rise of professionalism: A sociological analysis.* Berkeley: University of California Press.

MacNaughton, G. 2003. *Shaping early childhood. Learners, curriculum and contexts.* Maidenhead: Open University Press.

————. 2005. *Doing Foucault in early childhood studies: Applying poststructural ideas.* London: Routledge.

McCann, C. 2006. *Zoli.* London: Weidenfeld & Nicholson.

Mead, M. 1978. *Culture and commitment. The new relationships between the generations in the 1970s.* New York: Columbia University Press.

Ministry of Education. 2007. Centres of innovation. http://www.minedu.govt.nz/index.cfm?layout=document&documentid=10688&indexid=8303&indexparentid=10945.

Murray, C. 2006. The conceptualisation of diversity and equality in early childhood care and education. Unpublished MSc thesis, University College Dublin.

Murray, C., and A. O'Doherty. 2001. *Éist. Respecting diversity in early childhood care, education and training.* Dublin: Pavee Point.

Oberhuemer, P. 2005. Conceptualising the early childhood pedagogue: Policy approaches and issues of professionalism. *European Early Childhood Education Research Journal* 13, no. 1: 5–16.

Oberhuemer, P., and M. Ulich. 1997. *Working with young children in Europe: Provision and staff – training.* London: Paul Chapman.

Office of the Minister for Children. 2006. *Diversity and equality guidelines for childcare providers.* Dublin: The Stationery Office.

Oliver, M., and G. Conole. 2003. Evidence-based practice in e-learning and higher education: Can we and should we? *Research Papers in Education* 18, no. 4: 385–97.

Organization for Economic Co-operation and Development (OECD). 2001. *Starting strong. Early childhood education and care.* Paris: OECD.

————. 2004. *OECD thematic review of early childhood education and care policy in Ireland.* Dublin: The Stationery Office.

————. 2006. *Starting strong II. Early childhood education and care.* Paris: OECD.

Parsons, T. 1951. *The social system.* Glencoe, IL: Free Press.

————. 1968. Professions. In *International encyclopaedia of the social sciences,* vol. 12, ed. D.L. Sills, and R.K. Merton, 536–47. New York: Macmillan.

Peeters, J. 2005. Flanders: Improving inclusion policies and services. In *Learning with other countries: International models of early education and care,* 36–39. London: National Day Care Trust.

Pence, A.R., and P. Moss. 1994. *Valuing quality in early childhood services: New approaches to defining quality.* London: P. Chapman.

Preissing, C., ed. 2003. *Qualität im Situationsansatz: Qualitätskriterien und Materialien für die Qualitätsentwicklung in Kindertageseinrichtungen,* [Quality in contextually appropriate practice: quality criteria and resources for developing quality in early childhood services.] 1st ed. Weinheim und Basel: Beltz.

Rinaldi, C. 2005. *In dialogue with Reggio Emilia: Listening, researching, and learning.* London and New York: Routledge.

Schön, D.A. 1983. *The reflective practitioner. How professionals think in action.* New York: Basic Books.

Schwandt, T.A. 2004. Hermeneutics: A poetics of inquiry versus a methodology for research. In *Educational research: Difference and diversity,* ed. H. Piper, and I. Stronach, 31–44. Aldershot: Ashgate.

Siraj-Blatchford, I., and K. Sylva. 2004. Researching pedagogy in English pre-schools. *British Educational Research Journal* 30, no. 5: 713–39.

Siraj-Blatchford, I., K. Sylva, and S. Muttock. 2002. *Researching effective pedagogy in the early years.* London: Department for Education and Skills.

Taylor, C. 1995. *Philosophical arguments.* Cambridge, MA: Harvard University Press.

————. 2002. Gadamer on the human sciences. In *The Cambridge companion to Gadamer,* ed. R.J. Dostal, 126–42. Cambridge: Cambridge University Press.

Urban, M. 2003. From standardized quality towards "good enough" practice: A dialogic approach to evaluation and quality development in early childhood settings. Paper presented at the European Early Childhood Education Research Association (13th Annual Conference), at the University of Strathclyde, in Glasgow, 3–6 September 2003.

————. 2005a. Dealing with uncertainty. Paper presented at the European Early Childhood Education Research Association (15th Annual Conference), at St. Patrick's College, in Dublin, 31 August–3 September 2005.

————. 2005b. Quality, autonomy and the profession. In *Questions of quality,* ed. H. Schonfeld, S. O'Brien, and T. Walsh. Dublin: Centre for Early Childhood Development and Education.

————. 2006. *Strategies for change. Gesellschafts- und fachpolitische Strategien zur Reform des Systems frühkindlicher Bildung. Expertise für das Forum Frühkindliche Bildung der Bertelsmann Stiftung.* [Socio-political and professional strategies for reforming systems of early childhood education. Expert report to the early childhood education forum, Bertelsmann Foundation.] Halle: Martin-Luther-Universität.

————. 2007. Strategies for change: Reflections from a systemic, comparative research project. In *A decade of reflection. Early childhood care and education in Ireland: 1996–2006,* ed. N. Hayes, and S. Bradley, 44–64. Dublin: Centre for Social and Educational Research.

Urban, M., N. Huhn, and M. Schaaf. 2004. *Bildung: Elementar. Bildung als Programm für Kindertageseinrichtungen in Sachsen-Anhalt. Integrierter Abschlußbericht.* [The Bildung: Elementar Curriculum. Integrated final report.] Halle: Martin-Luther-Universität Halle-Wittenberg.

Urban, M., and C. Murray. 2005. Changing habit(u)s. Perspectives on change, resistance and professional development. Paper presented at the international conference 'Honoring the Child, Honoring Equity 5: Reconsidering Rights and Relationship', at the Centre for Equity and Innovation in Early Childhood, University of Melbourne, 16–19 November 2005 in Melbourne, Australia.

Vandenbroeck, M. 1999. *The view of the Yeti. Bringing up children in the spirit of self-awareness and kindredship.* The Hague: Bernard van Leer Foundation.

Winnicott, D.W. 1987. *The child, the family and the outside world.* Cambridge: Perseus.

Woodhead, M. 1996. *In search of the rainbow. Pathways to quality in large-scale programmes for young disadvantaged children.* The Hague: Bernhard van Leer Foundation.

Towards professionalism in early childhood practicum supervision – a personal journey

Yael Dayan

The Hebrew University of Jerusalem, Israel

ABSTRACT: The role of a practicum supervisor of early childhood students has received limited research attention in discussions of professional practice in this field. This article discusses four phases in the author's personal journey towards professionalism in this role. The phases reflect an ongoing research-practice cycle: Phase 1 involved a research study on the role perception of the early childhood practicum supervisor; the second phase corresponded to the implementation of findings from Phase 1 and involved a transition from a behaviourist approach to a humanistic-democratic approach in supervising, and the emergence of further research questions. The third phase comprised a research study on children's perspectives on early childhood teacher education and training; and the fourth phase included an attempt to facilitate the participation of children in the supervising process. The article shows how each of these phases has contributed to a framework for examining and enhancing the practicum supervisory process on the basis of humanistic-democratic values.

RÉSUMÉ: Le rôle du superviseur des pratiques d'étudiants en formation dans le champ de la petite enfance a peu suscité l'attention des chercheurs dans la discussion des pratiques professionnelles dans ce domaine. Cet article décrit les quatre étapes du parcours personnel de l'auteur vers le professionnalisme à travers ce rôle. Ces étapes reflètent un processus recherche - pratique en cours: la première étape repose sur une étude de la perception du rôle du superviseur des pratiques préscolaires; la deuxième étape correspond à la mise en œuvre de résultats de la première et au passage d'une approche behavioriste à une approche démocratique - humaniste de la supervision, et amène de nouvelles questions de recherche. La troisième étape comprend une étude des points de vue des enfants dans la formation des enseignants du préscolaire ; et la quatrième étape inclut une tentative pour faciliter la participation des enfants dans le processus de supervision. L'article montre comment chacune de ces étapes a contribué à la création d'un cadre permettant l'analyse et la mise en évidence du processus de supervision des pratiques sur la base de valeurs démocratiques et humanistes.

ZUSAMMENFASSUNG: Die Rolle der Praxisanleiterin von Studierenden der Frühpädagogik wurde in der Professionsforschung und der Fachdiskussion zur Professionalisierung bisher nur unzureichend beachtet. Der vorliegende Beitrag erörtert vier Phasen einer persönlichen Reise der Autorin hin zur Professionalität in dieser Rolle. Sie reflektieren Stationen in einem kontinuierlichen Praxis-Forschungs-Zyklus: Phase eins bestand in einer Forschungsstudie zur Rollenwahrnehmung von Praxisanleiterinnen in der Frühpädagogik; die zweite Phase entsprach der Umsetzung von Ergebnissen aus der ersten; sie war verbunden mit der Weiterentwicklung von einem behavioristischen zu einem humanistisch-demokratischen Ansatz in der Anleitung und der damit verbunden Entstehung weiterer Forschungsfragen. Die dritte Phase umfasste eine Studie zu Perspektiven von Kindern auf die Ausbildung von

Frühpädagoginnen; sie mündete in die vierte Phase, nämlich dem Versuch, die Beteiligung von Kindern am Anleitungsprozess zu ermöglichen. Der Artikel zeigt auf, wie jede dieser Phasen zur Entwicklung eines Rahmens zur Untersuchung und Weiterentwicklung des Prozesses von Praxisanleitung auf der Grundlage humanistisch-demokratischer Werte beigetragen hat.

RESUMEN: El rol del supervisor del período de práctica de estudiantes de educación pre-escolar ha recibido escasa atención en las discusiones acerca de la práctica profesional en esta área. Este artículo trata cuatro etapas en la travesía personal de la autora hacia el profesionalismo en el cumplimiento de este rol. Las etapas reflejan un ciclo continuo investigación- práctica: la primera etapa consiste de un estudio investigativo acerca de cómo percibe la supervisora pre-escolar su rol; la segunda etapa concuerda con la implementación de los resultados de la primera e incluye una transición desde el enfoque conductista hacia un enfoque humanista-democrático de la supervisión, junto con el surgimiento de nuevos temas de investigación. La tercera etapa consiste de un estudio investigativo acerca de la perspectiva infantil sobre la preparación y el entrenamiento de la educadora pre-escolar; la cuarta incluye un intento de facilitar la participación de los niños en el proceso de supervisión. El artículo muestra cómo cada una de estas etapas contribuyó a la creación de un marco de análisis y mejoramiento del proceso de supervisión del período de práctica, basándose en valores humanistas-democráticos.

This article describes my professional development as an early childhood teacher educator, and focuses on my role as a practicum supervisor. My professional development can be defined as a search for the best way to accompany and facilitate students in their own journey towards becoming early childhood professionals. Using insights from two research projects and reflections on my attempts to apply them in my practice, I propose a framework for examining and enhancing the practicum supervisory process in order that this may be transformed from one based on behaviouristic principles to one that forefronts humanistic-democratic values.

The context

My perceptions of my profession have evolved from two main sources: first, as a teacher educator at the David Yellin Teacher's College in Jerusalem, my goal is to prepare students to become professional teachers; second, as a faculty member in the Graduate Program in Early Childhood Education at the Hebrew University of Jerusalem, I am influenced by the university's mandate to conduct research. My perceptions of myself as a professional, as presented in this article, are thus constructed by the mutual influence of research and practice in both contexts. My practice as a practicum supervisor has raised questions that have stimulated several lines of research. The research findings have led me to consider new approaches and attitudes for the practice of teacher education and, in particular, practicum supervision. This practice–research cycle has become an ongoing activity that I consider to be the essence of my professionalism in this role. Both elements of the cycle (research and practice) are strongly influenced by a set of evolving values and principles, which both inform and are informed by the research–practice cycle. These values can be described as humanistic-democratic and are consistent with the notion of 'democratic professionalism' as described by Oberhuemer (2005): 'a concept based on participatory relationships and alliances' (13).

Early childhood teacher education

Early childhood teacher education has been conceptualised as mastery of a particular set of knowledge and skills that pre-service teachers should learn (Spodek and Saracho 1990; Bowman, Donovan, and Burns 2001; Hyson 2003; Ryan and Grieshaber 2005). The knowledge and skills usually contain a similar list of subjects such as child development, working with families and curriculum (McCarthy 1990; Ryan and Grieshaber 2005). This commonality of perspectives (Cannella 1997) has constructed the field of early childhood teacher training and preparation.

Whereas there is widespread agreement that teachers' education and training are important for achieving a higher quality of early childhood programmes, it is difficult to compare conclusions from different studies that have explored this issue (Early et al. 2006). Furthermore, while the relationship between early childhood teacher education and the quality of educare has been studied and documented (Bowman, Donovan, and Burns 2001), much less is known about the actual preparation of teachers, and which specific components in the training programme (e.g. the nature of the learning process; or the content of the education programme) might have the most influence on best practice (Early et al. 2006).

One of the key components of early childhood teacher preparation, which lacks documented practical or theoretical knowledge about best practice, is the domain of practicum and student supervision. In practicum situations, students engage in a developmental process of observing and experimenting with the practice of working with children, learning about skills, knowledge, philosophies and attitudes during their practica in preschool settings. While most teacher education programmes address the roles and expectations of practicum students, there is a need to explore the roles of the other key players, such as the cooperating teacher and the college/university supervisor (Walkington 2005). Few teacher education programmes examine the complexity of the supervisor's role (Slick 1998) and there is even less literature about the character, quality, and definition of this role. The few references to the supervisory roles generally allude to problems and difficulties, with few attempts at analysis and/or recommendations. This gap in the literature is surprising given the widely held assumption that the practicum is such an essential component of early childhood teacher preparation programmes.

Practicum supervision as a profession

The concept of professionalism has been used in a variety of ways and is subject to continual alterations (Krejsler 2005). According to commonly accepted characteristics of professionalism (e.g. Katz 1988; Spodek and Saracho 1990), practicum supervision in itself would not qualify as a profession because it lacks some specific characteristics. For example, there is no special training programme for supervisors or 'protracted period of preparation in university study' (Spodek and Saracho 1990, 60).

Usually, practicum supervisors are former teachers and, as such, their professional background relates to teaching children. Yet, as Caruso and Fawcett (1986) have shown, qualification for work with children is not necessarily a guarantee of ability to work with adults.

Given that the practicum supervisory role is not well defined by educational institutions, and that new supervisors receive insufficient instruction in their duties, supervisors tend to adopt their own individual methods, based on personal opinions, experiences and intuitions.

Another characteristic of professionalism is the theoretical knowledge base and skills needed for practice (Katz 1988; Spodek and Saracho 1990). It is not clear whether we can identify the body of knowledge that may be used to form a consensus regarding a definition of professional practicum supervision. My experience as a practicum supervisor has led me to agree with Sockett (1993), that 'we have no common epistemology on which professional expertise and knowledge can be based' (92). We lack a clear theory of practicum supervision as a basis for action within the supervisory relationship and research is one of the means to develop a theory of supervision (Strauss and Corbin 1990). In its absence, the role of practicum supervisor tends to be enacted on the basis of common sense and intuition.

Over the years, my experience and subsequent research have led me to identify three elements that have become an important part of my working definition of a professional practicum supervisor. These elements have guided my practice and indeed have become central to my own goals for development as a professional. These elements are:

(1) *Ongoing reflection on one's actions*: Professionals need to engage in an ongoing process of examining their own acts; raising difficult questions; doubting assumptions and conceptions and continuously learning (Phelps 2006). They recognise that the knowledge base which informs professional action is contestable (Oberhuemer 2005).

(2) *Promoting democratic relationships*: Professionalism should be understood as an attempt to decrease power relations between the supervisor and the students, and between students and children, and to promote democratic relationships in what is usually an undemocratic educational system. Participation and collaboration are means of developing and fostering a democratic personality and a democratic system (Oberhuemer 2005; Biesta 2007). The meaning of being professional in practicum supervision is to find the best way in which students, teachers and supervisors can engage in a democratic process of deliberation and discussion, aimed at advancing professionalism in early childhood education.

(3) *Constructing new knowledge for practice*: Professionals engage in a process of constructing new knowledge and applying it to practice. Understanding the complexity of professional knowledge and practice is an important step for all practitioners wishing to improve the quality of their practice. Choi-wa Dora (2006) has suggested that the issues of complexity can be approached from two perspectives: the source of the knowledge base and the context of knowledge use. For a practicum supervisor this means, for example, understanding the principles of a humanistic-democratic approach and the transformation of these principles to practicum supervision in the early childhood preschool context.

In the rest of this article I discuss two studies that have helped me identify these three elements. I also discuss how my reflections on these studies impacted my journey towards professionalism in my role as a practicum supervisor. I think of this journey as having four phases that evolved from an initial stage of practice. These phases are listed in the next section and each is elaborated on in subsequent sections.

Four phases in the evolution of my professionalism as a practicum supervisor

The four phases below reflect my development as a practicum supervisor over the last decade.

Phase 1. A research study on the role perception of the early childhood supervisor (my doctoral thesis);

Phase 2. Applying the findings from my doctoral research to my practice: this involved a transition from a behaviourist to a humanistic-democratic approach in supervising early childhood students, and the emergence of further research questions;

Phase 3. A research study on children's perspectives on early childhood teacher education and training; and

Phase 4. Applying the findings to practice: These findings led to an attempt to facilitate the participation of children in the supervising process.

In the rest of this article I discuss each of these phases and show how they have contributed to a framework for examining and enhancing the practicum supervisory process on the basis of humanistic-democratic values.

Phase 1. A research study of the role perception of the early childhood supervisor

As a novice practicum supervisor, many years ago, I worked within the framework of a lack of 'common epistemology' (Sockett 1993), as described above. There was no clear theory of supervision as a base for action, and my perception of the role was based mostly on common sense and intuition.

In order to improve my understanding and practice of my role as a supervisor, I conducted a study (Dayan 1999) aimed at examining, describing and analysing how practicum supervisors perceive their role, how they act and behave during their visit in the preschool, how they tutor their students, and the essential content and methods of the supervision sessions. My main research question was: How do practicum supervisors of students in early childhood settings perceive their role?

Research methods

The study followed the format of a descriptive multiple-case study (Yin 1993). The participants were six practicum supervisors from five different teachers' colleges in Israel. Data-gathering methods included observations and interviews. The data were gathered over the course of one school year. Each supervisor was observed for four working days. In total, I visited 40 preschools. During each of those visits, I observed the supervisor and followed up the observation period with an interview. The observation was focused entirely on the supervisor. It included the supervisor's entire stay at the location, from the moment of entry until her departure. The observation procedure included a detailed audio-taped description of the supervisor's actions. In general, whenever the supervisor talked to the student, the conversation was entirely taped. The process of data analysis in this research was based mainly on the proposals of Strauss and Corbin (1990) for categorical analysis.

Research findings – types of practicum supervisors

From the analysis it was clear that the practicum supervisor's visit to the preschool could be divided into three main stages: (i) wandering around the setting; (ii) observation of student's activity; and (iii) supervisory conference. Additionally, the analysis revealed that differences among the supervisors, as they emerged in the three stages of the preschool visit, could be conceptualised in terms of three principal types of supervision: *activity-oriented*; *child-oriented*; and *student-oriented*. The next three sections of this article elaborate on each of these types.

The *activity-oriented* practicum supervisor

The activity-oriented practicum supervisor perceived supervision mainly in the context of performing activities with the children in the preschool. During her visit to the preschool the supervisor expected the student to function as a teacher responsible for the daily schedule and activities of the setting. The student's role was seen to be that of learning the functions of the preschool teacher; the role of the supervisor was to transmit knowledge about the correct way of performing these functions. Supervision therefore consisted mainly of giving advice, correcting, giving positive feedback or helping the student to interpret the meaning of her actions. The phase of 'wandering around the setting' was devoted to evaluating the student's performance. Thus the supervisor observed and did not interfere in the activities of the children. She also observed the scheduling – that is, how the student arranged the order of activities and the materials necessary for their performance.

With this type of supervisor, the conference with the student focused mainly on the goals of the activity, the student's considerations in choosing an activity, and the ways in which the activity was implemented. The main consideration in determining the subject of the conference was the evaluation of the student's performance: the conversation focused on issues that needed improvement. The main characteristic of the 'activity-oriented' type conference was 'elicitation'. This meant that the supervisor introduced the subject of the conference and remained responsible for the course of the conversation around the subject. In general the supervisor asked the questions and the student replied (Blum-Kulka and Snow 1992).

The *child-oriented* practicum supervisor

The child-oriented supervisor performed her role in the context of activities with children. The supervision meetings were perceived as a mutual learning experience, for the supervisor and the student, concerning the children and the ways that the student related to the children's activities. The purpose of supervision was to enhance the student's ability to understand children, and to develop a special sensitivity towards them. The supervisor viewed the facilitation of change in the thinking and attitudes of the student as one of the elements of the supervision. Reflection on the students' activities was encouraged, as was the development of a deeper awareness of their reactions to the children with whom they worked. A greater involvement in both child- and adult-initiated activities, and sensitivity to the individual needs of the child, were expected by this type of supervisor. The period of 'wandering around the setting' was devoted to learning: about the preschool, the children, and the student.

The supervision conference, dubbed 'peer conversation', focused mainly on the children's behaviour during the activities and on the subsequent reactions of the student. The student and the supervisor acquired insight into the children together. The main characteristic of the 'child-oriented' type conference was 'collaboration'. In the collaboration mode the supervisor and the student both contributed to the course of the conversation. They listened and reacted to one another's discourse, introducing commentary and details in order to clarify (Blum-Kulka and Snow 1992). Both the supervisor and the student introduced new subjects to the dialogue.

The *student-oriented* practicum supervisor

The student-oriented supervisor defined her role as a variety of interactive relations with the student, and aimed to relate to the student on a basis of equality. The declared goal was to train the student to acquire a sense of self-worth while fostering attentiveness to the needs of the children. The principal aim of the role of supervisor was to enhance the students' awareness of their behaviour and of their personal characteristics. The supervisor saw the student as a mature person capable of making intelligent choices regarding suitable methods. Thus, she expected that the student would make independent choices as to what was an appropriate teaching strategy. She assumed that the student would independently acquaint herself with the different children, their special needs and with the programmes which were most appropriate for each of them. The period of 'wandering around the setting' was characterised mainly by interchanges between the supervisor and the student. The supervisor did not interact with the children. She assumes that by placing the student at the centre, and conversing with the student about herself, her work, and her feelings, the importance of the child-oriented approach would be demonstrated. This, in the opinion of the practicum supervisor, was more important than any activity that the student might perform. Observation of activities was thus less important during the visit.

The supervision conference focused mainly on the student. Guidelines for conducting the conference related primarily to better acquaintance with the student and her personality. The main element in a conference with a 'student-oriented' supervisor was 'collaboration'.

Having identified these three types of practicum supervision, one of the conclusions of my study (Dayan 1999) was that the identification of different practicum supervisory types opens up new perspectives on supervision of early childhood students during their practica and contributes to a clearer definition of the supervisor's role in this task. I suggested that this typology can assist practicum supervisors in reflecting on their perception of their professional role especially at the beginning of their supervisory careers.

Phase 2. Applying the research findings to practice: from a behaviourist to a humanistic-democratic approach to supervising early childhood students

Throughout my doctoral research I reflected on my own style of practicum supervision and asked myself which supervisory type I demonstrated, questioning the relevance of my research findings to my particular contexts and circumstances (Davis 2007). When I started to supervise students, my guidelines were to visit the student, observe her while she was involved in an activity with children, and then discuss with her what was 'good' and what she should improve. In my research, I argued that this style of conducting practicum supervision revealed a behaviourist approach and I termed the supervisor who used this approach the 'activity-oriented type'.

In my own practice, I found the behaviouristic approach philosophically problematic and I sought to develop a practice more founded on the principles of a humanistic-democratic approach which could be viewed as a combination of 'student-oriented type' and 'child-oriented type' of supervision. I wanted to explore how I could utilise the grounded theory I had developed through my doctoral research in order to practice in a manner more consistent with my humanistic-democratic belief system. The result was a conceptual and practical framework for examining and enhancing the supervisory process based on the following premises:

(1) Inherent in the role of practicum supervisor are two educational approaches. The first is an approach to working with children, and the second is an approach to working with adult students.
(2) The supervisor's approach to working with children, and her approach to working with students, should be examined for coherence and consistency.

(3) The most commonly favoured approach to working with children is a child-centred humanist democratic approach, and the predominant approach in working with students is behaviourist.
(4) The inconsistency of the approaches used with children and with students hampers the student's learning.
(5) It is possible to bridge these approaches through a different model of student practicum supervision.

Implicit in this framework is the notion that increased awareness of the supervisor's approach to working with students and with children, and enhancing the consistency between those approaches, can lead to significant improvement in the practice learning of students. Furthermore, increased awareness will provide supervisors with a framework for examining and reflecting on their practice. Each of the premises in my framework is explored more fully in the rest of this section.

Examining the practicum supervisor's educational approach to working with children

I argue that the facilitation of students' adoption of a child-centred approach is fundamental to supervision in early childhood education. This means 'that education should be oriented towards children's interests, needs and developmental growth and informed by an understanding of child development' (Burman 1994, 164). The underlying values of such an approach are essentially humanistic-democratic: They imply that in working with students, the practicum supervisor should emphasise:

- the significance of relating to children as independent human beings who have their own ideas, thoughts, and feelings which students need to respect;
- the need to have trust in the child's ability to take responsibility for his/her learning;
- the importance of cultivating the child's autonomy;
- the value of enabling children to choose activities according to their individual interests;
- the recognition of individual differences between children, as well as the uniqueness of each child.

Examining the supervisor's educational approach in supervising early childhood students

While there may be a recent trend to more student-centred approaches, the predominant approach in most teacher education programmes in colleges and universities is behaviourist-authoritative: 'professing' and 'testing' are the key strategies employed (Lunenberg and Korthagen 2003). In this context, teacher educators do not always 'teach as they preach' (29). They often use a cultural transmission model that allows them to transmit knowledge, information, and techniques, and they use this model to teach concepts in early childhood that are based on romanticism or progressivism. Usually students are expected to acquire domains of knowledge, specific skills and attitudes. Thus, students acquire an understanding of how they should teach using an ideology that they may understand cognitively, but have not experienced personally (Burts and Buchanan 1998). It is an educational environment that is focused on the reproduction of the subject matter of the curriculum – an environment focused on filling empty vessels instead of one that allows students to respond in their own unique ways to the learning opportunities provided (Biesta 2007).

My study on the role perception of the early childhood practicum supervisor showed that the supervisor's visits in the preschool are often constructed by her more as an assessment visit than for guidance purposes, and there is a tendency to focus on the student's performance and competence. The supervisor evaluates the student's abilities and level of knowledge. In general, supervisors do not encourage independent initiatives. Rather, they expect students to follow their guidelines.

By contrast, applying humanist-democratic principles to the supervision of students would mean that the practicum supervisor would focus on the three aims of:

(1) cultivating the students' sense of responsibility for their own learning and professional growth;
(2) strengthening the students' child-centred approach; and
(3) encouraging the students' autonomy.

I elaborate on each of these three aims in the rest of this section.

Aim 1: Cultivating the student's sense of responsibility for his/her own learning and professional growth

To implement this aim, the supervisor would guide the students in defining a topic for observing and learning according to their needs, interests and level of knowledge, so they can learn and discuss it together during the supervisor's visit. This strategy encourages students to think about their concerns and take responsibility for their own learning process. By choosing topics, students can better understand their own interests, learning styles and the way they interact with children. Learning then occurs according to the student's domains of interest and not according to the supervisor's subject knowledge, or any other external curriculum; this would be consistent with a student-centred approach. This approach also emphasises the meeting of the individual learning needs of students, and the provision of challenge and support to meet these needs. This would enable learning about a whole spectrum of teacher tasks. In each visit the student could define a different topic such as: children's behaviour; organising the curriculum; choosing appropriate activities; parent involvement; or personal issues like self-confidence and professional development. Choosing a topic for learning that emerges from the practicum experience facilitates integration across theoretical domains and subject-matter areas. As the student is responsible for choosing a topic for learning, the supervisor is not obliged to define a set list of learning topics. The supervisor can thus be much more attentive and sensitive to the students' learning requests, and will have many opportunities to learn about issues concerning students en route to becoming professionals. This strategy modifies the supervisor's role and has the potential of making it much more interesting and challenging.

Aim 2: Strengthening the students' child-centred approach

As stated previously, during supervisory visits, the student is usually observed while organising an activity with a group of children, followed by a discussion about the quality of her/his performance. This procedure emphasises an activity-centred approach (Dayan 1999). Supervision should aim at improving the student's capacity to learn about children rather than focusing exclusively on developing teaching performance. It is important, therefore, to move from an activity-centred approach to a child-centred approach. One strategy that shifts the focus from activity to child is to ask the student to choose a child that she would like to learn more about, and get to know better.

I see this strategy as having five stages:

(i) The student and supervisor engage in a joint observation for approximately ten minutes.

(ii) They share a description of the observation and construct a narrative of the child's behaviour during the observation time.

(iii) They analyse the narrative. The student chooses the criteria of analysis, which could be, for example, domains of development, categories of temperament, or social competences.

(iv) They summarise the knowledge collected on the child from the description of the observation, analysis and additional information known from previous experience. At this stage the cooperating teacher is invited to contribute other details about the child that are unknown to the student.

(v) The student and the practicum supervisor make plans for the child, based on the learning that has occurred.

This process enables the construction of the student's knowledge base as an early childhood teacher. The student is able to attain a deeper knowledge of the child and the child's context. The supervisor can contribute from theoretical knowledge and from her experience. This mutual sharing of knowledge and ideas constructs a new knowledge which is specific to an individual child but also demonstrates the idea of constructing a knowledge base as a general approach to education (Ott, Zeichner, and Price 1990). The last stage in this process enables the student to understand and implement her knowledge and skills in working with the child. This process integrates universal knowledge of child development and the uniqueness of this child, and combines theoretical principles of working with children and the capacity to work with this child in this context. This process is also an opportunity for both the supervisor and the student to benefit from the relationship, and to learn by exchange of knowledge, ideas, and strategies. Conversations that are concerned with helping children are respectful and caring. Professionalism is thus mirrored in teacher talk that seeks solutions (Phelps 2006).

There can be additional benefits when supervisor and student observe the child together and follow this observation with discussion, including:

- The focus of the learning process is the child; this demonstrates directly the meaning of a child-centred approach.
- It demonstrates the importance of observation as a means of knowing the child and utilising this knowledge in planning an appropriate programme.
- It enables a common basis for analysing the information which was collected during the observation.
- It fosters an enquiring stance towards working with young children.
- It supports the uniqueness of each child, recognising that children are best understood in their context.
- It doubles the information gathered and enables two points of view in understanding the child. The interpretations of the child's behaviour are discussed from both the perspective of the student as an 'insider' and that of the supervisor as 'outsider'.
- It gives the student an opportunity to express her 'voice' as equal to the supervisor's voice.

- It demonstrates to the student how to construct a theory of practice based on, for example, a theory of development.
- It constructs a deeper understanding of what can be done in a given situation and what to take into account in decisions on actions that need to be taken.
- It supports the student's hypotheses about the learning process as she tries to act according to the agreements reached during their discussions.
- It involves the supervisor, who is usually an outsider, in the daily life of the children.
- It minimises student anxiety by focusing on the child, thus enabling a positive learning climate and more student involvement in the learning experience.
- It fosters the triadic relationship and partnership between the student, the cooperating teacher, and the supervisor, thus modelling and facilitating teamwork.

Aim 3: Encouraging the student's autonomy

The behaviourist approach, by focusing on how external behaviour comes under environmental control, ignores both the inner world and urges toward independence (Crain 1992). According to the behaviourist approach, for students to learn and acquire knowledge, they must be given reinforcements. Studies show that when students are not generally exposed to other patterns of relationships, they adopt the authoritative models they experience and their roles within it (Van Dijk 1997). Therefore, when the supervisor visits the students, students are so used to being assessed and judged that they often expect to hear whether they are 'good' or 'bad', often asking for an evaluation. This kind of relationship fosters the student's dependence on a knowledgeable outsider, instead of supporting autonomy and encouraging self-evaluation.

In order to foster learning rather than evaluating the student's performance, the supervisor and the student can jointly define a list of criteria for assessment of the activity. For example, they would list the criteria for assessing the student's performance in the circle time or in interaction with the child. In this way the student acquires a tool for independent self-evaluation which can be used whenever the student wants to evaluate her/his performance.

This strategy, together with the strategy of choosing a learning topic, can encourage the student's autonomy and decrease dependence and reliance. Students are referred to as subjects. Subjectivity refers to the individual as a person who is able to act, who is in control of her or his life and who is able to take responsibility for their own deeds and actions (Biesta 2007).

The description of a supervisor's role presented in this section is one example which demonstrates a way of dealing with the contradiction which, on the one hand advocates for a democratic-humanistic approach in working with children, and on the other hand deals with students from a behaviourist-authoritative stance. This example presents the supervisor as a team member who, together with the facilitating cooperating teacher and student, collaborates and constructs new meanings of teaching and learning (Slick 1998). This is in line with the model of a teacher proposed by Freire (1970) when he wrote:

> The teacher [supervisor] is no longer merely the one-who-teaches, but one who is himself taught in dialogue with the students, who, in turn, while being taught, also teach. They become jointly responsible for a process in which all grow. (61)

I have argued that the behaviour of practicum supervisors must be congruent with their values; as Phelps (2006) has suggested, this congruency should be tested continually. I have argued elsewhere (Dayan 2003) that the transition from a behaviourist-authoritative approach to a democratic partnership approach will begin when supervisors view themselves not only as people who 'impart' knowledge, but as people who are learning, who view students as partners in the construction of new knowledge. This change in perception has the potential to allow greater democratic relations to develop.

Phase 3. A research study on children's perspective on early childhood teacher education

Reflecting on the practice model which I described above, I began to realise that to speak about a democratic partnership between students, teachers and supervisors excludes one important group of partners – the children. I further reflected that although the main goal of teacher education is to ensure the best for children, they are seldom, if ever, asked about their views on teacher education. I became convinced that children too should be heard about their perception of early childhood student training.

These realisations were key aspects of Phase 3 in my personal journey of development as a professional practicum supervisor. In this section, I describe a research study on children's perspectives in which I explored two questions with child participants: (i) What should an early childhood teacher know? And (ii) How could she learn it? (Dayan 2006).

Studying children's perspectives

In recent years, a growing number of early childhood researchers have argued that it is important and appropriate to listen to the voices of children. They have shown that there are important insights to be gained from asking children for their opinions on, and their experiences of, social issues (O'Kane 2000; Brooker 2001; Clark 2004).

Researchers have used a number of strategies to encourage children to express themselves in a research situation, such as the use of props, dolls, photos and drawings or other kinds of expressive art (Graue and Walsh 1998; Brooker 2001; Sumsion 2005). In current research, there is the notion that young children are social beings, competent and communicative, capable of reflecting on their lived experiences (Langston et al. 2004). However, the child has not been approached as an informant who can participate in a qualitative interview and contribute to new perspectives and knowledge on issues such as early childhood teacher education. Yet, children observe their teacher's work daily, so they have a lot of impressions, reflections, and interpretations to potentially describe and articulate on issues of teacher education.

Interviewing young children

In conducting a qualitative child interview, the guidelines for interviews with adults, like developing rapport, using clear and understandable questions, adopting the terms that informants use and attentive listening (Arksey and Knight 1999), are all relevant. But there are also some obstacles that need to be taken into account when interviewing young children (Hatch 1990). These obstacles arise from the inherently greater power that adults hold in their relationships with children (Cannella 1997), including the following:

- From an early age, children are used to adults asking them questions to which the adults already clearly know the answers. They learn that much of adult questioning is 'test' questioning (Hatch 1990; Brooker 2001). Thus, questions are likely to make children feel they are being challenged and tested rather than truly asked to voice their opinions. In research situations this can lead to children becoming suspicious about the intentions of the interviewer and this can inhibit them from cooperating and expressing their ideas.

- Children accumulate experiences of having their opinions ignored by adults, which might influence their motivation to share ideas and opinions.
- Children occasionally experience laughter as a response to a serious expression of their opinion on any issue that adults interpret as 'cute', funny or amusing. This insulting response might inhibit children from answering questions.
- Because of power relations between adults and children (Cannella 1997), children tend to respond to adult questioning whether they have an opinion or not. They wish to please adults and will produce 'right' answers even to nonsense questions (Hughes and Grieve 1981 as cited in Brooker 2001; Hatch 1990).

On the other hand, we also know that children speak much more when they are in a familiar environment with familiar adults (Tizard and Hughes 1984). Thus, in conducting the interviews for my study on children's perspectives on the early childhood teacher preparation, I chose to conduct the interview in a familiar environment, the preschool classroom, as part of the normal daily routine. A total of 35 children were interviewed in five preschools. Present in the environment were the regular classroom teacher, the student, the practicum supervisor and groups of two to four children aged four to five years old. According to Goodwin and Goodwin (1996) and Graue and Walsh (1998), this qualitative group interview encourages children to talk and assist each other.

Children could choose whether or not to participate in the interview and they had the opportunity to leave at any stage of the interview. The teacher was the interviewer, so there was already a relationship of rapport and trust (Hatch 1995). The teacher's serious and respectful approach helped to make it evident that the conversation was an important one, asking for real information, ideas and thoughts. It also convinced the children that we were genuinely asking for their opinion and that this was not some kind of manipulation to test them or to make fun of their 'cute' answers. The student's presence was important because the children could more easily relate to my request for their help in my efforts, as a teacher educator, to better prepare the student for her future role as an early childhood teacher.

The presence of a tape recorder helped to demonstrate the conversation as an important one and turned out to be a motivational means as we promised the children that they could hear themselves at the end of the conversation.

The opening question was: *'What does (name of practicum student) need to learn so she can be a teacher?'* The second question was: *'How should she learn it?'* (Dayan 2006).

Research findings

In response to the opening question, 'What does (name of student) need to learn so she can be a teacher?', three main categories of learning were identified: She needs to learn to: (i) do (Doing); (ii) to say (Saying/Telling); and (iii) to teach (Teaching). Each category of learning encapsulated several themes that were grouped as sub-categories under each main theme as listed below.

Doing

(A) Helping and supporting children
(B) Organising the environment and maintaining order
(C) Activities

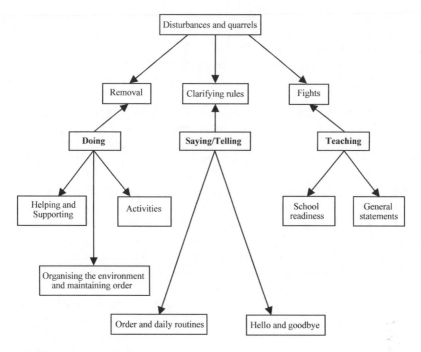

Figure 1.   Categories of learning.

Saying/Telling

    (A) Order and daily routine
    (B) Hello and goodbye

Teaching

    (A) General statements like: *she must learn how to teach the children everything, or to teach the children a lot.*
    (B) School readiness

An additional theme that appeared in all three categories of learning was 'disturbances and quarrels'. The chart shown in Figure 1 illustrates these findings.

The following is an example taken from one of the children's interview transcripts which could provide us with some new insights that could benefit teacher education:

Yuval:	They must also learn to laugh with children
Ofir:	But there are teachers who actually don't know how to laugh
Cooperating teacher:	Aaaahhh (non-committally)
Practicum supervisor:	Is it worth learning it?
Ofir:	Yes
Practicum supervisor:	How do you learn it?
Ofir:	From teachers who know.
(Laughter)	

In response to the second question, 'How should she learn it?', the children provided ideas that could be categorised around the three themes of: (i) by being and doing; (ii) by observing and showing; and (iii) by listening to us/by us telling her.

One child's answer captured the essence of the practicum from the children's perspective: 'she must practise and also watch what the teachers do and also try to do what the teacher does'.

One of the most interesting results of these interviews was that although the children were not asked about it directly, their answers demonstrated that they saw themselves as responsible for the student's training. For example, one child said: 'We will teach her. She will observe us and see what we are doing. And then she will know how to be a teacher.'

The children's role in training the student was perceived by them to be an active one. They saw themselves as able to teach her and to answer her questions; but when the children referred to the regular classroom/cooperating teacher, the person who is responsible for the training, her role was described as a passive one. The children suggested that the student should observe the regular teacher. For example, one child said: 'they should learn from another teacher. They should watch how other teachers are doing things and then they learn quickly.'

One of the benefits of this research is that it disturbs our taken-for-granted views about teacher education and training and enables us to reflect upon our own beliefs and practices so that we can rethink our current ideas. It provokes us to examine our knowledge, assumptions and beliefs to advance our understanding of the complexity of early childhood teacher education and training. As Krejsler (2005), has suggested:

> if we want to see something that we did not already know … we will have to consider whether we need to conceptualise in new ways in order to grasp what we are looking for or, at least, whether we need to empty and refill current dominating concepts with a different content or combine them in new and for our purposes, potentially more fruitful ways. (339)

One of the research results that impressed me most was the fact that children observed, in a very attentive way, the student's behaviour and her responses to children's conduct. They had a strong sense of feeling responsible for the learning of the student. This result led me to the conclusion that we should listen to them and involve them in the process of planning and reflection, and even the evaluation of the student's practice. I will discuss this further in the next section, where I focus on what I have called Phase 4 of my personal journey towards professionalism in early childhood practicum supervision.

Phase 4. Applying the research findings to practice: facilitating the participation of children in the practicum supervision process

In my experience of applying humanistic-democratic principles as a practicum supervisor, the involvement of children in the supervising process usually takes place when the student defines a topic for learning, as described in Phase 2. For example, during one of my practicum supervisory visits, the student expressed her difficulties with transitions in general and at tidy-up time in particular. She said: 'When the teacher asks the children to tidy up the room they do it immediately, but when I ask them they don't listen. I don't know what to do.' A girl approached us and I asked her if she wanted to join in our conversation. As she responded positively I repeated the question. The girl had some explanations and suggestions:

- 'You should speak louder and sometimes shout'
- 'The teacher plays with us. For example, she puts on music and tells us "who will be the first to finish", or she counts till 3'
- 'You can also do it with a drum'
- 'You can tell each one of the children to tidy up the room'
- 'You can ask one child to tell another child'

About two months later, during one of my visits in the preschool, this girl came to me and said, 'She is improving.'

Another example is an evaluation conversation that occurred at the end of a week in which the student had been in charge. Two children participated in this conversation as follows:

Lilach: I loved her activity. And she prepared sheets for us to colour in a butterfly and there was a lion and a lot of animals and I enjoyed the activities. She learned a little more about us, for example she learned to put things on the table and she learned the names of all the children. I liked her.

Another child said:

She is a good teacher. I absolutely think we can call her A TEACHER. Everything she is doing, she does it well. There are some things she does better than our teacher. Simply: she makes it fun for the children.

These insights lead me to conclude that as children were able to express their responsibility for the student's preparation, they should also take part in planning the training process. It seems to me that there is much to be gained from the supervisor encouraging the student to share ideas with the children about her practice and experiences. Sharing ideas with children can provide the student with an understanding of early childhood education from a different perspective, and offer alternative ways of seeing, understanding and acting in a given situation. She can learn about children's perspectives in the preschool context and their perceptions of the teacher's role.

Conclusion

In this article, I have described my journey in the development of professionalism, and raised questions and dilemmas concerning the concept of professionalism in the supervisor's role.

Experience tells us that the practice of education is one of ongoing decisions regarding what, when, and how. Most of the time practitioners make decisions about these questions intuitively. In this article, I have argued that we need to complement the intuitive knowledge by sound research. This means that we must first formulate the questions and then we need to try to answer those questions by developing new knowledge. This new knowledge becomes the basis for heightened professional practice from which new questions will emerge, and the cycle of the development of professionalism will continue.

The questions I have raised in this article are ones that have concerned me in my practice: What is really the role of the supervisor? How can I implement and teach more humanistic-democratic values in a system that is rooted in behaviourism? How can I work towards diminishing the power relationships between children and adults to ensure that I can learn from the children about the role of the supervisor? How can we involve children in the supervisory process?

One of the main paradoxes of asking such questions lies in the fact that the very concept of professionalism implies a reliance on the views of professionals to identify what is right, what is good, what is best practice. However, a humanistic-democratic ideology brings forth the awareness of the exclusion of key voices in those definitions. My research and practice have provided a step towards the integration of the diverse voices that need to be heard as we develop professionalism. I see the attempt to define and articulate professionalism as a stage, and certainly not as the end of the process. There is much more to learn from the participants in this field – the children, the students, the teachers, and the supervisors.

Acknowledgements

I wish to thank my friend and colleague Dr Rena Shimoni, Bow Valley College, Calgary, Canada, for her insightful comments and corrections on a draft of this article.

References

Arksey, H., and P. Knight. 1999. *Interviewing for social scientists.* Thousand Oaks, CA: Sage Publications.

Biesta, G. 2007. Education and the democratic person: Towards a political conception of democratic education. *Teachers College Record* 109, no. 3: 740–69.

Blum-Kulka, S., and C.E. Snow. 1992. Developing autonomy for tellers, tales and telling in family narrative events. *Journal of Narrative and Life History* 2, no. 3: 187–217.

Bowman, B.T., S. Donovan, and M.S. Burns, eds. 2001. *Eager to learn: Educating our preschoolers.* Washington, DC: National Academy Press.

Brooker, L. 2001. Interviewing children. In *Doing early childhood research. International perspectives on theory and practice,* ed. G. MacNaughton, S.A. Rolfe, and I. Siraj-Blatchford, 162–79. Buckingham: Open University Press.

Burman, E. 1994. *Deconstructing developmental psychology.* London: Routledge.

Burts, D.C., and T.K. Buchanan. 1998. Preparing teachers in developmentally appropriate ways to teach in developmentally appropriate classrooms. In *Continuing issues in early childhood education,* ed. C. Seefeldt and A. Galper, 129–58. Upper Saddle River, NJ: Merrill.

Cannella, G.S. 1997. *Deconstructing early childhood education: Social Justice and revolution.* New York: Peter Lang.

Caruso, J., and M.T. Fawcett. 1986. *Supervision in early childhood education.* New York: Teachers College Press.

Choi-wa Dora, H. 2006. Understanding the complexity of preschool teaching in Hong Kong: The way forward to professionalism. *International Journal of Educational Development* 26, no. 3, 305–14.

Clark, A. 2004. The mosaic approach and research with young children. In *The reality of research with children and young people,* ed. V. Lewis, M. Kellet, C. Robinson, S. Fraser, and S. Ding, 142–56. Thousand Oaks, CA: Sage Publications.

Crain, W. 1992. *Theories of development,* 3rd ed. Englewood Cliffs, NJ: Prentice Hall.

Davis, S.H. 2007. Bridging the gap between research and practice. *Phi Delta Kappan* April: 569–78.

Dayan, Y. 1999. The role perception of the field-work supervisor of early childhood student. Paper presented at the EECERA conference, in Helsinki, Finland, September.

———. 2003. The question as an indicator of power relationships in educational institutions. Paper presented at the EECERA conference, in Glasgow, Scotland, September.

———. 2006. Early childhood teacher education – children's perspective. Paper presented at the EECERA conference, in Reykjavik, Iceland, September.

Early, D.M., D.M. Bryant, R.C. Pianta, R.M. Clifford, M.R. Burchinal, S. Ritchie, C. Howes, and O. Barbarin. 2006. Are teachers' education, major, and credentials related to classroom quality and children's academic gains in pre-kindergarten? *Early Childhood Research Quarterly* 21: 174–95.

Freire, P. 1970. *Pedagogy of the oppressed.* New York: Continuum. 20th anniversary edition, 1993.

Goodwin, W.L., and L.D. Goodwin. 1996. *Understanding quantitative and qualitative research in early childhood education.* New York: Teachers College Press.

Graue, M.E., and D.J. Walsh. 1998. *Studying children in context: Theories, methods, and ethics.* Thousand Oaks, CA: Sage Publications.

Hatch, J.A. 1990. Young children as informants in classroom studies. *Early Childhood Research Quarterly,* 5: 251–64.

———. 1995. Studying childhood as a cultural invention: A rational and framework. In *Qualitative research in early childhood settings,* ed. J.H. Hatch, 117–33. Westport, CT: Praeger.

Hyson, M., ed. 2003. *Preparing early childhood professionals. NAEYC's standards for programs.* Washington, DC: National Association for the Education of Young Children (NAEYC).

Katz, L.G. 1988. Where is early childhood education as a profession? In *Professionalism and the early childhood practitioner,* ed. B. Spodek, O.N Saracho, and D.L. Peters, 75–83. New York: Teachers College Press.

Krejsler, J. 2005. Professions and their identities: How to explore professional development among (semi-) professions. *Scandinavian Journal of Educational Research* 49, no. 4: 335–57.

Langston, A., L. Abbot, V. Lewis, and M. Kellett. 2004. Early childhood. In *Doing research with children and young people,* ed. S. Fraser, V. Lewis, S. Ding, M. Kellett, and C. Robinson, 147–60. Thousand Oaks, CA: Sage Publications.

Lunenberg, M., and F.J. Korthagen. 2003. Teacher educators and student-directed learning. *Teaching and Teacher Education* 19, no. 1: 29–44.

McCarthy, J. 1990. The content of early childhood teacher education programs: Pedagogy. In *Early childhood teacher preparation,* ed. B. Spodek and O.N. Saracho, 82–101. New York: Teachers College Press.

Oberhuemer, P. 2005. Conceptualising the early childhood pedagogue: Policy approaches and issues of professionalism. *European Early Childhood Research Journal* 13, no. 1: 5–16.

O'Kane, C. 2000. The development of participatory techniques. Facilitating children's views about decisions which affect them. In *Research with children. Perspectives and practices,* ed. P. Christensen and A. James, 136–59. London: Falmer Press.

Ott, D.J., K.M. Zeichner, and G.G. Price. 1990. Research horizons and the quest for a knowledge base in early childhood teacher education. In *Early childhood teacher preparation,* ed. B. Spodek and O.N. Saracho, 118–37. New York: Teachers College Press.

Phelps, P.H. 2006. The three Rs of professionalism. *Kappa Delta Pi Record* Winter: 69–71.

Ryan, S., and S. Grieshaber. 2005. Shifting from developmental to postmodern practices in early childhood teacher education. *Journal of Teacher Education* 56, no. 1: 34–45.

Slick, S.K. 1998. The university supervisor: A disenfranchised outsider. *Teaching and Teacher Education* 14, no. 8: 821–35.

Sockett, H. 1993. *The moral base for professionalism.* New York: Teachers College Press.

Spodek, B., and O.N. Saracho. 1990. Preparing early childhood teachers. In *Early childhood teacher preparation,* ed. B. Spodek and O.N Saracho, 23–44. New York: Teachers College Press.

———. 1998. Professionalism in early childhood education. In *Professionalism and the early childhood practitioner,* ed. B. Spodek, O.N Saracho, and D.L. Peters, 59–74. New York: Teachers College Press.

Strauss, A., and J. Corbin. 1990. *Basics of qualitative research.* Newbury Park, CA: Sage Publications.

Sumsion, J. 2005. Preschool children's portrayals of their male teacher. A poststructuralist analysis. In *Critical issues in early childhood education,* ed. N. Yelland, 58–80. Buckingham: Open University Press.

Tizard, B, and M. Hughes. 1984. *Young children learning.* London: Fontana Press.

Van Dijk, T.A. 1997. Discourse as interaction in society. In *Discourse as social interaction,* ed. T.A. Van Dijk, 1–37. London: Sage.

Walkington, J.A. 2005. Mentoring preservice teachers in the preschool setting: Perceptions of the role. *Australian Journal of Early Childhood* 30, no. 8: 28–39.

Yin, R.K. 1993. *Applications of case study research.* Newbury Park, CA: Sage Publications.

Pedagogy, knowledge and collaboration: towards a ground-up perspective on professionalism†

Carmen Dalli

Victoria University of Wellington, New Zealand

ABSTRACT: Drawing on a national survey of New Zealand early childhood teachers' views on ethics and professionalism in their practice, this article discusses three key themes that emerged as core conceptual elements in how teachers in education and care settings defined professionalism. The three themes were: a distinct pedagogical style; specialist knowledge and practices; and collaborative relationships. Elements that were perceived as unprofessional or undesirable in an early childhood professional were also identified. It is argued that as the early childhood field debates the meaning of professionalism, teachers' views can contribute a 'ground-up' perspective that can enable the concept of professionalism to be reconceptualised in ways that reflect the reality of teachers' work experiences.

RÉSUMÉ: Cet article s'appuie sur une étude nationale des points de vue des enseignants de la petite enfance, en Nouvelle-Zélande, sur l'éthique et le professionnalisme dans leur pratique. Il en discute trois thèmes – clés qui ont émergé et apparaissent comme des éléments conceptuels au centre de la façon dont les enseignants du secteur de l'accueil et de l'éducation de la petite enfance définissent le professionnalisme. Les trois thèmes sont les suivants : un style pédagogique différent ; des relations de collaboration ; une connaissance spécifique. Des éléments perçus comme non professionnels ou indésirables pour un professionnel de la petite enfance ont également été identifiés. Nous défendons que, puisque le champ de la petite enfance débat de la signification du professionnalisme, les points de vue des enseignants peuvent contribuer à une mise en perspectives, ancrée sur le terrain, permettant au concept de professionnalisme d'être reconceptualisé en reflétant l'expérience professionnelle de ces derniers.

ZUSAMMENFASSUNG: In einer nationalen Studie wurden die Sichtweisen von Neuseeländischen Frühpädagoginnen zu Ethik und Professionalität in ihrer Praxis erhoben. Ausgehend von den Ergebnissen der Studie erörtert der Beitrag drei Schlüsselthemen, die als konzeptionelle Kerne sichtbar werden, wenn Praktiker in Bildungs- und Betreuungseinrichtungen ihre Professionalität definieren. Die drei Themen sind: ein deutlich erkennbarer pädagogischer Stil, kollaborative Beziehungen, sowie das Verfügen über Expertenwissen und –praxen. Elemente, die als unprofessionelle oder unerwünschte Eigenschaften wahrgenommen werden, wurden ebenfalls identifiziert. Es wird argumentiert, dass die Sichtweisen von Praktikerinnen in der aktuellen Diskussion zur Bedeutung von Professionalität im Feld der Frühpädagogik einen wichtigen Beitrag leisten können: Die grundständige Praxisperspektive ermöglicht es, Professionalität in einer Weise zu re-konzeptualisieren, die den real erfahrenen Arbeitserfahrungen entspricht.

---

†This article is a development and expansion from a presentation at the 2005 EECERA annual conference and has been developed into an article for the *Early Childhood Folio* (Dalli 2006a).

RESUMEN: Basado en una encuesta nacional acerca de las visiones éticas y profesionales de los profesores pre-escolares de Nueva Zelanda, este articulo discute tres temas claves que surgen como elementos centrales acerca de como los profesores definen profesionalismo. Los tres temas son: un estilo pedagógico distinto; relaciones de colaboración; y posesión de conocimientos y prácticas especialistas. También fueron identificados elementos percibidos como no profesionales o no deseables en la educación pre-escolar. Se argumenta que en tanto que en el campo de la educación pre-escolar se debate el significado del profesionalismo, las visiones de los profesores pueden contribuir con una perspectiva de terreno que haga posible que el concepto de profesionalismo sea reconceptualizado en forma que refleje la realidad laboral de los profesores.

Introduction

... when I went to Teachers' College ... we had a six week block where we talked about becoming a professional and [about] international concepts of professionalism and codes of ethics ... I wouldn't imagine anybody who graduated from that class would see themselves as anything less than professional.... . your training contributes to it and then you have to person-ally take ownership of it and accept that you are in that role. (Kindergarten teacher, interviewed July 2007, in Dalli 2007, August)

New Zealand can be considered to be leading the way in attaining a professionalised early childhood workforce. As a small nation with a centralised policy-making process, in 1986 it became the first country in the world (Moss 2000) to integrate policy and administrative responsibility for all childcare and preschool services within the Department of Education. Two years later, three-year integrated early childhood training was introduced in colleges of education. This created a qualifications track for early childhood practitioners that paralleled that of the compulsory school system; it also opened the way for three-year diploma and degree qualifications to become the benchmark qualification for employment in licensed early childhood services. At the same time, these measures abolished the *education vs. care* divide that still persists in many other countries (Bennett 2003). Integrated training also meant that despite historical, philosophical and organisational differences among services, by 1990, early childhood practitioners were entering the field with the same training background, meeting at cross-sector fora and conferences, and participating in professional development courses alongside colleagues from other parts of the sector.

The merging of the two major early childhood unions, the Early Childhood Workers' Union (ECWU) and the Kindergarten Teachers' Association (KTA), in 1990 further broke down lines of division with the subsequent integration of this amalgamated group into the primary teachers' union (the New Zealand Education Institute (NZEI) – Te Riu Roa) in 1993 creating a powerful alliance for the pay parity campaign of the late 1990s (Mitchell and Wells 1997). Introduced first for kindergarten teachers in 2002, pay parity with primary school teachers has now extended to qualified teachers working in education and care centres, or, as they were formerly called, 'childcare centres'. Along the way there have been perceptible shifts in the way that the early childhood sector has identified itself, with labels for the sector ranging from 'educare' (Smith 1988), to 'care and education' (e.g. Meade 1988), or 'education and care', and settling more recently as 'education'(e.g. Strategic Plan Working Group 2001; Ministry of Education 2005). Likewise, there has been a change in the terminology used to refer to the early childhood workforce, with the term 'teacher', previously reserved for practitioners working in state kindergartens, now applied to all qualified early childhood staff employed in licensed early childhood centres. The terms 'minders' and 'childcare workers', historically used to refer to the childcare workforce, have fallen out of use, reflecting both the effects of sixty years of sector advocacy as well as shifts in dominant 'political gazes' and policy blueprints (May 2007). A clear example of one of these shifts was evident at the 2005 annual conference of the New Zealand Childcare Association, Te Tari Puna Ora o Aotearoa, when the then Minister of Education, Trevor Mallard, commented: 'Early childhood people are being regarded as professionals. They have gone from "childcarers" to "educator": This was the debate of the 70s.'

The debate, three years on from Mallard's speech, is now about early childhood as a teacher-led profession. Government's 2002 ten-year strategic plan for early childhood education, *Pathways to the Future, Ngā Huarahi Arataki* (Ministry of Education 2002) has been crucial in positioning the early childhood sector more firmly within the field of education. Premised on the statement that the early childhood sector is 'the cornerstone of our education system' (1), the strategic plan includes two key provisions that have put the seal on the regulatory and legislative frameworks under which the sector now operates. One provision is the requirement that by 2012, all staff in licensed early childhood teacher-led services (*vs.* the voluntary parent-led one) must be registered teachers holding a benchmark qualification; the second is the requirement that all early childhood teachers be registered through the New Zealand Teachers' Council (NZTC). Together, these two provisions situate early childhood education as an integral part of the broader education sector, and early childhood teaching as part of the overall profession of teaching.

In the ten-year strategic plan (Ministry of Education 2002), early childhood education is perceived as a multi-disciplinary field that draws on knowledge/s from diverse areas. This is consistent with the ideas in *Te Whāriki*, the New Zealand curriculum document (Ministry of Education 1996) in which the early childhood curriculum is understood as a weaving (whāriki) of experiences that are not subject-bound but arise when professionally trained early childhood teachers, soundly grounded in the traditional specialist knowledge bases of child development and early childhood curriculum studies, are able to draw knowledgeably on insights from other disciplines and work collaboratively with professionals from related disciplines. It also reflects a worldwide trend (e.g. OECD 2001, 2006) and the massive expansion in early years scholarship which has re-positioned the field as a cross-disciplinary one with connections to fields such as social policy, health, cultural studies, family studies, and the social sciences more generally.

Within this context, New Zealand scholarly discussions of what it means to be 'professional' have not been extensive. An early paper by Dinniss (1974) considered whether early childhood work could be called a profession on the basis of criteria proposed by Lieberman (1956). Twenty years later, following a similar exercise using Lilian Katz' (1985) list of criteria of a profession, I concluded (Dalli 1993) that the structural components of a professionalised sector were beginning to bed down but raised questions about the criteria of 'autonomy' and 'optimal distance' between teacher and child in a sector where staff are expected to work collaboratively with parents, the community and other professionals, as well as about ways of continuing to value the contribution of untrained mothers (or other home adults) who work alongside their children in services like play centres or in the indigenous Māori Kohanga Reo. In a survey of 215 associate teachers[1] in the Auckland region, Cooper (1993) found that when the respondents were asked to nominate the skills, abilities, and attributes related to the word 'professional', their responses included: being highly paid and qualified; being competent; and being or having respectability. Cooper commented that the discourse of professionalism only emerged when respondents were specifically asked about this; she therefore concluded that 'the definition of what constitutes professionalism in early childhood education is still to be argued' (7).

Interest in the 'still to be argued' definition has increased in the past decade (e.g. Bruce 2000; Cherrington 2001; Dalli 2003a,b). Bruce, for example, used focus groups to explore how practitioners from different parts of the early childhood sector viewed the professionalism of staff in other parts of the sector: Her results showed that all practitioners valued qualifications as a marker of professionalism but that defining professional status in a very diverse early childhood sector is full of complexities. In illustration, Bruce drew attention to the case of home-based services where it is the network coordinators who are required to be qualified, not the actual caregivers (see also Dalli 2003b; Everiss and Dalli 2003). Bruce suggested that professionalism may need to be understood as a continuum ranging from professional status to para-professional status, and non-professional status.

Cherrington (2001), on the other hand, suggested four 'cornerstones of professionalism': professionalism of interpersonal actions; having and acting upon a professional knowledge base; acting in the child's best interest; and taking professional responsibility for the actions of one's colleagues. The cornerstones were identified from an analysis of data gathered as part of a national survey of ethically difficult situations in daily practice conducted during the development of the Early Childhood Code of Ethics in the mid-nineties (Dalli and Cherrington 1994).

Taking a different angle, I have argued that the traditional alignment of early childhood work with the role of mothering, and the attendant discourses of love and care, have acted to disempower early childhood practitioners from claiming professional status (Dalli 2002). At the same time, discourses of love and care persist in early childhood teachers' talk about their work. I have argued that these discourses should not be ignored in scholarly discussions on the nature of early childhood professionalism (Dalli 2003a,b); rather, it is timely to re-vision notions of love and care so that they may be transformed into pedagogical and political tools (Dalli 2006b). They can also contribute to a reconceptualised notion of professionalism that responds to the unique and evolving nature of quality early childhood practice (Dalli 2004).

In late 2003, an opportunity arose to explore more fully the evolving characteristics of early childhood professional practice as part of a national survey on how qualified staff in the early childhood sector were using the Early Childhood Code of Ethics developed in the mid-1990s (Dalli and Mitchell 1995). In the rest of this article, I discuss findings from this survey, and in particular the responses received from 139 teachers working in licensed care and education centres (45% of the total [$n = 285$] care and education centres sampled).[2] I argue that as interest grows in scholarly definitions of professionalism, teachers' views can contribute a ground-up perspective that can enable a reconceptualised view of professionalism that reflects the reality of early childhood work.

Method

The survey was conducted via a postal questionnaire sent to a random stratified sample of 594 early childhood centres across the range of licensed early childhood services[3] (education and care centres; kindergartens; kohanga reo; home-based centres; and playcentres). The questionnaire included the request that the respondent be qualified to the benchmark level of a three-year degree or diploma, or its equivalent. This was to ensure that the practitioner views accessed were informed by a background of teacher education. The overall response rate was 43%, with the highest return rate being from kindergarten centres (55%), followed by family daycare homes (51%) and education and care centres (45%). Lowest return rates were from kohanga reo (18%) and play centres (33%).

The questionnaire consisted of two sections. The first section focused on eliciting examples of situations that posed ethical difficulty for early childhood teachers, and ways they responded to them. The second section featured three questions that asked respondents to: (i) list the qualities they would expect to find in an early childhood teacher whom they would describe as 'professional'; (ii) describe how they would recognise professionalism in early childhood teachers' interactions across a range of workplace relationships; and (iii) make any other comment they wished about the issue of professionalism in early childhood practice.

Responses were coded using a set of thematic categories developed from the data. For the section on professionalism, 27 thematic categories were developed: Fourteen of these were stand-alone categories derived from the qualities listed by teachers as characteristic of a professional teacher. These were: advocacy; communication skills; confidentiality; respect for diversity/difference; emotions (e.g. passion) about teaching; high ideals/seeking excellence/true to profession; integrity/honesty/trustworthiness; leadership (providing and taking); appropriate pay-work conditions; personal qualities/style/personality; respect for personal and professional boundaries; caring about the public perception of early childhood education; self-management; and self-presentation. A fifteenth category was set aside for qualities/behaviours considered to be unprofessional. The other twelve thematic categories clustered around the three major themes of (i) pedagogy; (ii) professional knowledge and practice; and (iii) collaborative relationships.[4]

Results

This article focuses on findings from teachers working in education and care centres. It discusses statements they made about early childhood (i) pedagogy; (ii) professional knowledge and practice; and (iii) collaborative relationships. These three themes emerged as key ones in teachers' open-ended responses to the second question on professionalism where respondents were asked to reflect on how they would recognise professional behaviour in the context of teachers' interactions with children, other colleagues, parents/whanau/family, management and the wider community. The article also identifies qualities that education and care teachers nominated as unprofessional and thus to be avoided.

Table 1 presents the three major themes as clusters of related thematic categories; the table also sets out the numbers of teachers who mentioned the themes within their statements about professionalism.

Table 2 presents the un-clustered thematic categories in rank order of popularity. Of these categories, four were used by over 60% of the education and care teachers: (1) pedagogical strategies; (2) collaborative relationships generally; (3) collaborative relationships with management; and (4) professional knowledge and practice generally.

Table 3 lists injunctions about unprofessional behaviours that appeared in teachers' responses.

Discussion

Tables 1 and 2 show that the four most popular categories are spread across the three major thematic clusters (pedagogy; professional knowledge and practice; and collaborative relationships). This suggests that these themes are key conceptual components of any statement about 'professionalism' based on these data. I discuss each of these themes below.

Table 1.   Themes in teachers' statements about professionalism.

Thematic clusters and categories	Education and care teachers who mentioned the theme	
	#	% of total respondents
PEDAGOGY		
- pedagogical strategies	125	89
- pedagogy of care	47	34
- best/wise practice	3	2
PROFESSIONAL KNOWLEDGE AND PRACTICE		
- professional knowledge and practice generally	85	61
- qualifications and professional development	51	37
- content knowledge	33	24
- reflection on practice	21	15
COLLABORATIVE RELATIONSHIPS		
- collaborative relationships generally	105	75
- collaborative relationships with management	87	63
- collaborative relationships with parents	81	58
- collaborative relationships beyond the centre	71	51
- collaborative relationships in teaching team	55	40

By contrast, Table 3 lists behaviours that teachers felt were totally unprofessional. These are included in this article as a foil for the rest of the data: If a distinct pedagogy, specialist knowledge and practices, and collaborative relationships are essential components of a ground-up definition of professionalism, the list in Table 3 constitutes elements that a ground-up definition would exclude.

Table 2.   Un-clustered categories in rank order of popularity.

Rank order	Categories within three major thematic clusters	Teachers who mentioned the theme	
		#	% of total respondents
1	Pedagogical strategies	125	89
2	Collaborative relationships generally	105	75
3	Collaborative relationships with management	87	63
4	Professional knowledge and practice generally	85	61
5	Collaborative relationships with parents	81	58
6	Collaborative relationships beyond the centre	71	51
7	Collaborative relationships in teaching team	55	40
8	Qualifications and professional development	51	37
9	Pedagogy of care	47	34
10	Content knowledge	33	24
11	Reflection on practice	21	15
12	Best/wise practice	3	2

Table 3.   Injunctions about unprofessional behaviours.

Injunctions against unprofessional behaviours
No gossip
No favouritism
No talking behind back of people
No putdowns
No personal attacks
No negative comparisons between children
No personal involvement with parents
No extended conversations with other staff that draws them away from children
No running down of other centres
No stamping of feet in anger!
No discussing of personal details about the children
No scruffy clothing
No swearing or 'stupid behaviour'
Not hostile
Not patronising of parents
No discussing of personal issues with parents
No letting personal opinion get in the way of working with parents

1. Pedagogy: strategies and style

The category 'pedagogical strategies' was used whenever statements were made that articulated a specific strategy or an attitude to early childhood teaching which respondents saw as professionally desirable. 'Pedagogy' was understood in its traditional meaning of 'the art and science of teaching' and as 'any conscious action by one person designed to enhance learning in another' (Mortimore 1999, 3). At the same time, the analysis took on board the principle from New Zealand's early childhood curriculum, *Te Whāriki*, which states that 'children learn through responsive and reciprocal relationships with people, places and things' (Ministry of Education 1996, 14). Thus pedagogy was understood as embodying the idea that teaching involves relationships and a stance or approach to the learner that goes beyond a focus on subject knowledge or expertise; it includes practice based on respect, care (Noddings 1984); and wise practice (Goodfellow 2001).

As a set of strategies, the pedagogy of the professional teacher was seen by respondents to include a focus on listening to children and the strategies of engagement, tuning in, and speaking 'at the child's level'. As style, the key elements were an attitude of respect and fairness to all children. Typically, statements that fell into any of the 'Pedagogy' cluster of categories incorporated reference to both strategy and style. This is evident in the following statement, one of many that emphasised professional behaviour as involving interactions 'at the child's level' and cautioned against using a belittling manner or tone of voice:

> Professional people interact with children at the children's level, without imposing their own ideas, keeping things on a child's level, not the adult's, nor using a belittling manner.

A pedagogical style of 'respect' and 'fairness' had many dimensions. Many teachers emphasised respect for each child's individuality; and 'being fair and developing a sense of trust and caring with each child' were qualities that often went hand in hand. In the following statements, a respectful and fair style included the components of a calm approach and an inclusive attitude alongside the use of open-ended questions that extend children's thinking and encourage self-esteem. The professional teacher:

is respectful, positive, calm, informed; interacts without discrimination, is able to listen to the children and follow their interests building on their knowledge, skills and ability by providing opportunities and experiences that are culturally, emotionally and physically appropriate.

... should get down to the child's level; use open-ended questions to extend the child's learning and thinking ... respecting all children(inclusiveness), greeting and farewelling all children; no belittling of children when encouraging appropriate behaviours; building a child's self-esteem through encouragement, scaffolding and guidance.

... works to extend and draw out the interests of children by bonding, understanding the child, the responsive interactions, understanding the child's wellbeing.

In similar vein, other teachers described a particular:

... manner and tone and the ability to listen and to respond to their[children] needs; ... down to their level and not dominating situations, allowing children to speak without interruptions, being respectful of their thoughts and opinions

while

... working towards the common goal of 'best practice' and acting in the best interests of children.

Respect as an attitude, and interest in children, were additionally articulated in the specific strategies of:

speaking to the child not *at* the child

... encouraging and building on the child's ideas. Educating the children, i.e., discussing what is happening at that time. Planning, scaffolding, evaluating, reflecting on practice, appropriate touching and affection.

These statements emphasise sensitivity and responsiveness to children's 'cues' or messages about who they are and where they are at. They emphasise engagement with children's interests and an attitude of 'being present' to the child, an attitude characteristic of an 'ethics of care' approach to teaching (e.g. Goldstein 1998). Additionally, the specific strategies of planning, scaffolding, evaluating, and reflecting on practice are articulated as professionally desirable in the same phrase as 'appropriate touching and affection', suggesting that to be professional as an early childhood teacher includes an affective dimension and its appropriate physical demonstration.

2.   *Professional knowledge and practice*

Four thematic categories were used to code statements about content knowledge and practices that a professional early childhood teacher was perceived to need: (i) 'professional knowledge and practice generally'; (ii) 'qualifications and professional development'; (iii) 'content knowledge'; and (iv) 'reflective practice'.

Professional knowledge and practice generally

Respondents saw general knowledge about children and about the 'theory of early childhood education' as central to professionalism, with qualifications, training and ongoing professional development being the route to achieving these. Many statements also supported the need to 'have current knowledge of legislation, regulations, policies' and 'being aware of the different roles of outside agencies' and how to access them for support.

Alongside existing knowledge and skills, teachers valued an attitude of openness to new learning. They identified as professional a teacher who:

> ... keeps up to date with current theory, practice and research, is aware, and has knowledge of regulations, Acts, DoPs [Statement of Desirable Objectives and Practices] etc; it's very important.

For some, professional knowledge and practice was also associated with an orientation to leadership and management, as well as engagement with the broader political context in which teachers operate. Thus, the professional teacher was seen to demonstrate:

> leadership and management knowledge and skills, ... able to articulate any concerns in a confident manner, demonstrates a knowledge of current educational research, someone who is aware of the education political environment.

Qualifications and professional development

Coding statements that mentioned qualifications and professional development into a specific category clarified the keen support among the respondents for the current policy direction to upgrade teacher qualifications, and to ensuring all teachers meet the registration guidelines of the New Zealand Teachers' Council (Ministry of Education 2002). Strong support for these goals was evident in statements such as:

> All teachers need to be trained and must continue to keep updated with changes and develop-ments in early childhood education e.g.: be conversant with EC regulations, code of ethics, Te Whāriki.

> Registration ensures professionalism; we need to have more structured guidelines to ensure equal standards for all teachers.

> Professionalism comes with training and working within the early childhood setting. Personal and professional development is ongoing throughout one's life and it never stops.

Another teacher put it a different way:

> It can be very difficult with varying degrees of untrained and trained staff in centres, as well as experience, which means varying degrees of professional knowledge.

Some saw the current policies as also holding the promise of enhancing the public image of early childhood teaching:

> As all early childhood educators achieve teacher registration, hopefully professionalism will increase and this will impact on public opinion and the early childhood educator's image.

Content knowledge

Statements referring to documents in use in the local early childhood context, or to other recognisably early childhood domain knowledge such as the early childhood curriculum document, Te Whāriki, the early childhood regulations, and the *Statement of Desirable*

Objectives and Practices (DoPs),[5] were categorised as 'content knowledge' that respondents saw as marking out professional practice. Thus, professional teachers were expected to:

> Be aware of and operate within the early childhood regulations; be conversant with early childhood curriculum Te Whāriki.

> keep up to date with current theory, practice and research, is aware and has knowledge of regulations, Acts, DOPs etc.

> be knowledgeable about compliance and regulation requirements

Reflective practice

Statements in the category 'reflective practice' without exception emphasised the ability 'to observe, analyse and critically evaluate' one's professional practice, with some also commenting on the need to formally recognise that time of no contact with children needs to be set aside to enable this to happen. One respondent wrote that teachers needed:

> More time and space ... to work on administration in relation to planning/assessment and evaluation. I feel this is one of the big issues that childcare centres are tackling now. My centre staff deal with other issues positively and we often have regular meetings where we set scenarios on how to deal with issues properly.

Some saw the potential for these issues to be solved through the current policies to upgrade all teachers' qualifications:

> I am really pleased that the sector is aiming for all teachers to be qualified with Dip Tchg ECE and for all qualified teachers to gain their teacher registration. It enables teachers to continue reflecting on their teaching and keeps them in touch with professional development.

Overall, these data indicate that education and care teachers were very clear about the content knowledge and type of practice that they would deem essential in a professional early childhood teacher; they were also very clear about their support for early childhood specific qualifications and the recently introduced requirement for professional registration with the NZTC.

3.   Collaborative relationships

The five thematic categories clustered around the theme of 'collaborative relationships' (see Table 1) were used to code statements in which attitudes, skills or behaviours were mentioned that were aimed at joint action to advance a common goal. Statements of this kind were made in relation to the full range of teachers' workplace relationships about which they were prompted to think by the survey questions: within the teaching team; beyond the centre; with parents; and with management.

Collaborative relationships generally

Generic statements about 'working together', being 'supportive', working in a 'consultative' way, or networking with others were all coded under the general category of collaborative relationships. The aim of such collaboration was not always explicitly stated but, in most cases, could be assumed to be the collective or 'general good'. One explicit statement that collaborative relationships had holistic beneficial impact was in the following description of the professional teacher as:

> Able to work side by side for the advantage of children, staff, management and community of the centre.

In the next set of statements, collaboration is explained more fully and emerges as a mixture of behaviours, attitudes and skills underpinned by the common values of support for colleagues; respect for others; non-discriminative working relationships; and aspirations for a working environment that is democratic, respectful and pleasant:

> Working together as a team, enjoying their company; supportive and assists when needed; 'caring and sharing' attitude; respectful

> Knowledgeable about the wider community, responsible, cooperative, welcoming and interactive, culturally aware and sensitive, confident in promoting the value of early childhood education

> Discusses and consults with other staff, has skills in working with others in a team, warm, friendly (not gossipy); accentuates the positive work of teachers, help others in areas they may feel inadequate, be honest/have integrity, values others

> Communicates, discusses and consults with other staff and informs them of their intentions so everyone is always aware of what is going on, raising issues as they arise instead of letting them build.

Collaborative relationships with management

Respondents in education and care centres thought that a professional teacher would respect management as part of the overall team of the centre; being respectful stood alongside an awareness of one's right to fair employment practices.

The following statements highlight the respondents' awareness of the difficulties that might arise from the hierarchical (and power) differences between staff and management and suggest that respect, responsiveness, honesty and openness are key to successful management of this professional relationship:

> Treat management with the respect they deserve – no gossiping. If you have an issue then go straight to management first; be open to criticism on how you can improve as an educator.

> Treat them with respect, being honest and open, by not becoming defensive in a tricky situation. Respecting them enough to know they are your employers, but knowing they are there if you need to talk to them about an awkward situation.

Working with management was also seen to require:

> Someone who can contribute ideas/ views in a collaborative manner; someone who values others' diverse contributions; someone who has knowledge of, and contributes to policies, procedures, management plans, strategic plans and is supportive and open.

Collaborative relationships with parents and within teaching team

Respect, honesty and open communication were also valued in professional relationships with parents and within teaching teams. With parents, the education and care teachers expected professional teachers to be:

respectful and non-judgemental; prepared to listen and be supportive to them in their parenting, sharing special moments and events; offering alternatives if a parent shares a home problem (e.g. child's sleeping, eating, toileting)

Not patronising, listening to what parents are saying, not lying or telling the parent what they want to hear. Discuss sensitive issues without upsetting the parents (and in an appropriate time or place); cultural awareness and respect.

When working with colleagues, the desired quality emphasised by teachers was teamwork. This phrase dominated the statements of most teachers; the following is a good example of the overall range:

Working together as a team through listening to other points of view, modelling good practices, using good interpersonal skills, sharing the workload, planning together and sharing information.

Collaborative relationships beyond the centre

Teachers saw their professional role as including being part of the community, making links with schools and other early childhood services in the areas, networking with relevant agencies and making use of valuable community resources. They saw benefits from this community engagement accruing to the children and their families as well as in creating community support for the centre, including, as one respondent said, 'with fund raising'. Beyond gaining support from the community, professional teachers support the life of the community. One respondent illustrated how the teachers in her centre demonstrated this, when she wrote:

our community house has a vege co-op and op-shop, we support this by using it ourselves and making parents aware of its existence.

Professional teachers were also:

willing to learn the community beliefs/values; respectful and sensitive to their culture; meeting the community needs, welcoming, encouraging their participation and valuing their contributions; consulting them in decision-making.

In dealing with agencies beyond the centre, being professional also meant:

… not being intimidated; recognising that the goal is the same …

… if you don't agree with something, being able to say in a professional manner. Using facts only, owning your statements. Respect what they have to say and being able to put your view across. Respect for everyone's job and what they do

The image of the professional early childhood teacher that emerges from these statements is that of a collaborative person of sound personal integrity. The professional teacher is warm and friendly and does not gossip; instead, she/he accentuates the positive side of others rather than undermines them. Openness to learning, good communication skills, and having knowledge alongside humility: these are all part of the general mix of attitudes, skills and dispositions that the respondents identified as characteristics of the professional early childhood teacher.

Towards a ground-up perspective on early childhood professionalism

As I stated at the beginning, one of the aims of this study was to contribute to ongoing debate about how professionalism might be reconceptualised in a way that reflects the reality of teachers' experiences.

It is clear from the analysis in this article that the reality of the respondents' practice was vibrant and complex. It is also clear that the teachers had very clear views about the behaviours, attitudes and skills that a professional teacher would use in response to this context. Equally, the respondents were clear about behaviours and attitudes that were unprofessional.

This analysis makes it reasonable to conclude that the teachers' ground-up perspective on early childhood professionalism presented in this article adds a rich dimension to existing scholarly discussions on professionalism which have tended to 'express expectations' about practitioners (see Urban, this issue) rather than express their professional reality.

I note also that the respondents cited in this article viewed professionalism as valuable, desirable and entirely achievable. On the basis of the data in this article, I suggest that a reconceptualised definition of professionalism is likewise not only valuable and desirable, but entirely achievable. Such a definition could be conceptually structured around the three themes discussed in this article: (i) a distinct pedagogical style; (ii) (specialist) professional knowledge and practices; and (iii) collaborative relationships.

I suggest that in a local policy context which has moved purposefully to 'professionalise' the sector (e.g. Ministry of Education 2002; Dalli and Te One 2003), it is timely that teachers' ground-up perspectives contribute to constructing a fuller understanding of what being professional means in this continually evolving sector.

Acknowledgement

I wish to acknowledge Sue Cherrington as my co-researcher on the national survey on ethics and professionalism from which this article draws data. The national survey was funded by a grant from the Faculty of Humanities and Social Sciences of Victoria University of Wellington in 2003.

Notes

1. Associate teachers are responsible for supervising early childhood teacher trainees on practicum.
2. The 285 education and care centres comprised 48% of the total national sample of 594 centres used in the study.
3. The total number of licensed early childhood services in New Zealand in 2003 was 3523. The survey was sent to one in every six centres in the country.
4. A statement could be coded to more than one category.
5. Early childhood centres are audited by the Education Review Office against the DoPs on a roughly three-yearly cycle.

References

Bennett, J. 2003. Starting strong. The persistent division between care and education. *Journal of Early Childhood Research* 1, no. 1: 21–48.
Bruce, L. 2000. A debate on the professionalisation of early childhood education in Aotearoa New Zealand. Unpublished research paper for MEd degree, Victoria University of Wellington, School of Education.
Cherrington, S. 2001. Dealing with difficult situations in early childhood education: Stories of professional practice. Occasional Paper No. 10. Wellington: Institute for Early Childhood Studies.

Cooper, D. 1993. Perceptions of issues in early childhood teacher education. Paper presented at the NZ Association for Research in Education Conference, December, at University of Waikato, New Zealand.

Dalli, C. 1993. Are we a profession? The contribution of the national curriculum guidelines and the need for a code of ethics. Keynote address. In *Early childhood education: Papers presented at the CECUA National Curriculum Conference,* October. Wellington: New Zealand Education Institute (NZEI).

———. 2002. Being an early childhood teacher: Images of professional practice and professional identity during the experience of starting childcare. *New Zealand Journal of Educational Studies* 37, no. 1: 73–85.

———. 2003a. The challenges of professionalism. Keynote address at the Early Childhood Council's annual conference, April, in Christchurch, New Zealand.

———. 2003b. Mothering, caring and professionalism in family day care: unpacking the debates in family day care. Paper presented at the 3rd International Family Day Care Conference, February 19–23, in Wellington, New Zealand.

———. 2004. Teachers' thinking about professionalism in early childhood practice. Paper presented at the EECERA conference, September 1–4, in Malta.

———. 2006a. Redefining professionalism in early childhood practice: a ground-up approach. Views from teachers in care and education settings. *Early Childhood Folio* 10: 6–11.

———. 2006b. Re-visioning love and care in early childhood: Constructing the future of our profession. *The First Years. New Zealand Journal of Infant and Toddler Education* 8, no. 1: 5–11.

———. 2007. A day in the life of an early years practitioner: The New Zealand case study. Symposium presentation at 17th EECERA conference, August 30, in Prague, Czech Republic.

Dalli, C., and S. Cherrington. 1994. Survey of ethical concerns faced by early childhood educators in Aotearoa/New Zealand: preliminary results. Paper presented at the New Zealand Association for Research in Education Conference, December, in Christchurch, New Zealand.

Dalli, C., and L. Mitchell. 1995. The early childhood code of ethics or how you can prise yourself from between a rock and a hard place. Keynote address. *Proceedings of the 6th Early Childhood Convention* 1: 63–76. September 5–8, in Auckland, New Zealand.

Dalli, C., and S. Te One. 2003. Early childhood education in 2002: Pathways to the future. *New Zealand Annual Review of Education* 12 (2002): 177–202.

Dinniss, P. 1974. Professionalism in early childhood education: Some trends. In *Trends and issues in early childhood education,* ed. M. Bell, P.E. Dinniss, and G. McDonald. Wellington: New Zealand Council for Educational Research.

Everiss, E., and C. Dalli. 2003. Family day care in New Zealand: Issues of professionalism, training and quality. In *Family Day Care: International Perspectives on Policy, Practice and Quality.* Chapter 4 pp. 59–77, ed. J. Statham and A. Mooney. London: Jessica Kingsley Publishers.

Goldstein, L. 1998. More than gentle smiles and warm hugs: Applying the ethic of care to early childhood education. *Journal of Research in Childhood Education* 12, no. 2: 244–71.

Goodfellow, J. 2001. Wise practice: The need to move beyond best practice in early childhood education. *Australian Journal of Early Childhood Research* 26, no. 3: 1–6.

Katz, L. 1985. The nature of professions: Where is early childhood education? Address presented at the Early Childhood Organisation Conference in honour of Miss E. Marianne Parry, OBE, September, at Bristol Polytechnic, UK. Printed in *Talks with teachers of young children,* 219–35. New Jersey: Ablex Publishing Corp.

Lieberman, M.H. 1956. *Education as a profession.* Englewood Cliffs, NJ: Prentice Hall.

May, H. 1987. Childcare activism in the seventies. Interview with Diulia Rendall. *Childcare Quarterly* 7, no. 2: 22–31.

———. 2007. "Minding", "working", "teaching": Childcare in Aotearoa/New Zealand, 1940s–2000s. *Contemporary Issues in Early Childhood* 8, no. 2: 133–43.

Meade, A. 1988. Education to be more. Report of the Early Childhood Care and Education Working Group. Wellington: Government Print.

Ministry of Education. 1996. Te Whāriki: He Whāriki Mātauranga mō ngā Mokopuna o Aotearoa: Early Childhood Curriculum. Wellington: Learning Media. http://www.minedu.govt.nz/web/downloadable/dl3567_v1/whariki.pdf.

———. 2002. *Pathways to the Future – Ngā Huarahi Arataki.* Wellington: Learning Media.

————. 2005. *Early childhood education funding handbook.* Wellington: Resourcing Division, Ministry of Education.

Mitchell, L., and C. Wells. 1997. Negotiating pay parity in the early childhood sector. *Proceedings of the Closing of the Gap Forum on Equal Pay,* 1630172, pp. 163–172. Wellington: New Zealand Council of Trade Unions.

Mortimore, P., ed. 1999. *Understanding pedagogy and its impact on learning.* London: Paul Chapman Publishing.

Moss, P. 2000. Training and education of early childhood education and care staff. Report prepared for the Organisation for Economic Co-operation and Development (OECD). London: Thomas Coram Research Unit, Institute of Education, University of London.

Noddings, N. 1984. *Caring: A feminine approach to ethics and moral education.* Berkeley: University of California Press.

Organisation for Economic Co-operation and Development (OECD). 2001. *Starting strong. Early childhood education and care.* Paris: OECD.

————. 2006. *Starting strong II. Early childhood education and care.* Paris: OECD.

Smith, A. B. 1988. Education and care components in New Zealand childcare centres and kindergartens. *Australian Journal of Early Childhood* 13, no. 3: 31–36.

Strategic Plan Working Group. 2001. *Strategic plan for early childhood education.* Wellington: Ministry of Education.

Preschool teachers' and student preschool teachers' thoughts about professionalism in Sweden

Marja Kuisma[a] and Anette Sandberg[b]

[a]Uppsala University, Uppsala, Sweden; [b]Mälardalen University, Västerås, Sweden

ABSTRACT: This article discusses the different ways in which students and preschool teachers at two Swedish universities interpret the concept of professionalism. Data for this article are drawn from a study conducted in two different urban areas of Sweden which explored the following four questions: (1) What does the concept of professionalism imply for preschool teachers and students? (2) What does a professional teacher do in a pre-school/school/after-school recreation centre? (3) How is professionalism developed? (4) What does preschool teachers' professionalism mean in comparison with professionalism in other closely related professions such as day-care attendants or recreational pedagogues? The survey was conducted using a questionnaire that students completed during a lesson at the university and by their supervisors at preschools. Data from the study are interpreted against a theoretical background that problematises the concept of 'professionalism' within the societal context of preschools in Sweden.

RÉSUMÉ: Cet article examine les différentes manières dont les enseignants du préscolaire en activité et en formation dans deux universités suédoises interprètent le concept de professionnalisme. Les données présentées proviennent d'une étude conduite dans deux zones urbaines différentes de Suède, autour des questions suivantes : (1) Qu'implique le concept de professionnalisme pour des enseignants du préscolaire en activité et en formation ? (2) Quel est le rôle de l'enseignant professionnel à la pré-école/ à l'école /au centre de loisirs ? (3) Comment se développe le professionnalisme ? (4) Que signifie le professionnalisme des enseignants du préscolaire par rapport au professionnalisme d'autres groupes professionnels proches, tels que le personnel de service ou les animateurs ? Les données de l'étude sont interprétées à partir d'un cadre théorique problématisant le concept de « professionnalisme » dans le contexte sociétal des pré-écoles suédoises.

ZUSAMMENFASSUNG: Dieser Artikel diskutiert die unterschiedlichen Weisen, in denen Studierende zweier schwedischer Universitäten und erfahrene Praktiker Konzepte von Professionalität interpretieren. Die Daten für den Beitrag stammen aus einer Studie, die in zwei unterschiedlichen städtischen Gebieten Schwedens durchgeführt wurde und folgenden vier Fragen nachging: (1) Was impliziert das Konzept 'Professionalität' für Vorschul-Lehrer und Studierende? (2) Was tut ein professioneller Vorschul-Lehrer in der Vorschule/Schule/außerschulischem Freizeitzentrum? (3) Wie wird Professionalität entwickelt? (4) Was bedeutet die Professionalität der Vorschul-Lehrer im Vergleich zu der nahe verwandter Berufsgruppen wie Freizeitpädagogen oder anderer Betreuungskräfte? Interpretiert werden die Daten vor einem theoretischen Hintergrund, der das Konzept 'Professionalität' im gesellschaftlichen Kontext der Schwedischen Vorschule problematisiert.

RESUMEN: Este artículo discute la forma en que estudiantes y profesores pre-escolares en dos universidades suecas interpretan el concepto de profesionalismo. Los datos se basan en un estudio conducido en dos áreas urbanas suecas, y que explora las siguientes preguntas: 1) Que implica el concepto de profesionalismo para profesores y estudiantes pre-escolares? 2) Que hace un profesor profesional en la pre-escuela/escuela/centro recreativo? 3) Como se desarrolla el profesionalismo? 4) Que significa el profesionalismo del profesor pre-escolar en comparación con el profesionalismo de otras profesiones cercanas, tales como cuidadores de niños y pedagogos recreativos? Los datos son interpretados a partir de una base teórica que problematiza el concepto de 'profesionalismo' dentro del contexto social sueco.

Introduction

This article describes a study which aims to identify and analyse the different ways in which student and preschool teachers interpret the concept of professionalism. It explores their perspectives on professionalism in the institutional context of the Swedish preschool.

Early childhood education in Sweden

Early childhood education in Sweden is specified as being part of the education system. The curriculum (Swedish National Agency for Education 1998) identifies fundamental values such as democracy and children's rights, the importance of children's contributions and activities, cooperation, and partnership between professionals, families and compulsory schooling. Approximately 77% of Swedish children aged one to five years old attend preschool if they have special needs, or while their parents are working, studying, or on parental leave (Swedish National Agency for Education 2006). There are two staff categories in Swedish preschools: Preschool teachers and day-care attendants. Over half of all preschool employees have university degrees in early childhood education. The day-care attendants have a vocational qualification at post-secondary level. In Sweden, preschool teachers work with children aged one to seven years. Preschool is an educational group activity for enrolled children between the ages of one and five years. Preschool class, as a distinct programme, begins at the age of six, and compulsory schooling starts at the age of seven.

Professionalism

The professional field for the preschool teacher's role can be understood by the connection between the society and its development (Carlgren and Marton 2000). The society formulates expectations (the arena for formulation), which preschool teachers realise in their daily work (the arena of realisation) (Lindensjö and Lundgren 2000). Traditions formed by different cultures influence the free space of action that exists to realise these expectations. The curriculum for the preschool, (Swedish National Agency for Education 1998) gives a clear task to preschool teachers. The public function of the preschool in Swedish society is to be a first step in the education system and to influence lifelong learning. According to Carlgren and Marton (2000), the first step in the profession is to problematise things usually taken for granted and to question what it means to learn different things, and to unite concepts of 'how' and 'what' to learn. The teacher should handle groups of children and encourage situations that promote learning. This is the teacher's pedagogical task. Carlgren and Marton (2000) write about progression in the teacher's profession, highlighting the ways in which teachers deal with changes over time. For example, factual meanings may change depending on different circumstances existing in schools, or mental meanings may change in accordance with how the teacher interprets and reacts differently to new demands. One of the mechanisms through which the profession is developing is the unequal division of teachers' professional status. Some teachers take more progressive positions and innovate through new solutions, while others struggle against change and development in the profession.

The sociological perspective on professionalism relates to the professional group striving for status and position, and dealing with power. The pedagogical perspective describes professionalism as being the same as competence. Professionalism is constructed in the teacher training programme in a dual sense (Moore 2007). First, it develops in connection with theories and perspectives at the university, and then in practical periods in preschools with supervisory teachers. The supervisors have constructed their professionalism once, and have then re-constructed it with their new experiences, in response to the changing demands in their society and working area.

The Swedish National Agency for Education (1999) states that the pedagogical activities, derived from the curriculum, require professional competence. They are formulated through employing three basic ideas. These ideas are:

- *competence* to concretise the aims of the curriculum, select and organise the content, and to be able to evaluate the activities and learning processes;
- *teaching*, to create good conditions for learning, to create situations that promote learning, and to know how to lead the teaching towards its educational aims;
- to formulate an *ethical stance* and subsequently have a clear *ethical attitude*.

Methodology

Fifty-seven students and preschool teachers chose to participate in this survey. The sample consisted of 30 student teachers at university and 27 preschool teachers. The students were between 21 and 46 years old, and the preschool teachers were between 26 and 64 years old. They took their teacher diplomas between 1964 and 2003.

The students completed the questionnaire during a lesson at their university and distributed the questionnaires to their supervisors at the preschools. For the analysis, every question is considered from two perspectives – from the student teachers' and teachers' viewpoints.

Both groups answered a questionnaire with questions that were formulated in accordance with the aim of this study: What does the concept of professionalism imply for you? What does a professional teacher do in preschool? How does professionalism develop? What does preschool teachers' professionalism mean in comparison with professionalism in other closely related professional categories, such as day-care attendants or recreational pedagogues? The focus lay on the respondents' thoughts in variations of experiences and concepts. The inquiry areas were broad, allowing the preschool teachers and students to express their thoughts with as little influence as possible. The questionnaire also covered the background areas of age and gender, and place of work for preschool teachers. The questionnaire was chosen to get a larger coverage of preschool teachers and students in the study.

The qualitative analysis was carried out based on a latent content analysis approach (Graneheim and Lundman 2003). The analysis began with a read-through of the material. During the initial phase, the questionnaire answers were read repeatedly in order to gain an overall impression and to find patterns in the answers given. After this general analysis, the main analysis was undertaken with the initial aim of identifying and describing generic conceptions of professionalism – that is, what was common to all participants. The material was read through and the quotations that indicated the significance of professionalism were marked. A second aim was to identify and describe conceptions of professionalism specific to students and to preschool teachers, respectively. Therefore, in the next reading, quotations demonstrating similarities and differences were marked. The different replies were marked out from the material and spread over a large surface to obtain totality. Once more, similar replies formed categories and remaining quotations were compared with each other through similarities and differences until all quotations were categorised.

Findings

The findings presented from the four themes in the study are based on students' and preschool teachers' conceptions of (a) professionalism, (b) acting like a professional teacher, (c) professionalism in development, and (d) professionalism in relation to other professions. The findings have been categorised further and sub-categories are presented in sub-headings.

Students' and preschool teachers' conceptions of professionalism

In this study, the concept of professionalism was expressed in the two categories of *attitude* and *knowledge*. Within the category 'attitude', both the preschool teachers and the students focused on their professional actions. They deliberately assumed the children's perspective. Furthermore, the teachers felt satisfaction and pride in their profession. It was also found that the teachers were professional in their workplace relationships, without entering into personal relations.

> One practises the profession in a competent, objective and ethically respectable way. Reflection, self-knowledge and empathy.[1] (Teacher)

The second category that they expressed was 'knowledge' – that is, what preschool teachers knew when they taught. Those preschool teachers were skilful; they knew how preschool teachers should treat and respond to children, and how to formulate activities with their perspective in mind. They were able to apply their knowledge in response to different situations. The preschool teachers were able to collaborate with both parents and other staff. They also emphasised the social function of the profession. This can be illustrated by the following quotation:

> Complete knowledge within theory that can be put into practice. To see the children and arrange pedagogical activities from their perspectives. That I can work with all and with everything that belongs to the profession in an individual way. (Teacher)

Act like a professional teacher

The preschool teachers perceived themselves as acting professionally according to two sub-categories. The first sub-category was about observing themselves and children from a contextual developmental perspective. The second sub-category dealt with pedagogical activities in their entirety, with a theoretical base towards practical acting.

Teachers observing themselves and children from a contextual developmental perspective

In this category, the participants expressed that preschool teachers worked from the intentions of the curriculum. They created documentation and reflected together with the children in order to develop learning. Children's thoughts, questions and ideas were taken seriously. Preschool teachers found it easy to cooperate with colleagues and parents. Preschool teachers were sensitive and responsible.

> Preschool teachers behave with children, parents and colleagues in ways in which they encounter reciprocal respect for their work. Make preparations for activities with a goal and purpose. Documentation and reflection. Responsibility for the didactic. (Student)

The pedagogical activities in their entirety with a theoretical base towards practical acting

The content in this category meant that the preschool teachers had knowledge, which increased the potential capabilities for children's lifelong learning. The theoretical base made it possible for the teacher to support the children in their quest for knowledge, in their learning and development. The preschool teachers emphasised the focus on children's capacity, needs and development.

> Consider the children from their needs, competencies and developmental level. Use a warm heart in combination with a cold brain. (Teacher)

Children were considered to be equally valuable individuals. Preschool teachers wanted to observe and perceive children's well-being and to become a role model. They also wanted to meet each child's needs with the same respect as the needs of the whole group. The teacher assumed a pedagogical way of thinking. Through theoretical competence, the teacher worked in a goal-oriented way and developed further in her/his work.

> A professional teacher knows what she stands for, which values she has, how she shall act, design teaching to reach each child and teaching which is based on the curriculum. (Student)

Professionalism in development

From the preschool teachers' and the students' descriptions, three sub-categories emerged, that focused on developing professionalism – that is, *further training, collective reflection* on further development and *experience*.

Further training

In their descriptions, both the preschool teachers and the students emphasised that the core of their profession developed with further training, but that knowledge changed with time and that teachers could never become skilled enough. Furthermore, the teachers pointed out that professionalism developed through discussion forums where pedagogical questions arose, through the pedagogical network and through action research in groups of children. Therefore it was seen as important that the teacher wanted to learn new things and was eager to attend new courses.

> Professionalism develops through an interplay between education, reflection and further training. It keeps pedagogical awareness alive. (Teacher)

Reflection as a collective phenomenon

It was shown that professionalism developed through preschool teachers learning together with their colleagues and the children while reflecting with them on preschool activities. It was also noteworthy that preschool teachers conveyed what made them professional in different contexts:

> The team can revise their skills together through improving theories, laws, policy documents, and reflections. I will never become fully trained, as knowledge changes with time. (Student)

Experience

Both preschool teachers and students pointed out that professionalism developed through practical experiences in the profession. They emphasised that teachers should be open to new ideas, and to continuing to conduct evaluation which should lead to development.

> Through the experience of the profession and its individuals. (Student)

Professionalism – relation to other professions

While the responses under the previous categories reflect views on the participants' own profession, preschool teachers and students showed a variety of perspectives on other related professions. Day-care attendants or recreational pedagogues were perceived as either *disparate* or *equivalent*, compared with the preschool teacher profession. An additional perspective dealt with common practice – that is, that *cooperation* was considered to enrich different professions. However, the majority of the preschool teachers and the students considered that preschool teachers' professionalism was markedly different in relation to other professions.

Dissimilarities in representations

In this sub-category, the preschool teachers and the students considered that all groups had different competencies in their own areas.

It was significant that preschool teachers had a higher education and a wider pedagogical base of knowledge compared with day-care attendants. They had a deeper theoretical base, and more didactic knowledge. The preschool teachers were seen as responsible for the pedagogical activities and showing an analytical attitude even though their tasks were similar. Furthermore, the students pointed out that the preschool teachers had a different attitude towards children.

> A preschool teacher and recreational pedagogue perform most of the pedagogical work, while a day-care attendant takes care of the practical aspects. Preschool teachers are needed to increase professionalism in preschools. Through their higher knowledge and education, they are able to offer support and confidence to day-care attendants. (Student)

The preschool teachers pointed out that there were no differences between the professions of a recreational pedagogue and a preschool teacher, as they had an equivalent education and performed pedagogical work. However, the difference between preschool teachers and day-care attendants was that the main focus in day-care attendants' work was care. A preschool teacher described it thus:

Day-care attendants' and preschool teachers' professionalism differs in that preschool teachers have university education, they have learned more about children's development and learning. (Teacher)

Equivalent perspective towards tasks

The responses under this sub-category emphasised that there were different professions that did the same work. Students asserted that education had great importance, but that preschool teachers' professionalism had equal value with other professions. A day-care attendant's professionalism can be equally high as a teacher's. Furthermore, they maintained that all work within the preschool area should strive for the same goals.

No profession is better than another! Multiplicity and different ideas and experiences are absolutely necessary ingredients if we are to have good schools for our children. (Student)

Cooperation that enriches mutually

The preschool teachers and the students emphasised the fact that all professions should enrich one another, which means that collaboration is a necessity. It was seen as important to have a common view of knowledge in the team.

Collaboration, each person contributes with whatever the person is able to and does a revision together with the others. It requires good knowledge of development and learning proportionately to each other. Day-care attendants' professionalism builds on experiences and reflections, while knowledge interchanges between preschool teachers and their colleagues. (Teacher)

Conclusions

How do Swedish students and preschool teachers regard professionalism today? The aim of this study was to investigate, identify and describe different ways in which Swedish students and preschool teachers interpret the concept of professionalism. This study investigated how participants understand professionalism in an institutional context as well as in comparison with other closely related professional categories.

The concept of professionalism

In this study, the results from both preschool teachers and students strengthened the notion that the concept of professionalism stems from the possession of knowledge. Professionalism also deals with practical actions in a competent way. Furthermore, 'ability and experience' were in focus. Therefore the concept of professionalism could be considered in two ways. On the one hand, ability can be seen as knowledge gained at a scientific level as a teacher qualification. On the other hand, ability can be measured through experiences gained through practical activities with several associates such as children, colleagues, and parents, and through cooperation with social services in the community.

Professionalism according to Colnerud and Granström (1996) consists of the teacher being able to concretely describe their professional area with the help of language and professional concepts. This language makes communication in the profession easier, and it has an important function in developing identity. The teacher has the ability to describe the professional area with essential concepts. Aims, teaching, learning, and the process of planning and ethical attitude are included in this area. None of the participants in this study focused on professional language and its importance for professionalism. In order to know how to communicate her/his knowledge in the professional field, the teacher needs to possess a well-developed language skill set. Today, this is even more important, due to every teacher constructing their own practice out of the arena of formulation from the expectations of the curriculum. A potential risk is that preschool teachers can become private if they do not share a common understanding of professional language. To obtain status and legitimacy in society, professional competencies need to be articulated and communicated to the public.

According to Colnerud and Granström (1996) and Forslund and Jacobsen (2000), actions in the teaching profession are restrictive with a clear ethical perspective. This aspect is visible in the results of this study, as it was seen that ethical attitudes in the workplace must not become private or personal. To gain this dimension requires self-knowledge and knowledge of the public function of the task. Both categories in this study focused on taking an empathetic ethical attitude. Work is based on creating close relationships in order to know how partners can influence each other. This new progressive perspective and these methods of working can influence professional areas holistically, reconstructing existing concepts.

How does a professional teacher act?

In this study, the preschool teachers and the students expressed what a professional teacher did in preschool in two sub-categories – namely, to see themselves and children in a contextual developmental perspective, and the pedagogical activities as a whole with a theoretical base towards practical conduct. In the first sub-category, the curriculum for the preschool (Swedish National Agency for Education 1998) was used actively as a basis for reflection for both preschool teachers and students. In order to be able to use reflection as a tool, a theory base, a perspective and knowledge are needed within several areas in the organisation: in the contents, in conversation and in social relations (Colnerud and Granström 1996; Forslund and Jacobsen 2000). The students were more aware than the preschool teachers of the comprehensive picture of the ethical attitude and the holistic pedagogical contents. Both preschool teachers and students saw the importance of the entire sphere of collaboration with children, colleagues, parents and supervisors. The second sub-category emphasised the overall picture that educational activities derive from an ethical attitude towards fundamental values and the pedagogical content that exists in the curriculum (Swedish National Agency for Education 1998). Preschool teachers' views on children, as expressed in the survey, were more in the shape of the psychological theory including developmental stages. Students see the child as a construction, thus adopting a perspective derived for postmodern theory (e.g. Dahlberg, Moss, and Pence 1999). Children are seen as constructions in pedagogical activities and in different situations which are planned and accomplished. What happens when these two different views meet during common activities, where the students encounter the preschool teachers in their practical study periods? Will the preschool teachers' viewpoints act as a model for the students, or will the preschool teachers become influenced by the new theory presented by students, thus supporting their point of view and subsequent endeavours? Synthesising different ideas may lead to reflection. If the teacher has to reframe her/his existing thoughts, strength in new knowledge can be cultivated.

How does professionalism develop?

The importance of reflection is emphasised in the responses to this study. Schön's concept of reflection is seen to be a tool towards creating 'the reflective practitioner' (Schön 1987). In this way, professionalism can become a goal for developing the preschool teachers' actual practice with the concepts 'reflection-on-action' and 'reflection-in-action' that assume reflection over and in actual practical situations. Lidholt (1999) points out that knowledge in action develops through a reflective discussion of the situation. Preschool teachers can develop these reflective discussions in situations consisting of 'uncertainty, instability, uniqueness, and value conflict' (25). Other concepts that influence development in professionalism are teachers' thinking and reframing. When teachers become conscious of their own frames, according to Lidholt (1999), they also become conscious about alternative ways of framing practical situations. Reflections have led to change and renewal in work. To be able to use reflection for this purpose, preschool teachers need a basis in the form of theories, perspectives and knowledge in several fields, in the organisation, in content, in discussions and in social relationships in preschools.

How do preschool teachers and students see the relationships with other professions within the same field?

Berntsson (1999) states that that a characteristic of a profession today is that its members carry a specific base of knowledge to which they have the sole right, which should be worthwhile and meaningful. It can therefore be seen that this could lead to conflicts between different professional groups – for example, preschool teachers and day-care attendants (cf. Kinos in this volume). In this study it became clear that both preschool teachers and students often benefit from an inclusion theory – that is, that preschool teachers and day-care attendants carry out the same work. However, preschool teachers possess the pedagogical responsibility and didactic knowledge together with a longer and higher education. The findings allude to the fact that all the different professions within the preschool are welcomed and that staff collaborate to combine their competencies. But even if all employees have the same basic education, different competencies exist at a personal level. Does this mean that tasks can be accomplished with different depth and quality depending on the individual's way of thinking? What does this mean for the team? Some of the preschool teachers in this study assert everybody's equal competencies and value in their work. A day-care attendant with a post-secondary education can be equally competent as a preschool teacher with university education. Some saw preschool activities as divided into two parts: the day-care attendants should be more responsible for educare and the teacher for the pedagogical work. This may be due to the preschool teachers' difficulties in claiming their professionalism and legitimacy in society. They cannot, for instance, achieve adequate status in the form of wages. Subsequently, they do not receive proper acknowledgment for their responsibilities, nor is their required education valued.

However, the fundamental question remains: How can a qualitative difference between staff become visible and valued in preschool? Preschools are built on democracy, and therefore everybody is considered to have equal value in the working team, although having qualitatively different educations.

Note

1. Since the study was carried out in Sweden, all quotations presented in this article were translated into English by the authors.

References

Berntsson, P. 1999. Förskolans läroplan och förskolläraryrkets professionalisering. [The Curriculum of the pre-school and the professionalization of the pre-school teachers' profession]. *Pedagogisk forskning i Sverige* 4: 198–211.

Carlgren, I., and F. Marton. 2000. *Lärare av i morgon* [Teacher of tomorrow]. Kristianstad: Lärarförbundet.

Colnerud, G., and K. Granström. 1996. *Respekt för lärare. Om lärares professionella verktyg – yrkesspråk och yrkesetik* [Respect for teachers. About teachers' professional tools – professional language and professional ethic]. Stockholm: HLS Förlag.

Dahlberg, G., P. Moss, and A. Pence. 1999. *Beyond quality in early childhood education and care.* London: Falmer.

Forslund, K., and M. Jacobsen. 2000. *Professionell kompetens hos pedagoger inom förskolan* [Preschool pedagogues' professional competence]. Linköping: Linköpings Universitet.

Graneheim, M.Q., and B. Lundman. 2003. Qualitative content analysis in nursing research: Concepts, procedures and measures to achieve trustworthiness. *Nurse Education Today* 24: 105–12.

Lidholt, B. 1999. *Adjustment, fight and escape: How preschool staff cope with effects of financial cutbacks and other changes in preschool.* Acta Upsaliensis. Uppsala Studies in Education 83.

Lindensjö, B., and U. Lundgren. 2000. *Utbildningsreformer och politisk styrning* [Reforms of education and political steering]. Stockholm: HLS förlag.

Moore, A. 2007. Understanding the social self: The role and importance of reflexivity in school/ preschool teachers' professional learning. In *Handbook of teacher education. Globalization, standards and professionalism in time change,* ed. T. Townsend and R. Bates. Dordrecht: Springer.

Schön, D.A. 1987. *Educating the reflective practitioner: Towards a new design for teaching and learning in the professions.* San Francisco: Jossey-Bass.

Swedish National Agency for Education. 1998. *Curriculum for the preschool, Lpfö 98.* Stockholm: Fritzes.

———. 1999. *Ständigt. Alltid! Skolans värdegrund. Kommentar till läroplanen* [Constantly. Always! Comments to the curriculum]. Stockholm: Liber.

———. 2006. *Descriptive data about preschool activities, school-age child care, and adult education in Sweden.* Stockholm: Liber.

What's in a name? Seeking professional status through degree studies within the Scottish early years context

Kate Adams

University of Strathclyde, Glasgow, Scotland

ABSTRACT: This article draws on two small-scale pieces of research that investigated the views of twenty-five final year students in the BA Early Childhood Studies programme at a Scottish university, and the views of ten recent graduates about early years job titles and perceptions of professionalism. Pen-and-paper questionnaires were used in both studies, with one study also including an analysis of texts from a final-year reflective assignment on professionalism. The article also discusses the impact of recent changes in the Scottish context, including: the introduction of a regulatory body, Scottish Social Services Council (SSSC); the National Review of the Early Years and Childcare Workforce; and changes in required qualifications for the future of an early years profession on early years workers' aspirations for professional status. It argues that the 'new' early years profession is in danger of being stillborn or dissipated across such a wide age range that the 'early' focus is lost.

RÉSUMÉ: Cet article s'appuie sur deux petites recherches sur les opinions de vingt cinq étudiants en dernière année d'étude pour devenir professionnel de la petite enfance dans une université écossaise, et les opinions de dix diplômés récents à propos des intitulés des métiers de la petite enfance et des perceptions du professionnalisme. Des questionnaires papier - crayon sont utilisés dans les deux études, l'une d'elles comportant aussi une analyse de textes produits à la fin d'une année d'un travail réflexif sur le professionnalisme. L'article discute également l'impact des changements récents sur les attentes des professionnels de la petite enfance quant au statut professionnel dans le contexte écossais: l'introduction du Conseil des Services Sociaux Ecossais; la Revue Nationale de la Petite Enfance et des Professionnels; et les changements dans les qualifications requises pour la future profession de la petite enfance. Il montre que la nouvelle profession de la petite enfance est en danger d'être 'mort-née' ou noyée dans une période d'âge si large que la centration sur les plus jeunes risque de se perdre.

ZUSAMMENFASSUNG: Dieser Beitrag wurde von zwei kleineren Studien inspiriert, in denen die Ansichten von fünfundzwanzig Studierenden im Abschlussjahr des BA Studiengangs 'Childhood Studies' einer schottischen Universität, sowie die von zehn Absolventinnen, zu Berufsbezeichnungen und Professionalität untersucht wurden. Schriftliche Befragungen wurden in beiden Studien eingesetzt; in eine wurden zusätzlich Textanalysen einer reflexiven Studienarbeit zu Professionalität einbezogen. Der Artikel diskutiert auch die Auswirkungen aktueller Veränderungen – wie die Einführung einer Aufsichtsbehörde, des "Scottish Social Services Council (SSSC), eines nationalen Berichts zur Personalsituation in der Frühpädagogik und Kinderbetreuung sowie veränderter Anforderungen and die Qualifikation für zukünftige Fachkräfte – auf das Streben der Beschäftigten nach professionellem Status. Es wird argumentiert, dass die "neue" frühpädagogische Profession Gefahr läuft, entweder totgeboren zu werden oder durch die Zuständigkeit für eine zu weite Altersspanne zu" verwässern' und den frühpädagogischen Fokus zu verlieren.

RESUMEN: Este artículo se basa en dos pequeños estudios que investigan la perspectiva de veinticinco estudiantes del último curso del programa de Educación Pre-escolar en una universidad escocesa, y la perspectiva de diez recientemente graduados, acerca de su trabajo y percepciones de profesionalismo. Cuestionarios de lápiz y papel fueron usados en ambos estudios, y un estudio incluyo también el análisis de textos sobre una reflexión en el último ano acerca del profesionalismo. El artículo discute también el impacto de cambios recientes para las aspiraciones profesionales, en contexto escoses, que incluyen: introducción de reglamentación; Consejo Escoses de Servicio Social; Estudio Nacional de la Fuerza de Trabajo Pre-escolar; y cambios en las calificaciones requeridas para la futura profesión pre-escolar. Se argumenta que la 'nueva' profesión pre-escolar corre peligro de ser disipada en un periodo de edad tan amplio, que el foco específico de interés 'pre-escolar' se pierde.

Introduction

Names matter:

> What's in a name? That which we call a rose by any other name would smell as sweet. (Romeo & Juliet, Act II, scene ii, 1–2 [http://www.allshakespeare.com/shakespeare.masters/276])

Juliet tells Romeo that a name is an artificial convention and that she loves the person called Montague, not the name or the family. Romeo rejects his family name and vows to 'be new baptised' as Juliet's lover. Therein lies the central struggle and tragedy of this most famous of Shakespeare's plays because the name carried with it so many other connections.

Romeo and Juliet's tragic dilemma may not, at first glance, appear to have much relevance to the issue of how early years practitioners are referred to in Scotland. Yet the question of 'what's in a name?' is an issue because it has relevance for how work with young children is perceived in Scottish society and the value accorded to people who choose to work with young children. Industrially, a variety of job titles may help or hinder employment prospects, while from a parental perspective, these may confuse parents and cause unnecessary difficulties. The data in this article show that early years workers who seek professional status through study are limited in the return they get for their efforts by the misconceptions that surround their job, and by the terminology around job titles used by governments and employers.

Professionalism in the Scottish early years context

Professional status for early years workers is not a well-defined concept in the Scottish context. Egan (2004) has used the term 'professionality' to refer to the understanding of oneself as a professional in terms of constructing, holding, re-evaluating and re-constructing a set of professional values which affect the ways in which s/he carries out work in a practice setting: Professionality is clearly much more than the outward signs of status. Scottish early years workers who are studying to degree level are, in Egan's terms, developing values and applying them to their work. However, as will be apparent from the contextual description in this section, early years workers need to be particularly strong to protect their developing professional values in the face of pervasive societal undervaluing of their work.

Recent history

During 2003 and 2004 Scotland experienced a long strike by nursery nurses who were pursuing a national agreement on pay and conditions. Industrial action of this kind may not immediately suggest a workforce with professional commitment. However, for many early years workers, the strike was an emotionally difficult plea for recognition of the importance of nursery education for children, which, as Moss and Penn (1996) have argued, should be accompanied by recognition of the people who work with them. Analysing the changing Scottish context in which early years practitioners have worked in recent years can help explain the phenomenon of carers apparently abandoning those they care for.

Since 1996/7, when the Conservative government introduced vouchers to enable all four-year-olds to access places in any available provision (including private nurseries and playgroups), politicians, parents and professionals alike have welcomed the expansion of nursery provision in the United Kingdom. Subsequently, the Labour government increased funding to local authorities to expand the number of nursery places. Following the initial rush for places by parents of four-year-olds, a number of authorities developed services to target 'priority 3' (inclusion and equality) of the Scottish Executive's National Priorities for Education (Scottish Executive 2002)[1] as well as to extend provision for under-threes. A falling school population in primary schools provided physical space for new nursery classes and some opportunities for integrating other early years services. While in some areas integrated campuses appeared that provided all levels of service, in smaller localities many early years or family centres were developed, with services for children from birth to five, and some after-school-care provision for young primary school children. These centres have generally been staffed and managed by nursery nurses holding a Nursery Nurse Examination Board certificate (NNEB) or a Higher National Certificate (HNC) in Early Childcare and Education (a one- or two-year further education qualification designed for school leavers, with minimal entry requirements). The policy decision not to appoint teachers to these centres provided an unprecedented career opportunity for nursery nurses as they were now able to apply for management posts previously reserved for teachers.

While these developments were unfolding, the Scottish Executive's revision of the Schools (Scotland) Code in 2002 had complicated repercussions for the early years sector. The revision was intended to 'give local authorities greater flexibility in deploying teachers in pre-school centres' (HMIE 2007, 2) by removing the statutory requirement to have a set ratio of one teacher to twenty children in nursery classes. This prompted some authorities to re-deploy qualified teachers out of direct work with children in nursery classes or schools into support, coordination, or teaching roles in primary classes to cover a shortage of primary teachers. The resultant replacement of the teachers by nursery nurses seemed a good career advancement opportunity for nursery nurses, but had some unwelcome side effects: Many establishments were left with no employees qualified to degree level; early years expertise was lost; and a number of nursery classes found themselves being nominally led by the primary head teacher, or depute,[2] who knew little of nursery pedagogy. In these situations, the quality of nursery education became solely dependent on the practice of nursery nurses.

The increased funding given to parents for nursery children's places since 1996 has suited entrepreneurs, and many private nurseries have sprung up to meet the widespread needs for full-time and extended day places. Many of these establishments keep costs manageable by training their staff on the job. This has led to a third type of early years worker, which previously only existed in the voluntary sector: the unqualified employee. Few private nursery schools can afford a full-time teacher, and their partnership with local authorities provides access to in-service courses for all early years workers, and access to an advisory part-time teacher.

The political commitment of all parties to the expansion of nursery school provision in the late 1990s also provided an opportunity for universities across the United Kingdom to introduce early childhood studies degrees, and many early years workers all over the country enrolled in these on a mainly part-time basis. Taking on further study arguably exhibits both a desire for public recognition of one's abilities and a desire for up-to-date knowledge and self-improvement: both characteristics that are generally ascribed to a professional attitude. When degree courses began in 1997, there were very few opportunities for promotion within individual nursery schools, but family centres, and an expansion of provisions for 0–3 year olds, have meant that these opportunities have increased. The increased responsibility expected of early years staff through these developments, and a desire within the sector for formal recognition of extra study, were part of the background to the strike of 2003–2004.

However, unfortunately for the nursery workers, the strike did not deliver the desired outcome of a national collective agreement on pay and conditions. A key factor in this was that the Scottish Executive was conscious of the costs of early childcare and education for rural and small local authorities and therefore chose not to step into pay negotiations to support a national agreement. This led to the single thing the union had been trying to avoid: separate negotiations by each local authority. The Scottish Executive justified its hands-off approach as encouraging flexible services with differing staffing models to meet differing needs. In reality, the separate negotiations resulted in a variety of pay and conditions of service across the different education authorities and a correspondingly wide array of job titles for what was previously known as the 'nursery nurse'. This array is illustrated by the following list of job titles gathered from students who completed an early childhood studies degree in 2004; all of the students held the same basic qualification and all were involved, to some degree, in working with children:

- Nursery Nurse
- Childhood Development Officer
- Early Childhood Development Officer
- Early Years Worker
- Early Years Practitioner
- Early Childhood Worker
- Early Childhood Practitioner
- Play Leader
- Senior Practitioner
- Team Leader
- Crèche Manager

In Scotland as a whole, the number of different titles for similar early childhood jobs totalled 44 in 2005, as evidenced by two members of the group developing the Workforce Consultation document (Scottish Executive 2006a). In practice, these terms are often reduced to acronyms by management and workers alike, compounding the already numerous misunderstandings of parents and society about the nature of the job once called 'nursery nursing'. Yet, paradoxically, despite (or perhaps because of) the efforts of each authority to find a suitable title for the early years workers they employ, national newspapers still refer to 'nursery nurses' when they write about the early years workforce and, while acknowledging that a range of titles is currently used to refer to early years workers who are not trained teachers, a recent HMIE document (HMIE 2007) used 'nursery nurse' to enable the authors to discuss the national situation.

The variety of job titles for early years workers in Scotland provides fertile ground for a possible fragmentation of the concept of an early years profession at a time when this concept is only just emerging locally and beginning to be more widely explored internationally. Research on professional identity in the health sector which, like the early years sector, is staffed by two differently qualified sets of employees (doctors and nurses), shows a concern about the changing discourse of work and working cultures caused by what Leonard (2003) has called the new managerialism of the health service. Leonard has suggested that managerial attempts to effect organisational change also involve concerted efforts to change individual workers themselves. Yet, 'new managerialism' ignores the fact that the process of change itself produces new self-perceptions and new 'subjectivities' in the workers that compete with pre-existing self-perceptions and discourses of professionalism, gender, home and performance. These previously established self-perceptions act to undermine the managerial image of the worker as someone who will fit the stereotypic 'box' and do precisely what they are told. From an early years perspective, this raises the question: If this is the case with doctors and nurses who have a well-established and recognised professional identity, how much more likely are early years workers, who are just beginning to establish a professional identity, to perceive their job differently from those who manage the system in which they work? Furthermore, could it be that in expanding and changing early years provision, the educational reforms have subverted the sector's chances for professionalism by allowing such a range of names for the job?

A real danger of multiple titles is that they disperse the focus for professionalism in an area. Bernstein (2000, cited in Beck and Young 2005, 184) introduced the concept that particular structurings of knowledge may be related to the formation of occupational identities through 'inwardness' and 'inner dedication'. He used these terms to stress the humane relationship between a body of knowledge and the professional who creates and uses it. In other words, feeling 'part of a profession' is more likely to be related to the inner dedication of a significant group of people who share a body of recognisable knowledge and have a similar occupation. For the early years sector, this would suggest that the development of a profession that is committed to working with young children would therefore require an inclusive and coherent, versus a fragmented, occupational identity. It would also be important that the profession is clear about what workers are doing *with* young children: Doctors practise medicine; lawyers practise law; but it is children who practise childhood. The adult working with the child is practising care and education. Yet in many of the new early years job titles a clear statement of the educative role within the job is missing and this could well be central to the struggle for professionalism in the sector.

The establishment of the Scottish Social Services Council (SSSC) in April 2003 with the explicit aim to develop the regulation and registration of the early education and child-care workforce in Scotland, and the subsequent National Review of the Early Years and Childcare Workforce in 2006 were both expected to yield better clarity in the way that the early years workforce will be defined as a profession. However, these expectations have not yet been realised. Indeed, the remit of the National Review of the early years workforce included within it the review of out-of-school care and play-work as well as childminders and early years care and learning workers, making this a very broad workforce indeed. The report's comment that 'currently few of those working in early years and childcare would consider themselves part of a single workforce' (Scottish Executive 2006a, 16) is therefore unsurprising. Nonetheless, the concept of a different kind of professional, one who works in partnership and collaboration with others, is signalled in the earlier statement that 'each worker should recognise they are part of a wider workforce working in partnership with others to support delivery of an agreed set of outcomes for all children' (Scottish Executive 2006a, 10).

Signs of the development of a 'wider workforce' were already evident in changes made in 2006 to the basic level qualification needed for work in early years settings: the Higher National Certificate (HNC). The changes extended the age range of children at which the HNC programme was targeted: the traditional age range of birth to 8 years was changed to the new range of birth to 12 years. This means that in order to complete the HNC qualification, students now can do their required two placements working with children from a choice of four age ranges: 0–3 years; 3–5 years; 5–8 years; 8–12 years. This laid the foundations for linking academic routes to learning with workplace roles as follows:

- HNC level qualification: Support Workers, requiring some non-directive supervision
- HND/Diploma in Higher Education/Scottish Vocational Qualification Level 4: Practitioner, professional autonomy with some guidance
- Ordinary degree level: Lead Practitioner/Manager, leading the work of others.

The wider age range of children for which the HNC qualification now prepares students suits workforce planning and prepares for the integrated way government plans for services to be delivered in the future. However, free movement across the services may prove to be challenging to basic grade support workers whose concept of the work, or, in Bernstein's (2000, cited in Beck and Young 2005) terms, 'inner dedication', was definable by a particular age range of children.

On a more positive side, one hope for consolidating the position and status of a new early years profession arises from Foucault's (1972) conception of discourse as enabling those individuals with access to it to re-work it to create a new identity or subject position. From this perspective it is possible to see the changed career structure that the new family and children's centres have opened up for nursery nurses as creating a whole new range of 'ways of being', which could provide a sound basis for the development of a professional identity. Previously trained to be subservient to teachers in the education of children aged from 3 to 5 years, many nursery nurses are now the main professionals in family and children's centres, giving them a new autonomy of management that positions them as leaders of staff and the service, responsible for quality, direct communication with parents and other agencies, and answerable directly to the employing authority. However, in centres where teachers continue to be employed, teachers are less than willing to relinquish power to differently qualified personnel. Here again, the parallel with the health sector applies, with doctors reported as very reluctant to relinquish their traditional power to other medical colleagues (Danes 2000, cited in Leonard 2003).

The professional distance between nursery nurses and teachers has not been lessened by statements such as those made by the Labour Scottish Minister for Education and Young People in setting up the National Review of the Early Years and Childcare Workforce in 2004: In briefing the panel, the minister asked the members to 'consider the issues relating to non-teaching staff in early years and childcare settings' (Scottish Executive 2006a), justifying this on the basis that there already had been a review of teachers in 2000. The minister further added: 'Not every early years setting currently has a teacher and this is not going to change. Indeed the balance is likely to shift towards more non-teaching staff managing centres in the future.' The clear distinction between the two workforces drawn by the minister not only mirrors the public perception of a different professional role for nursery nurses and for teachers, but simultaneously denies the recognition of the educative role played by the early years workforce, a role expressly articulated by my research participants as integral to being an early years professional.

More positively, a sign of the health of the new profession has been the increasing numbers of early years' workers achieving degree qualifications. Since 1998, five Scottish universities have introduced degree courses for early childhood practitioners and these are consistently over-subscribed. In the final learning journal assignments of students enrolled in one early childhood degree programme at my university, students acknowledged that the reasons they gave in the opening statements of their learning journal for enrolling were somewhat naïve and often related to a desire for promotion or 'to show everybody I have a brain'. For example, one student clearly wished to change what people thought of her:

> My reason for participating in the BA degree is to prove to myself that I can achieve such an accolade. To be able to say 'I have a degree' rather than people presume that I baby-sit for 35 hours a week. I hate that people stereotype me.

However, towards the end of her programme, this student wrote that she realised later there was more to be gained than that: 'I can see from reading my reflective journal that I have done a lot of growing up and I am not as naïve.' Another student initially wanted to gain the degree because she felt people 'look down on a nursery nurse qualification', but at the end of study reflected: 'I wanted to better my HNC so that other people would value my profession more than they do currently, but the effect has been that *I* now realise how valuable my profession is.'

Valuing of the work by the workers is a first essential step for an emergent profession. This is highlighted in Osgood's (2004) research which describes how workers resisted the marketisation and economisation of early years education and childcare. Rather than valuing a business approach to professionalism, the participants in Osgood's study wanted to heighten their professionalism through collaborative ways of working which acknowledge the emotional investment and personal sacrifices they make.

Examples of this type of personal commitment appear frequently in the final reflective essays of students at my university. Students acknowledge the responsibilities of professionalism in attitude; in challenging their own thinking through reading; in inspiring others; in initiating and facilitating change; in promoting quality; and in involving practitioners in understanding why the quality of provision should be the best possible. The impact of study, and of training in reflective skills, on professional practice is well exemplified by the following statement from a final-year student:

> I always thought I was quite good at reflecting on practice, but I wasn't really. When I wasn't happy with an area of the nursery I would stand and look at the area, thinking about how the children used it, trying to analyse the problem and come up with ideas for improvement by perhaps entering into discussion with my colleagues (or perhaps not if I had a hunch they might not agree with my thoughts). Now, when I am not happy with workplace practices, I reflect by using many more processes such as: identifying and noting problems and aims; reading literature; devising an action plan to include review and evaluation. I also discuss issues with my tutors and fellow students, and I am no longer afraid to discuss ideas with work colleagues because I now know I can explain and justify my thoughts.

These students fit easily into the definition of a professional given in the National Review of the Early Years and Childcare Workforce (Scottish Executive 2006a, 54) as a person possessing 'a unique set of skills, knowledge and values'. Carr (2000) stresses the importance of judgment, based on objective evidence, between several possibly competing strategies as the keystone of the argument for considering teaching a profession. MacNaughton

(2003) describes an early childhood professional as: 'strategic and reflective because he or she uses specialised knowledge as the basis for actions, and questions the effects of specialised knowledge in action' (293). In an example of this type of professional behaviour, one BA student wrote, 'While I value others' viewpoints I now look for evidence to support my thinking. I feel better equipped to justify actions and decisions.'

Examples like these of the emerging culture of professionalism within one early years degree programme suggest that while societal perceptions might be no closer to identifying early years workers as professionals, within the qualified early years workforce a shift in self-perception is taking place. Given Pascal's (1992) argument that self-perception is the key to the ability of educarers to be influential, the period immediately after the Scottish nursery nurses' unsuccessful strike and the subsequent proliferation of new job titles seemed a good time to explore the sector's emerging sense of being a professional workforce.

In the rest of this article I draw on two small studies to illustrate my argument that the 'new' early years profession is in danger of being stillborn as the government broadens the age range at which qualifications are targeted and possibly loses the focus of the specialist knowledge which might create a professional area of work.

Study 1: A name for the new early years professional

In May 2004, a simple questionnaire was given to the twenty-five final-year students of the part-time BA in early childhood studies programme at my university with the aim of establishing the views of committed practitioners on the effects of the multiplication of job titles. Questions explored key features of students' current work, their views about the proliferation of job titles, and their preferred job title. The students had considerable experience and had been employed full time in early years establishments during the period of their study.

Results and discussion

Twenty-three of the twenty-five final-year students responded to the questionnaire. In answer to the first question, 'What's in a name? Choose a title that reflects your job', fourteen respondents chose the term 'Early Years or Early Childhood Practitioner', four chose 'Nursery Nurse' or 'Early Childhood Development Officer', four said their actual work had no relationship to any of the titles, and one added 'Early Childhood Educator' to the list.

At the time that the questionnaire was administered, the job titles 'Nursery Nurse' and 'Early Childhood Development Officer' were the current employee titles of those who worked either in a private nursery or for Glasgow Council.

The second question asked the students to nominate the key features of their current job. The following aspects were identified by the respondents:

(1) Working with children (including planning, observing and assessing);
(2) Working with parents/other agencies/community;
(3) Professional report writing;
(4) Administration, staff development, curriculum monitoring and evaluation, development planning, covering for lunch and tea breaks, staff sickness and so on (predominantly, but not exclusively, managers);
(5) Supporting other staff or students;
(6) Tidying, cleaning, organisation of resources (exclusively basic grade staff and some as much as 20% of their time).

For eleven respondents, working with children took up 50% to 95% of their working time, while for nine respondents, this aspect took up less than 50% of their time; of the nine who gave this answer, eight were managers or deputy managers and one had a social work post in family support. Three respondents did not complete this section.

Asked to nominate personal and professional disadvantages of the lack of a clearly recognisable job title, all respondents ($n = 23$) indicated that a name for the profession was necessary.

The personal disadvantages experienced by the respondents were of four types: being confused with medical personnel in social settings; realising that key stakeholders lacked a clear understanding of their job; not being respected or valued for the work they did; and others finding their work difficult to categorise.

The three students who reported their position being confused with health nurses said that they had been asked medical questions in social situations and four others said that they regularly encountered faulty assumptions about the breadth and range of their job from parents, other professionals and society. Of the twenty-three respondents, thirteen stated that the nature of the job and its importance was underestimated and undervalued by society and other professionals and this was evident in statements that were made to them such as: 'It must be great playing with children all day', 'Lack of a title makes it seem not like a "proper" job', and 'People's opinions of titles reflect on how they treat you'. Other comments related to the difficulties of form completion for car insurance and for job applications because the current job title did not fit into any of the pre-specified lists held by insurance companies. The overall plea of the respondents is captured in the following statement: 'I would like to be categorised under "education", not "general" or "caring".'

In reporting professional disadvantages, respondents again nominated the confusion of their profession with medical personnel and lack of understanding of the true nature of the job as issues, but a few new issues were also reported. In particular, seven respondents felt it was professionally disadvantageous for the educator role not to be acknowledged in job titles and three reported that the job title variation had caused a divide between professionals in their workplace, or confusion in moving from one employer to another; additionally, these respondents said that this made career progress more difficult. Ten students felt there was no recognition of their work or its value. They also said that the lack of professional identity, being ignored or patronised, and work colleagues' suspicion of further study all undermined their professional status. One respondent wrote: 'Society perceives an early years care and education certificate as a Mickey Mouse qualification.' The antidote to this was articulated by one respondent who wrote: 'a professional name will bring people together, gain more respect and understanding from people outside the profession'.

The third question asked respondents to state which of three possible job titles they would prefer: 'early years teacher'; 'pedagogue'; or 'educarer'. Eighteen of the twenty-three respondents indicated they would prefer a changed job title; three said they did not want a change, and two did not respond to this question. Of those who said they would prefer a change ($n = 18$), five chose 'teacher', one chose 'pedagogue', three chose 'educarer', and two respondents made a point of adding the term 'educator'. The remaining seven did not indicate a chosen title but wanted a change, mostly because they wanted recognition for the degree to differentiate themselves from non-graduate early years workers.

The justifications for the preferred job titles were interesting: The respondent who chose 'pedagogue' as her preferred title suggested this as a title for degree-qualified workers only. By contrast, the two respondents who added 'educator' justified this term as being inclusive of all early years workers and noted that all are educators of young children. The choice of 'educarer' was also for inclusive reasons, with the respondent arguing that the term highlighted the importance of both education and care and provided one title for all early years workers. 'Early years teacher' was argued for 'because we are teaching children in the early years'. At the same time, an element of resentment against the current system was discernible in statements in which BA graduates showed that they wanted to have the same status as primary teachers. These statements argued that the title 'teacher' would be recognised more by parents and other professionals. Two of the three respondents who said they did not want a change of job title may have been constrained by the current understanding in Scotland of the title 'teacher'; they stated that teachers have a different qualification. One respondent looked to other avenues of employment by stating that 'professionals with a BA in Early Childhood Studies may choose not to be a practitioner'. All of the respondents who agreed that a change in job title was desirable (*n* = 18), except those who had chosen educarer and educator for inclusive reasons (*n* = 5), wanted a special name for early years graduates (*n* = 13). Twelve of the thirteen felt that the job title should depend on the nature of employment, emphasising the 'promoted' status.

A final opportunity was given to students to suggest their own name for the profession. This question yielded five terms, as shown in Table 1.

Overall, the results of this study suggest that students who have been employed while studying understandably want some acknowledgement of their degree by their employers as well as some recognition from their colleagues. It would seem that the challenge of this finding is to achieve this result without exacerbating an already hierarchical system, for surely the ideal would be to encourage more colleagues to study to degree level. Yet there are tensions in this ideal. For example, in studying the paradoxes of professionalism in relation to substitute teachers in North America, Weems (2003) highlighted the tension between teacher identity and teacher role and concluded that the acknowledgement of teachers as professionals by their qualifications status alone directs attention away from the interactive, situated nature of effective teaching. Strengthening the argument for non-hierarchical relationships in teaching, another American study (Shim, Hestenes, and Cassidy 2004) has pointed out that higher quality childcare may be associated with a co-teacher structure rather than a hierarchical teacher structure, a finding congruent with those of Stephen, Brown, Cope, and Waterhouse (1997, cited in Wilson and Ogden Smith 1999, 41–57), who found that the behaviours of teachers and nursery nurses in Scottish pre-school classrooms were very similar. At the same time, the findings of the Effective Provision of Pre-School Education (EPPE) project (Sylva et al. 2004) have emphasised the importance of highly qualified staff to provide teaching input for effective learning in pre-schools, as well as the importance of working relationships for quality childcare and education. The clear message from these combined studies is that good early years provision does not need differentiated staff, but more highly qualified staff who can work together with professional respect and collaboration.

A further clear finding from this study is that the students in the BA in early childhood studies programme felt that educating children is such a large part of their work that it

Table 1.   Suggested name for the profession.

	Number of respondents
Educator	5
Practitioner	4
Educarer	3
Teacher	1
Development Officer	1

should be recognised as such. Fumoto, Hargreaves, and Maxwell's (2004) analysis of what is involved in 'teaching' in early education and childcare concluded that: 'the activity of teaching, broadly defined, might be said to concern all adults who work in this area and occur in all phases of the educational system' (187). They highlighted that:

> The decision to use a particular term to address a certain profession can have important consequences for the definition and status of that profession, because a term consists of constructs that represent its underlying meaning. (182)

Study 2: Do time and workplace culture affect personal views of professionality?

The second study I want to draw on in this article was a small-scale exploration of early year workers' perceptions of how having a degree impacted on the way that their work role was valued. The study involved a postal questionnaire sent in June 2005 to a sample of ten BA students who had graduated five or six years previously. As a further source of data, the final reflection assignments of an equal number of students from 2004 and 2005 were also used. The 2004 and 2005 graduates each had a minimum of 10 years' work experience before embarking on degree study and since their final assignment required students to discuss the requirements for early years professionalism as well as review their progress towards that goal, their material provided a good match for the questionnaire data.

The postal questionnaire explored the graduates' ideas about any differences between a graduate early years professional when compared with a basic level early years worker. Class discussions had suggested that some students perceived that the degree or a management post conferred the title 'professional', implying that less qualified basic level workers were not yet professional. Questions were asked about features that respondents saw as meriting the title of 'early years professional'; elements which could be seen to be part of the responsibilities of a 'basic grade professional' or which were reserved to management: and signs of recognition as a professional experienced by respondents since graduation. Content analysis of the reflection assignments also focused on these topics.

The results of the postal questionnaire indicated that the achievement of a degree proved worthwhile for many BA students in terms of job change or salary improvement, but recognition as a professional appeared to differ greatly from one workplace to another. Those graduates who had moved into lecturing positions perceived themselves as having achieved respect, but those who were directly working with children claimed they were no more respected by colleagues or other professionals as a result of their degree. A clear job title and a role of responsibility, as well as any level of promotion, were seen as important signs of having been recognised as a professional. Being invited to be part of a working party was likewise viewed as a significant indicator of recognition as a professional, but opportunities for this were strongly dependent on workplace and employing authority. Personal signs of professional recognition which emerged were sometimes more subtle and included:

- head teacher acknowledgement that ideas being suggested were topical, important and could be trusted to the graduate to develop (e.g. in an Additional Support Needs situation where individual educational programmes (IEPs) are often within the nursery nurse's responsibility);
- encouragement and support to share learning from the degree course with management, colleagues and parents and through making presentations at area in-service sessions;

- awareness that other professionals were not simplifying technical language or requiring to 'talk down' in multi-professional meetings to discuss individual children;
- being asked for advice by colleagues;
- receiving positive feedback from service providers following meetings (this from someone who moved into a support role for a variety of centres);
- the fact that at least one local authority now has a degree in early childhood studies as an essential criterion for a head of centre or deputy's post;
- the ability to exercise autonomy in the professional work setting (e.g. while in college lecturing positions).

A strong suggestion from the questionnaire responses was that opportunities to behave professionally were limited and circumscribed by workplaces. For example, a respondent who worked in a private nursery attributed all of the elements of early childhood professionals identified by Oberhuemer (2000, cited in Ebbeck and Waniganayake 2003, 29) to the manager, and did not attribute any freedom of professional judgement and decision-making to other staff except in a very basic way. Conversely, a different respondent noted that in a large fee-paying primary and secondary school which planned to expand its nursery section to a new building comprising five nursery classes, a wraparound[3] and an out-of-school care facility, a BA graduate was given the responsibility to create the design for the new building. The BA graduate was also given leadership of the 27 staff employed on the wraparound and out-of-school care provision, as well as continuing her duties as a key worker in the nursery where she worked alongside teachers. People who had moved into lecturing positions reported that they had appreciated the change in status because they were now working in an environment where the students were adults, but also because they now had time to think about values and principles, had autonomy to plan their work, and were expected to communicate their beliefs and values.

These data indicate that views of professionalism, and growth as a professional, are strongly linked to workplace context and to collective identities which, as Foster and Newman (2005) point out, 'are formed within structures, invite certain behaviours and circumscribe individual agency' (346). Lave (1991, cited in Altrichter 2005, 15) similarly argued that 'the construction of practitioners' identities is a collective enterprise and is only partly a matter of an individual's sense of self, biography and substance'. Thus, while ministerial proposals to broaden the experience of trainees across a range of types of establishments may help to establish a collective identity for early years and childcare workers by creating an occupation that is 'a large enough group to be noticed' (Scottish Executive 2006a, 39), this broadening may not be the full answer as some early years practitioners may be located in workplaces which do not allow them to increase their sense of professional status. These practitioners will be entitled to question the worth of being part of such a broader 'profession'.

Conclusion

These two small studies highlight a quandary for early years workers: While many are undertaking degree studies with a focus on their area of expertise of working with children aged birth to 8 years, they are finding that the educative nature of their role continues to be under-acknowledged and recognition as a professional appears to be more likely if they move into related fields such as preparing the next generation of early years workers.

The studies further show that the graduates acknowledged that their work had many common features with different forms of care, and that they had begun to appreciate the work of colleagues in different branches of early years work. This would suggest that these graduates had attained what Hargreaves (1994) described as a sense of obligation towards, and responsibility for, colleagues which he identified as a hallmark of professionals. Such an outcome is good news for Scottish policymakers who have stated that a sense of collective identity will be essential for collaborative working to deliver agreed outcomes for children (Scottish Executive 2006a), a goal embedded also in Scotland's new Curriculum for Excellence (Scottish Executive 2003b) for use by all those who work with children in the age range 3–18. Entrusting those who work with this age group with a curriculum positions those workers as educators, especially when the 2006 early years enquiry (http://www.scottish.parliament.uk/business/committees/education/reports-06/edr06-07.htm)   of the Scottish Parliament Education Committee identified the improvement of the cognitive element of 0–3 provision as a key area for development. Her Majesty's Inspectorate for Education (HMIE 2007) similarly acknowledges the educative nature of the early childhood workforce and has advocated the employment of degree-qualified staff, with a particular preference for teachers. Clearly, official documentation has high expectations for the early years workforce: the argument for a job title that reflects that role is strong. Recently, Boddy et al. (2007) have suggested that advocacy for pedagogues as generic workers across a wide age range may bring about a cohesive view of a new 'profession'. It may be that while the workforce consultation exercise between 2004 and 2006 found 'pedagogue' too strange for a Scottish context, the time may have come to reconsider the usefulness of this term if the early years workforce is to achieve the clarity and focus needed to allow the 'inner dedication' of the professional to develop.

Postscript

In June 2007 the Scottish National Party (SNP) was elected to government in the Scottish Parliament. The SNP promised an increase in the number of teachers in nursery education and acted on this promise almost immediately, specifying priority for schools in areas of disadvantage. A potentially more significant announcement has been the statement that proposals for a new BEd degree, that would prepare teachers to work with children aged from birth to eight years, are to be submitted by 2009. This suggests that two professions, related but differently qualified, will be involved in working with young children in Scotland for many years to come, whether it is a profession of pedagogues or a profession of nursery nurses alongside teachers.

Notes

1. The five priorities are: (1) Achievement and Attainment; (2) Framework for Learning; (3) Inclusion and Equality; (4) Values and Citizenship; and (5) Learning for Life.
2. Scottish usage meaning 'deputy'.
3. 'Wraparound' care refers to childcare that is additional to core entitlement to free pre-school education – for example, a core entitlement of 12.5 hours per week may be supplemented by additional hours paid by parents.

References

Altrichter, H. 2005. The role of the "professional community" in action research. *Educational Action Research* 13, no. 1: 11–26.

Beck, J., and M.F.D. Young. 2005. The assault on the professions and the restructuring of academic and professional identities: A Bernsteinian analysis. *British Journal of Sociology of Education* 26, no. 2 (April): 183–97.

Boddy, J., C. Cameron, P. Moss, A. Mooney, P. Petrie, and J. Statham. 2007. *Introducing pedagogy into the children's workforce.* London: Thomas Coram Research Unit.

Carr, D. 2000. *Professionalism and ethics in teaching.* London: Routledge.

Codd, J. 2005. Teachers as managed professionals in the global education industry: The New Zealand experience. *Educational Review* 57, no. 2: 193–206.

Ebbeck, M., and M. Waniganayake. 2003. *Early childhood professionals: Leading today and tomorrow.* London: Elsevier.

Egan, B. 2004. Constructing a professional identity: Some preliminary findings from students of early years education. *European Early Childhood Research Education Research Journal* 12, no. 2: 21–32.

Foster, T., and E. Newman. 2005. Just a knock back? Identity bruising on the route to becoming a male primary school teacher. *Teachers and Teaching* 11, no. 4: 341–58.

Foucault, M. 1972. *The archaeology of knowledge.* London: Routledge.

Fumoto, H., D. Hargreaves, and S. Maxwell. 2004. The concept of teaching: A reappraisal. *Early Years* 24, no. 2: 179–91.

Hargreaves, A. 1994. *Changing teachers, changing times: Teachers' work and culture in the post modern age.* London: Cassell.

Her Majesty's Inspectorate for Education (HMIE). 2007. *The key role of staff in providing quality pre-school education.* Livingston: HMIE.

Leonard, P. 2003. "Playing" doctors and nurses? Competing discourses of gender, power and identity in the British National Health Service. *Sociological Review* 51, no. 2: 218–37.

MacNaughton, G. 2003. *Shaping early childhood.* Maidenhead: Open University Press.

Moss, P. and H. Penn. 1996. *Transforming nursery education.* London: Paul Chapman Publishing.

Osgood, J. 2004. Time to get down to business. *Journal of Early Childhood Research* 2, no. 1: 5–24.

Pascal, C. 1992. Advocacy, quality and the education of the young child. *Early Years: An International Journal of Research and Development* 13, no. 1: 5–11.

Scottish Executive. 2002. *National Priorities in Education Newsletter* 1. http://www.scotland.gov.uk/Resource/Doc/46905/0024044.pdf.

———. 2003a. A curriculum for excellence. Curriculum Review Group. http://www.scotland.gov.uk/Publications/2004/11/20178/45862.

———. 2003b. A curriculum for excellence. Ministerial response. http://www.scotland.gov.uk/Publications/2004/11/20175/45848.

———. 2006a. *National review of the early years and childcare workforce, report and consultation.* Edinburgh: Blackwell.

———. 2006b. *Investing in children's futures – Scottish Executive response to national review of the early years and childcare workforce.* Edinburgh: Blackwell.

Scottish Parliament Education Committee – Early Years Inquiry. June 2006. http://www.scottish.parliament.uk/business/committees/education/reports-06/edr06-07.htm.

Shim, J., L. Hestenes, and L. Cassidy. 2004. Teacher structure and childcare quality in pre-school classrooms. *Journal of Research in Childhood Education* 19, no. 2: 143–59.

Sylva, K., E.C. Melhuish, P. Sammons, I. Siraj-Blatchford, and B. Taggart. 2004. The effective provision of pre-school education (EPPE) project. Technical Paper 12 – the final report: Effective pre-school education. London: Department for Education and Skills (DfES)/Institute of Education, University of London.

Weems, L. (2003) Representation of substitute teachers and the paradoxes of professionalism. *Journal of Teacher Education* 54, no. 3: 254–65.

Wilson, V., and J. Ogden-Smith, eds. 1999. *Pre-school educational research: Linking policy with practice.* Edinburgh: Scottish Executive, Education Department.

Website

http://www.allshakespeare.com/shakespeare.masters/276.

A Finnish viewpoint on professionalism in early childhood education

Kirsti Karila

University of Jyväskylä, Finland

ABSTRACT: This article discusses professionalism in early childhood education through the analytical tool of a research-based multi-level perspective that sees this as a cultural, communal, organisational, and individual phenomenon. Starting from an understanding of professionalism derived from a model of professional expertise, the article discusses the Finnish day-care context at the social and cultural level, followed by a discussion of field-specific knowledge as a tool for building professionalism. Professionalism is further examined as it plays out in the employees' working environment, the day-care centre and its working culture and from the perspective of the professionals themselves. Key characteristics of professionalism in the Finnish early childhood education sector are also summarised.

RÉSUMÉ: Cet article traite du professionnalisme dans le champ de la petite enfance grâce à un outil d'analyse inscrit dans une recherche, à plusieurs niveaux, qui le conçoit comme un phénomène culturel, commun, organisationnel et individuel. Fondée sur une compréhension du professionnalisme provenant d'un modèle d'expertise professionnelle, cette contribution concerne le contexte finlandais de l'accueil de la petite enfance, au niveau social et culturel. S'ensuit une discusssion de connaissances spécifiques à ce champ, comme instrument pour construire le professionnalisme. Cette notion est ensuite examinée dans la façon dont elle ressort des conditions de travail des employés, des lieux d'accueil et de leur culture professionnelle, ainsi que du point de vue des professionnels eux-mêmes. Les caractéristiques clefs du professionnalisme dans le secteur de l'éducation préscolaire finlandais sont également récapitulées.

ZUSAMMENFASSUNG: Dieser Artikel diskutiert Professionalität in der Frühpädagogik aus einer forschungsbasierten Mehrebenen-Perspektive, die Professionalität als kulturelles, soziales, organisationales und individuelles Phänomen analysiert. Ausgehend von einem Verständnis von Professionalität als Expertise erörtert der Beitrag den sozialen und kulturellen Kontext der Kindertageserziehung in Finnland um dann feldspezifisches Wissen als Mittel zur Entwicklung von Professionalität zu diskutieren. Professionalität wird zudem aus weiteren Perspektiven untersucht: in der Arbeitsumgebung der Kindertageseinrichtung und ihrer Arbeitskultur, wie auch aus der Perspektive der Fachkräfte selbst. Schlüsselcharakteristika von Professionalität in der Finnischen Frühpädagogik werden ebenfalls benannt.

RESUMEN: El artículo discute el profesionalismo en la educación preescolar a través de un instrumento de análisis de una perspectiva investigativa de niveles múltiples que la entiende como un fenómeno cultural, comunal, orgánico e individual. A partir de una comprensión del profesionalismo derivada del modelo de experto profesional, el articulo discute la enseñanza parvularia finlandesa en su nivel social y cultural, seguida de una discusión del conocimiento de terreno especifico como instrumente para construir profesionalismo. El profesionalismo es además examinado desde el punto de vista del ambiente laboral de los empleados, de la cultura laboral de las instituciones y de la perspectiva propia de los profesionales. Además se presentan características claves del profesionalismo en la educación parvularia finlandesa.

Professionalism as professional expertise

Professionalism can be understood and defined in a number of ways. I regard it as a multi-level and multifaceted phenomenon involving socio-cultural issues, issues related to national regulation and policy decision-making, as well as issues related to work communities and the individuals within them. Sorel and Wittorski (2005) also refer to such a multi-level definition of professionalism in which the process of professionalisation includes professionalisation of individuals, professionalisation of activities, and professionalisation of organisations.

In an earlier study (Karila 1997), I discussed the phenomenon of early childhood professionalism in the context of expertise research. Traditional expertise research is related to the study of intelligence and sees the characteristics of experts as related to a person's abilities or aptitudes (de Groot 1965; Glaser 1992). Another more recent approach to the study of how expertise develops addresses the question of the type of social environment that provides a proper context for learning. According to the theory of situated learning, learning takes place in a participatory framework, not in an individual mind. Development is the result of inter-action between the person and the context (e.g. Lave and Wenger 1991). In most recent writings professional expertise and professionalism are often discussed in the context of professional identity (e.g. Eteläpelto and Vähäsantanen 2006, 26–49). This includes my own study (Karila 1997) in which I argued that professional expertise is a situational and cultural phenomenon in which there is also a personal dimension. Since I interpret professionalism and professional expertise as the same phenomenon, I will use the concepts side by side in this article.

In studying professional expertise (Karila 1997), I noted that three main elements are essential in the construction and development of expertise and argued that these constitute a relevant unit of analysis for the notion of professionalism: (a) the personal dimension, hereafter called 'Myself and life history'; (b) the domain-specific knowledge; and (c) the working environment. Additionally, the interaction between the three elements is significant for both the construction and the development process of expertise. The interaction takes place in the cultural context of society, which also provides a frame for the interaction (see also Karila 1998).

Another way to define professionalism is to discuss the core aspects of work that are significant for the very nature of professionalism in a given field. Oberhuemer (2005, 13) succeeds well in describing the current trends in discussions of the concept of professionalism in the early childhood education field and suggests the use of the term 'democratic professionalism'. She argues that there are at least three compelling reasons to consider this concept:

First, there is evidence in many countries of an increasing diversity of user groups, raising questions about the participation of different groups and individuals. Second, and closely related to the first, there is an acknowledged need for more effective links between early childhood settings, families and the local community. And third, there is a growing body of literature which questions traditional notions of professionalism, notions which distance professionals from those they serve and prioritise one group's knowledge over another's. (Oberhuemer 2005, 13)

Oberhuemer's (2005) thoughts on democratic professionalism, or the similar thoughts by Ebbeck and Waniganayake (2003) on shared leadership, would not be possible at all times and in all cultures. As an ideal of professionalism, they represent a typically western view that emphasises an equal and reciprocal relationship between professionals and their partners. Such ideals of professionalism are clearly visible in, for example, the contents of the Finnish early childhood education policy documents in which multiprofessionalism and educational partnership with parents are strongly emphasised (see e.g. Ministry of Social Welfare and Health [2002]; National Research and Development Centre for Welfare and Health [2003]).

In the following sections I present my perspective on the current state of professionalism in the Finnish early childhood education sector. I begin my description from the macro level, highlighting the importance of the social and cultural context as a significant element in defining the nature of professionalism.

Finnish society and culture as the context of professionalism in early childhood education

The socio-cultural contexts in different countries, with their different governance, legal and regulatory frameworks, are one macro-level definer of professionalism. MacNaughton (2003, 283) has argued, for example, that documents such as regulations will provide early childhood professionals and employers with the legislative frameworks for understanding what constitutes minimum standards within early childhood educational programmes. In Finland, the key documents that provide these definitions are:

(1) Act on Children's Day Care 367/1973 and Decree on Children's Day Care 239/ 1973;
(2) Act on Qualification Requirements for Social Welfare Professionals 272/2005 and Decree on Qualification Requirements for Social Welfare Professionals 608/2005;
(3) Decision in Principle of the Council of State Concerning the National Policy Definition on Early Childhood Education and Care (Ministry of Social Welfare and Health 2002); and
(4) The National Curriculum Guidelines on Early Childhood Education and Care in Finland, 2003 and 2005 (National Research and Development Centre for Welfare and Health 2003, 2005).

I refer to these documents and their role in shaping professionalism in Finnish early childhood education in the rest of my discussion.

In the Finnish context, the roots of the day-care system are embedded in the development of Finnish society. Hujala et al. (1998) suggest that the provision of early childhood education services in Finland should be understood as part of the welfare society. In Finland, day care is the central form of public early childhood education. Two tasks have been defined for the Finnish day-care sector in the legislation (Act on Children's Day Care 367/1973). They are: (1) the comprehensive support for the development of the child; and (2) support for the parents in nurturing and educating their child. In legislation, these tasks have been defined in such a general fashion that they allow a variety of interpretations. Thus, in Finland, day care has been considered a part of the social and the family policy and, only more recently, as part of the educational policy (Hujala et al. 1998, 148). Legislative changes have also emphasised the child's subjective right to day care and the municipalities' duty to make preschool education available for all children aged six years of age. In the process, these changes have also highlighted the function of teaching and educating as part of day care (Hujala et al. 1998). This re-positioning of the function of day care seems to be increasingly accepted even by parents who are frequently enrolling their children in day care not because of a custodial need occasioned, for example, by the parents' working hours but rather because of their subjective right as citizens to early childhood education and teaching. This parental practice is growing more popular and it has ignited heated debate in Finland. A part of the citizenry, politicians, and even early childhood practitioners, are in favour of limiting or dissolving the subjective right to day care, because they consider the practice a threat to parenthood (e.g. newspaper articles in *Helsingin Sanomat* 2007). This suggests that despite legislative changes and some shifts in parental perceptions, the educational function of early childhood services has not yet become an established part of how citizens perceive the sector. In other words, among sections of the population, the perception persists that day care is a care-taking service for the families rather than an educational child-oriented teaching service.

How do the Finnish policy documents position early childhood education and the professional work in the field? The central principles and foci for practice in the Finnish early childhood education and care sector have been gathered together in the national policy document on early childhood education and care, 'Decision in Principle of the Council of State Concerning the National Policy Definition on Early Childhood Education and Care' (Ministry of Social Affairs and Health 2002). These have been summarised as follows:

> Early childhood education and care is a part of life-long learning. The primary right and responsibility for children's education lies with the parents. It is society's role to support parents in their educational task. Care, education and teaching should form a seamless whole, which flexibly supports the individual development of each child. The aim is to develop the service system from the point of view of the needs of children and families. (Ministry of Social Affairs and Health 2002, 4)

The 'National Curriculum Guidelines on Early Childhood Education and Care in Finland' (National Research and Development Centre for Welfare and Health 2003) positions care, education, and teaching as an integrated whole:

> ECEC is a whole comprising the intertwining dimensions of care, education and teaching. These dimensions receive a different emphasis according to the age of the child and the situation. The younger the child is, the greater the extent to which interactions between the child and educators take place in care situations. These situations also involve education, teaching and guidance, being important for both the child's general well being and learning. (15)

Furthermore, the policy documents stress the educational partnership between the parents and the professionals. In particular, the two documents, 'Decision in Principle of the Council of State Concerning the National Policy Definition on Early Childhood Education and Care' (Ministry of Social Affairs and Health 2002) and the 'National Curriculum Guidelines on Early Childhood Education and Care in Finland' (National Research and Development Centre for Welfare and Health 2003), highlight the obligation set by the Act on Children's Day Care (367/1973) to support parents in nurturing and educating their child through formally organised early childhood education services. This emphasis can be attributed to a number of reasons, including an increase in the economic and social difficulties of families with small children (Törrönen 2001) and, at the same time, an increasingly voiced concern by the authorities about the weakening role of parenthood. For example, some recent studies have suggested that parents trust practitioners more than themselves when it comes to education (Alasuutari 2003). It has thus been interpreted that families need more support to become involved in their child's education. Additionally, a more general attempt in the Finnish administrative culture towards listening to the 'customers' has led to the emphasis of cooperation with parents in the educational sector. There is an ongoing inclination to shift from a working culture that highlights the power of expert authorities, towards a culture of participating and participation (Karila 2006). Thus, in the Finnish early childhood education context, the 'old' idea of supporting the education offered to children by their parents in the home has been supplanted by the idea that early childhood education and care is a partnership (Karila 2006).

At document level, such a partnership first appeared in the 2002 'Decision in Principle of the Council of State Concerning the National Policy Definition on Early Childhood Education and Care' (Ministry of Social Affairs and Health 2002). A year later, the 'National Curriculum Guidelines' (National Research and Development Centre for Welfare and Health 2003) sought to emphasise this new, more engaged approach, which involves participation that goes further than cooperation. The 'National Curriculum Guidelines on Early Childhood Education and Care in Finland' (3, 29) note that the journey from cooperation to partnership in early childhood education and care requires mutual, continuous, and committed interaction on all matters concerning the child; the guidelines note also that the experience of being heard, and mutual respect, are essential for attaining shared understanding.

Macro-level regulation has also addressed itself to the type and qualification level of the early childhood education professionals. In Finnish day-care centres both teachers (qualified at degree level) and nursery nurses (qualified with a secondary school level qualification) work with the children. In the past, there were general recommendations on the roles and responsibilities of each occupational group defined by the state administration (National Board of Social Welfare 1984). Due to the decentralisation[1] process that occurred at the beginning of the nineties, however, the decisions concerning the division of labour among different occupational groups working in the sector are now made in the day-care centres themselves (Hujala et al. 1998).

Recent policy documents (e.g. Ministry of Social Affairs and Health 2002; National Research and Development Centre for Welfare and Health 2003) have also emphasised multiprofessionalism. This term refers to both the cooperation of early childhood education and day-care centre professionals with professionals in other sectors (social work, comprehensive schools, maternity and child health), and to the multiprofessional operations within day-care centres between kindergarten teachers[2] with varying educational backgrounds and the nursery nurses (National Research and Development Centre for Welfare and Health 2003). Multiprofessionalism has also emerged as an analytic concept in research on the work-life of early childhood practitioners. In this context, multiprofessionalism is seen as a solution for the increasingly complex problems faced by practitioners: The shared expertise of various occupations has been regarded as a possible solution as it suggests that professionals from various fields may contribute via their own expertise to shared problem-solving so that decisions might acquire a higher quality via shared expertise (Karila and Nummenmaa 2001). In the working practices of early childhood education, however, internal multiprofessionalism in particular has been interpreted in differing ways.

The Finnish regulations (Decree on Children's Day Care 239/1973; Act on Qualification Requirement for Social Welfare Professionals 272/2005; Decree on Qualification Requirements for Social Welfare Professionals 608/2005) specify that one (kindergarten teacher) in three of the staff in any day-care centre must have a post-secondary level degree (Bachelor of Education, Master of Education, Bachelor of Social Sciences) and two staff members (nursery nurses) in three in any day-care centre are expected to have a secondary level qualification in the field of social welfare and healthcare. Currently, 30% of those working in

Finnish day-care centres are trained kindergarten teachers. This percentage is low compared with the situation in other Nordic countries: the percentage is 60 in Denmark, 50 in Sweden, and over 30 in Iceland and Norway. In addition, Finnish statistics show that the number of early childhood staff with a kindergarten teacher's degree working in day-care centres has dropped by almost 10% during the past five years (Unpublished statement for the Ministry of Social Affairs and Health 2005).

The situation is a result of the change in the qualification requirements that came into force in 1988. The change meant that the proportion of kindergarten teachers out of the total day-care staff working with the children in day-care centres was reduced. The direction of the change is paradoxical: while early childhood education has become an increasingly challenging scholarly field in the past decade, the educational level of day-care centre employees has been lowered via statutory regulations about qualification requirements (Karila 2004).

The qualifications levels for day-care centre directors are another topic of debate in Finland. University level teacher education programmes (Bachelor of Education) for early childhood teaching were launched in Finland in 1995. At the same time the universities started offering new postgraduate programmes in early childhood education (Master of Education). A masters level degree is widely understood to be the expected level of qualification for directors of day-care centres (e.g. in the report of the sub-committee of the Advisory Board for Early Childhood Education and Care, Ministry of Social Affairs and Health 2007, 58). However, this expectation has not been mandated as a requirement. The unclear market value of the masters level qualification within the early childhood world has already caused many early childhood professionals who hold the degree to move to primary education. This has resulted in the loss of valuable expertise to the early childhood sector.

Administratively, early childhood education is the responsibility of a number of agencies. At the national level, the Ministry of Social Affairs and Health is responsible for childcare and education services outside the compulsory school system. At the same time, an ongoing process of change is resulting in a move away from centralised regulation and responsibility for funding, management, and monitoring of services, to a system where these responsibilities lie with regional and local authorities. Thus, in today's welfare society the municipalities are responsible for organising day-care services. Kröger (1997) has argued that the concept 'welfare society' needs to be replaced by the concept 'welfare municipalities'. The variations in municipalities' political, organisational and economical situations result in variations in the municipal-level solutions and thus variations in the working environments for early childhood staff.

Municipal variations that affect the working context of early childhood staff stem, first, from the differing interpretations that municipalities make about the functions of day care and early childhood education more broadly. This is evident in the administrative arrangements municipalities make for early childhood provisions: Since the beginning of 2007, municipalities have been able to choose the administrative agency under which they organise their early childhood education services (Act on Social Welfare 710/1982). Approximately 10% of all municipalities (which number 415) in Finland have placed children's day care alongside the pedagogical and educational services (http://varttua.stakes.fi/ FI/Ajankohtaista/PHhallinto/phhallinto/ajankohtainen_phhallinto.htm), while the remaining municipalities have located early childhood education with either the social services or the social and healthcare services.

Second, recruitment policies in municipalities likewise vary. For example, while some municipalities are following the new regulations with their lower qualifications requirements for early childhood staff, others have opted to keep to the old regulations when recruiting new staff. There is also evidence that the operating policies of municipalities vary in which degree they favour from among the Bachelor of Education, the Master of Education, or a Bachelor of Social Sciences when recruiting kindergarten teachers. This means that there exist Finnish day-care centres today that have no staff with a pedagogical qualification. Furthermore, recruitment decisions of municipalities are inevitably affected by the quality of the job seekers available in the area.

Finally, the municipalities interpret the national regulations in different ways. These regulations can, for the most part, be considered to be of high quality. The problem is that there is no systematic monitoring of how the regulations are implemented and thus it is easy for the regulations to not be adhered to in practice (Karila 2002). It is known anecdotally, for example, that the child–adult ratio is not always maintained in practice. This poses grave problems for professionalism, as employees have to develop their professional operations in situations that are in breach of the regulations. Clearly, the different municipal environments provide the professionals with working contexts that are very diverse.

In sum, I have argued that the expectations for professionalism, and the way that professionals should operate, are set on the macro level. On a day-to-day- basis, however, these expectations are operationalised by municipalities which implement them in diverse ways. This diversity makes it problematic to articulate the core of professionalism within the Finnish day-care context. Care, education, and teaching are considered an integrated monolith, but differing opinions hold sway on the weight and the importance of each area. Joint operations with other professionals and the parents are strongly emphasised in official documentation intended for the guidance of municipalities. These macro-level operations seem, however, internally contradictory: while information steering documents and education policies set ever more demanding and educationally weighted expectations on early childhood education, the employee structure in day-care centres is putting more emphasis on nursery nursing expertise, and the educational requirements for the employees have been lowered. Furthermore, the municipal system is able to subvert the intentions of official steering and policy documents: it is difficult to be confident about the kind of professionalism that can be achieved in this complex context.

In the following section, I examine the changing nature of domain-specific knowledge.

Domain-specific knowledge and core competencies

Domain-specific knowledge is always historical, contextual, and situational in its nature. In the past few years, there has been discussion in Finland on the professional expertise required by early childhood education work in the present as well as for the future. Clarifications have been sought about the required professional expertise of all members of the multiprofessional working community alongside the special expertise of each occupation.

In Finland it has been broadly accepted that the best quality provision comes from well-trained staff with ongoing access to professional development opportunities. Each key staff member of day-care centres (nurses, teachers, directors) is required to have the appropriate training. The requirement to train is not in question, but the content of domain-specific knowledge required in the field is vigorously debated.

Table 1 summarises the central competence areas and the core competencies seen to be required in the field of early childhood education (Karila and Nummenmaa 2001, 33). The competence areas and competencies presented in the table were constructed as part of a research project (Karila and Nummenmaa 2001) that focused on the Finnish day-care centre work from the multiprofessionalism point of view, and were later accepted more widely in

Table 1.   The central knowledge and competency areas and the core competencies.

Central knowledge and competence areas	Core competencies
Contexts of early childhood education	Contextual competencies
Early childhood education	Educational competencies
	Competencies in caring
	Pedagogical competencies
Cooperation and interaction	Interaction competencies
	Cooperation competencies
Continuous development	Reflective competencies
	Knowledge management

the field, including in the report of the sub-committee on the development of staff education and skills within the Advisory Board for Early Childhood Education and Care (Ministry of Social Affairs and Health 2007, 28–32).

As mentioned earlier, multiprofessionalism is seen as important in Finland. Therefore, debate on the special domain-specific knowledge of each occupational group that works in day-care centres (teachers, nurses) has been vigorous. I have argued elsewhere (Karila and Nummenmaa 2001) that knowledge related to the contexts of early childhood education; co-operation and interaction; and continuous development is considered to comprise common areas of expertise for all early childhood education professionals. But there are differences in the depth of expertise that different occupation groups have, and these arise from their educational background. It is perhaps not surprising that the particular area where the special expertise of teachers and the nurses differs is in the competency area of early childhood education (Karila and Nummenmaa 2001).

The building of professional knowledge starts during one's training. As noted earlier in this article, during the past decade, the training of early childhood education professionals has changed: training courses for nursery nurses have changed from their focus on childhood and child welfare to a more broadly based focus on social care and community work with different age-groups in diverse settings (see Oberhuemer and Ulich 1997, 71). At the same time, kindergarten teacher training and early childhood education qualifications have shifted to universities, with new Bachelor and Master of Education degrees being developed. A Bachelor of Social Sciences degree has also been created at the polytechnic level, and this degree is now one of the qualifications accepted for working as a kindergarten teacher. This is a remarkably broad range of qualifications, which differ greatly in terms of subjects studied and curricula, as an entry point to becoming a kindergarten teacher. Since the interpretation of professionalism inevitably varies with the type of training one receives (Karila et al. 2005), interesting questions arise about the significance of this variety of training backgrounds for professionalism in early childhood work.

In an unpublished statement submitted to the Ministry of Social Affairs and Health in the spring of 2005, the representatives of the university-level early childhood education programmes evaluated the current situation of domain-specific knowledge in early childhood education and alerted the Ministry to what they saw as weaknesses in work practices related to the competence areas and core competencies presented in Table 1:

> We regard as a weakness the fact that pedagogical[3] expertise is alarmingly disappearing from early childhood education/day care, not to mention the shortfall in teaching expertise. We rate the knowledge of child development and learning as weak in a number of early childhood education organisations. Grave problems also emerge in professional expertise related to the children's individual guidance as well as supervising whole groups of children. The writing of

early childhood education curricula and pre-school curricula has proved that the theoretical mastery of the work (planning and mastering the pedagogical contents, the growing and learning environments etc.) is deficient, and the knowledge of the basic terminology necessary for creating various curricula is in many places poor or nonexistent. According to our view, there are major gaps in the communication, interaction, and evaluation skills, as well as in the cultural literacy of the employees. This poses problems for the co-operation in education and teaching as well as their implementation.

According to our evaluation, sufficient attention has not been paid to the pedagogical, financial, and personnel management of the early childhood education organisations. The scope of the directors' work has constantly widened and become fragmented. The actual pedagogical leadership is lost in the work of a number of day care centre directors. A holistic and goal-oriented vision for the challenges to be set for leadership is missing. (Unpublished statement for the Ministry of Social Affairs and Health by the representatives of the university-level early childhood education 2005)

It is widely accepted that professional expertise does not only develop in pre-service training or teacher education, but also in working life. In the next section, I will describe of the types of work cultures in which 'learning at work' takes place.

The working culture in day-care centres as a context for building and developing professionalism

Professionalism or professional expertise is not built and developed solely in a macro-level cultural and social environment, as described in the previous section. The everyday working environment – the workplace and its culture – forms a considerable context for building expertise (Karila 1997). In day-care centres, the organisational culture is made up of work practices and education practices which Wenger (1998) would describe through the concept of 'community of practice'. The ideas of Sorel and Wittorski (2005) related to the professionalisation of organisations (which determine who can operate in the profession, who can organise the activities, and who can communicate the professional expertise of the organisation) are also relevant to this dimension of professionalism.

As many have noted (e.g. Geertz 1973; Vygotsky 1978; Rogoff 2003), culture is an ever-present condition, and it has its effect on the cognitive structures of the members of the working community, as well as on all the activities within that community (Allaire and Firisotu 1984 ; Quinn and Holland 1987). The working reality is expressed and produced in a meaning-making process. Key meanings for professionalism are those related to interpreting the basic tasks of day care and early childhood education, and the distribution of work between various professionals. Interpretations of professionalism related to cooperating with parents are also of importance.

Anna Raija Nummenmaa and I (Nummenmaa and Karila 2005) have studied the working reality and the working culture of the Finnish day-care centre as a conceptual system – as meanings allotted (e.g. Lakoff and Johnson 1980) to the day-care centre and day-care centre work by Finnish nursery nurses, kindergarten teachers, and day-care centre directors. In our research we explored metaphors that participants used in talking about their work and found that three multiprofessional metaphorical landscapes appeared to dominate the way that the participants described the day-care centre and their work within it. The first metaphor that emerged for the daily work in a day-care centre was that it was a place of 'hustle and bustle', surmounted only by flexible attitudes and ways of working and by carrying out a variety of simultaneous tasks. Second, the day-care centre was described as a 'garden' in which adults nourish growth and development; and third, the day-care centre was seen as a 'second home' to provide shelter and care for children and adults alike. These metaphors reflect the employees' conceptions about education and children, including some quite personal interpretations of professionalism.

Our experience beyond the research (Nummenmaa and Karila 2005) suggests that these metaphors also seem to be handed down from generation to generation: They clearly appear in the speech of first-year students of early childhood education, and, again in our experience, they seem to change very little during the training. While these results (Nummenmaa and Karila 2005) cannot be generalised, they are thought-provoking. For example, it is reasonable to ask where the scientific approaches related to the modern developmental psychology and learning are in the practitioners' discourse. Likewise, it is reasonable to ask what the highlighting of the day-care centre as 'the second home' says about early childhood work. Where is the day-care centre's special pedagogical task? The metaphor of the day-care centre as a second home also implies that the work required of early childhood professionals is similar to the work of mothers and fathers, who thus are arguably both equal and similar experts of education. This strengthens the point that the prerequisites for the professional expertise in early childhood education are not explicitly expressed (Karila and Nummenmaa 2001; Nummenmaa and Karila 2005, 377). The metaphors, or the beliefs behind them, do not in any way refer to the day-care centre as a place of learning, even though the continuum of learning from early childhood education to comprehensive school has been strongly emphasised in connection with the pre-school education reform (Finnish National Board of Education 2000).

I have argued elsewhere that for professionalism to emerge, the working culture of the professionals plays a key role: it creates both boundaries and opportunities for developing professionalism (Karila 1997). In the working cultures of Finnish day-care centres, multi-professionalism seems to have developed a unique interpretation. Instead of clarifying the special expertise of the professionals working in day-care centres and developing a new kind of shared expertise based on it (Karila and Nummenmaa 2001), we have reached a situation where using special expertise in work is not taken for granted (Karila 2000). Kinos (1997) has argued that this has resulted in territorial fights between the occupations which may even lead to the disappearance of pedagogical special expertise in particular from day-care centres. Where previously the job descriptions, the responsibilities, and the obligations of professionals were defined on the basis of the qualification of the occupational groups, during the last decade, we have experienced a shift from clearly defined tasks for different job roles in early childhood settings, to an increasing 'everybody does everything' work distribution (Karila 1997). In such a system, a situation may arise in which a kindergarten teacher with a university degree takes care of putting the children's clothes to dry while a nursery nurse with a lower level qualification supervises the children's music session or another learning situation. It is evident that the roles and responsibilities of different occupations are not clearly defined (see also Puroila 2004). Additionally, as responsibilities and obligations of the various occupations vary within day-care centres, professionalism is realised differently from one working culture to another. A worrying finding from a project which looked at working practices in early childhood centres (Karila 2000) is that in an 'everybody does everything' working culture, the standard of professional operations has very often been set according to the skills of the weakest employee. If it is true that, as Lortie (1975) has argued, young employees often adopt the cultural working practices of their first workplace, then we must be concerned about the future of a young employee with a university degree: how could a new graduate learn to consolidate reflective professional practices based on scientific knowledge in such a situation?

The interpretation of multiprofessionalism as realised in working cultures has been considered alarming at the national level as well. The sub-committee on the development of staff education and skills within the Advisory Board for Early Childhood Education and Care (Ministry of Social Affairs and Health 2007, 59) has noted that the implementation of multiprofessionalism requires corrective measures. The sub-committee consists of representatives of various interest groups and has recently completed its report and recommended that the responsibilities and the obligations of the various day-care professions be clarified (see also Sarvimäki and Siltaniemi 2007).

Within this context it would appear that the idea of a close integration of care, education, and teaching may be lending a functional interpretation to multiprofessionalism that is weakening the definition of professionalism rather than strengthening it. The educare mentality requires strong and versatile professional expertise. I suggest that restrictions are necessary in the responsibilities and the obligations of each profession in order to enable the implementation of the educare ideal in a way that also promotes professionalism.

Myself and life history

I want now to examine the interpretations of professionalism expressed by individual employees because personal beliefs and interpretations of professional expertise, and of the profession, also strongly contribute to the shaping of the history of the profession. The ideas of Sorel and Wittorski (2005) on the formation of professionalism as a process of professionalisation of the individuals' identity construction also relate to this dimension of professionalism (see also Eteläpelto and Vähäsantanen 2006).

As MacNaughton (2003, 283) has noted, early childhood professionals are often required to translate social policy into practice in their community. The way the translation occurs is very much connected to the personal dimension of professionalism. In my thinking the 'Myself and life history' viewpoint is related to both the biographical elements of an individual, the previous significant experiences, and the individual's unique way of interacting with the environment. This is additional to the point noted earlier that the interpretations of the employees are shaped by history, and varying interpretations of professionalism (representing several eras and corresponding conceptions) are always present in any work community (Karila 1997). Additionally, people's own interpretations of professionalism may often be far removed from the interpretations of independent, reflective professionals.

In our metaphor research (Nummenmaa and Karila 2005), we examined the employees' relationship to their work and to their identity with the help of the 'In my work, I am like . . .' metaphor. Our analysis of the data showed that a central theme in describing one's working role was adaptation – being flexible and adapting to the prevailing circumstances, or 'going with the flow'. Respondents reported feeling like a 'bath sponge', a 'jack-in-the-box', or a traffic policeman; or even as one who has lost control of one's work – this is described as being 'a weathercock in the wind or a fish in a tank that tries to swim downstream'. Furthermore, in our data, multiprofessionalism emerged as a requirement of multiple expertises. Day-care centre work was seen to hold a variety of expectations and professional challenges for the practitioners. These were described with such metaphors as a 'jack-of-all-trades', a 'multiply-skilled person', or 'an errand boy'. Descriptions such as Captain, Gardener, nourishing Mother Earth, and a 'piece in a puzzle' were used to describe rather different significations in the working reality. For example, a captain steers his ship; he holds the wheel and has the course of the vessel firmly under control; Mother Nature nurtures and nourishes, and provides shelter. Describing one's work as a 'piece of the puzzle' emerged as a metaphor of a 'worker ant', or as 'being one of a crowd'. Furthermore, a key theme within the metaphors of the experience of day-care work seemed to be one of strong individuality and separate operations.

These are interesting findings that contribute yet another dimension through which to understand the development of professionalism in the early childhood sector in Finland. If, as I've argued above, professionals are constructing their sense of professionalism and their professional competences in different environments, and also as a function of their individual learning paths, then this is yet another significant reason for the wide variation of understandings that exist about the phenomenon of expertise or professionalism (Karila 1997).

Summary

I have discussed professionalism as a multi-level phenomenon, and aimed at describing the dynamics of its different aspects from the Finnish perspective. This description reveals the complexity of talking about professionalism in the specific local context of Finland. The Finnish story gives evidence to the conception that the interaction between the different elements of professionalism is significant for the construction, as well as for the development process, of expertise, or professionalism. The interaction takes place in the culture of society which also provides a frame for the interaction. Therefore, one would expect the processes of professionalism to differ in different countries.

The picture I have presented of professionalism in the Finnish early childhood education sector indicates that the sector is facing a period of transition. It is fair to say that the sector is experiencing a struggle in which the pedagogical core of professionalism traditionally associated with kindergarten teachers is facing the risk of weakening. As a corollary to this view, it would appear that the dimensions of care taking and nursery nursing are strengthening; the social science dimension, meanwhile, continues searching for its place in the picture.

I have argued that there are new expectations for professionalism in the early childhood field due to the changes in society and work life. The macro-level policy solution has sought to meet the changed expectations by numerically equal but educationally lower level employees. Meanwhile, cultural and historical ideals of professionalism continue to be reflected in the work practices of early childhood practitioners who use metaphors about their work that suggest an experience-based dimension to the way they view their professional identity.

In Finland, professionalism in early childhood education is characterised by variation, whether on the municipal or the individual level, or the level of the working unit. The definers of professionalism operating on different levels do not seem to share the interpretations of professionalism in practice. This makes it difficult to be clear about what professionalism means in early childhood education in Finland. A wider mutual understanding is needed on the interpretation of the basic tasks of day care, and of early childhood education generally, as well as on the responsibilities and the obligations of the various professionals who make up the early childhood workforce.

Notes

1. In the early part of the 1990s, Finland went through extensive deregulation. Decision-making powers were increasingly delegated to the local level (see OECD 2000, 40) Furthermore, at the turn of 1990s, steering and regulation by the central government were relieved both in the educational and the social sector. Regulation was increasingly redirected towards steering by information (see OECD 2000, 62.) At the beginning of this period the information steering in the field of early childhood education was quite scanty. The national project of curriculum in ECEC (since the year 2003) has changed the situation and nowadays the 'National Curriculum Guidelines on

Early Childhood Education and Care in Finland' (National Research and Development Centre for Welfare and Health 2003) are a significant means of information steering.
2. In Finland the teachers working in day-care centres and preschool settings are usually called *kindergarten teachers* (lastentarhanopettaja). The title comes from the Fröebelian tradition and has remained in use even after kindergartens were re-named *day-care centres* in 1973 through the Act on Children's Day Care (367/1973). Nowadays the day-care centres are sometimes called early *childhood centres*. The current names indicate the change in the cultural and historical interpretations of the functions of the centres.
3. Pedagogical expertise in this context includes the knowledge of child development and learning, the knowledge of curriculum and the knowledge of teaching and pedagogical guidance.

References

Act on Children's Day Care 367/1973.
Act on Qualification Requirement for Social Welfare Professionals 272/2005.
Act on Social Welfare 710/1982.
Alasuutari, M. 2003. *Kuka lasta kasvattaa? Vanhemmuuden ja yhteiskunnallisen kasvatuksen suhde vanhempien puheessa.* [Who is raising the child? Mothers and fathers constructing the role of parents and professionals in child development]. Helsinki: Gaudeamus.
Allaire, Y., and E. Firisotu. 1984. Theories of organisational culture. *Organisational Studies* 5, no. 3, 193–226.
Decree on Children's Day Care 239/1973.
Decree on Qualification Requirements for Social Welfare Professionals 608/2005.
de Groot, A. 1965. *Thought and choice in chess.* The Hague: Mouton.
Ebbeck, M., and M. Waniganayake, M. 2003. *Early childhood professionals: Leading today and tomorrow.* Sydney: MacIennan & Petty.
Eteläpelto, A., and K. Vähäsantanen, 2006, Ammatillinen identitetti persoonallisena ja sosiaalisena konstruktiona. [Professional Identity as a Personal and Social Construction] In *Ammatillisuus ja ammatillinen kasvu,* [Professional Expertise and Professional Development] ed. A. Eteläpelto and J. Onnismaa. Aikuiskasvatuksen 46. vuosikirja. Kansanvalistusseura ja Aikuiskasvatuksen tutkimusseura. (Vantaa: Dark Oy), 26–49.
Finnish National Board of Education. 2000. *Core curriculum for pre-school education in Finland.* Helsinki: Yliopistopaino.
Geertz, C. 1973. *The interpretations of cultures.* New York: Basic Books.
Glaser, R. 1992. Learning, cognition and education: Then and now. In *Cognition: Conceptual and methodological issues,* ed. H.L. Pick et al. Washington, DC: American Psychological Association.
Helsingin Sanomat. 2007. http://hs.fi/uutiset/arkisto/ subjektiivinen päivähoitooikeus http://varttua. stakes.fi/FI/Ajankohtaista/ PHhallinto/phhallinto/ajankohtainen_phhallinto.htm.
Hujala, E., K. Karila, V. Nivala, and A.-M. Puroila. 1998. Towards understanding leadership in Finnish context of early childhood education. In *Towards understanding leadership in context of early childhood. Cross-cultural perspectives,* ed. E. Hujala and A.-M. Puroila. Acta Universitatis Ouluensis. E35, 147–70. Oulu: Oulu University Press.
Karila, K. 1997. *Lastentarhanopettajan kehittyvä asiantuntijuus. Lapsirakkaasta opiskelijasta kasvatuksen asiantuntijaksi.* [Kindergarten teacher's developing expertise. From student fond of children to expert of education]. Helsinki: Oy Edita Ab.
———. 1998. Contextual and situational perspectives on leadership in early education centres. In *Towards understanding leadership in context of early childhood. Cross-cultural perspectives,* ed. E. Hujala and A.-M. Puroila. Acta Universitatis Ouluensis. E35, 63–70. Oulu: Oulu University Press.
———. 2000. Esiopetus työyhteisöjen ja työntekijöiden oppimismahdollisuutena. [Preschool education as a learning possibility for the early years professionals]. In *Omat opetussuunnitelmat esiopetukseen,* ed. M. Kangassalo, K. Karila, and J. Virtanen, 99–147. Helsinki: Tammi.
———. 2002. How does society regulate work in early childhood and what impacts do regulations have on leadership. In *Leadership in early childhood education,* ed. E. Hujala and V. Nivala. Acta Universtitatis Ouluensis. E 57, 65–74. Oulu: Oulu University Press.
———. 2004. Monimuotoistuva työ haaste päiväkodin johtajille. [The challenges for day-care directors' work]. In *Päiväkodin johtaja on monitaituri. Kurkistus päiväkodin johtajien työn arkeen,* ed. L. Seretin, 16–19. Lastentarhanopettajaliiton julkaisu.

92   *Professionalism in Early Childhood Education and Care*

————. 2006. The significance of parent–practitioner interaction in early childhood education. *Zeitschrift fur Qualitative Bildungs-, Betratungs- und Sozialforschung.* Heft 1/2006: 7–24.

Karila, K., J. Kinos, P. Niiranen, and J. Virtanen. 2005. Curricula of Finnish kindergarten teacher education: Interpretations of early childhood education, professional competencies and educational theory. *European Early Childhood Research Journal* 13, no. 2.

Karila, K., and A.R. Nummenmaa. 2001. *Matkalla moniammatillisuuteen. Kuvauskohteena päiväkoti.* [Towards multiprofessionalism in early childhood education]. Helsinki: WSOY.

Kinos, J. 1997. *Päiväkoti ammattikuntien kamppailujen kenttänä.* Turun yliopiston julkaisuja. [Kindergarten as a field for struggle for professional groups]. C: 133.

Kröger, T. 1997. *Hyvinvointikunnan aika.* [The welfare municipality] Vammala: Vammalan kirjapaino.

Lakoff, G., and M. Johnson. 1980. *Metaphors we live by.* Chicago: University of Chicago Press.

Lave, J., and E. Wenger. 1991. *Situated learning: Legitimate peripheral participation.* Cambridge: Cambridge University Press.

Lortie, D.C. 1975. *Schoolteacher. A sociological study.* Chicago: University of Chicago Press.

MacNaughton, G. 2003. *Shaping early childhood. Learners, curriculum and contexts.* Glasgow: Open University Press.

Ministry of Social Affairs and Health. 2002. Decision in principle of the council of state concerning the national policy definition on early childhood education and care. Helsinki: Publications of the Ministry of Social Affairs and Health 2002: 9.

————. 2007. Education and skills of early childhood education and care staff – the present state and development needs. Report of the sub-committee on of the Advisory Board for Early Childhood Education and Care, 2007: 7. Helsinki: Ministry of Social Welfare and Health.

National Board of Social Welfare. 1984. Circular A3/1984/pe. Children's day care. Helsinki: National Board of Social Welfare.

National Research and Development Centre for Welfare and Health. 2003. National curriculum guidelines on early childhood education and care in Finland. http://www.stakes.fi/varttua/english/e_vasu.pdf.

————. 2005. Varhaiskasvatussuunnitelman perusteet [National curriculum guidelines on early childhood education and care in Finland]. Stakesin oppaita 56. Saarijärvi: Sosiaalialan tutkimus- ja kehittämiskeskus.

Nummenmaa, A.R., and K Karila. 2005. Metaforat moniammatillisen päiväkotikulttuurin tulkkeina ja tuottajina. [What metaphors tell us about the working reality of the day-care centre] *Kasvatus* 36, no. 5: 373–82.

Oberhuemer, P. 2005. Conceptualising the early childhood pedagogue: Policy approaches and issues of professionalism. *European Early Childhood Research Journal* 13, no. 1: 5–16.

Oberhuemer, P., and M. Ulich. 1997. *Working with young children in Europe. Provision and staff training.* London: Paul Chapman Publishing.

Organisation for Economic Co-operation and Development (OECD). 2000. Early childhood education and care policy in Finland. Background Report Prepared for the OECD Thematic Review of Early Childhood Education and Care Policy.

Puroila, A.-M. 2004. Työ varhaiskasvatuksessa muuttunut yhä vaativammaksi. [The changes in day care work]. In *Päiväkodin johtaja on monitaituri. Kurkistus päiväkodin johtajien työn arkeen,* ed. L. Seretin, 20–23. Lastentarhanopettajaliiton julkaisu.

Quinn, N., and D. Holland. 1987. Culture and cognition. In *Cultural models in language and thought,* ed. D. Holland and N. Quinn, 3–40. Cambridge: Cambridge University Press.

Rogoff, B. 2003. *The cultural nature of human development.* Oxford: Oxford University Press.

Sarvimäki, P., and A. Siltaniemi, eds. 2007. Recommendations for the task structure of professional social service staff. Publications of the Ministry of Social Affairs and Health 2007: 14.

Sorel, M., and R. Wittorski, eds. 2005. *La Professionnalisation en actes et en questions.* [The professionalisation in acts and in questions] Paris: Editions L'Harmattan.

Törrönen, M., ed. 2001. Lapsuuden hyvinvointi. Yhteiskuntapoliittinen puheenvuoro. [Childrens'welfare] Helsinki: Pelastakaa lapsetry.

Unpublished statement for the Ministry of Social Affairs and Health by the representatives of the university-level early childhood education. 2005. April 30.

Vygotsky, L.S. 1978. *Mind in society.* London: Harvard University Press.

Wenger, E. 1998. *Communities of practice: Learning, meaning and identity.* Cambridge: Cambridge University Press.

Professionalism – a breeding ground for struggle. The example of the Finnish day-care centre

Jarmo Kinos

University of Turku, Finland

ABSTRACT: This article examines the Finnish day-care centre out of a neo-Weberian-Bourdieuan frame of reference. The leading idea is that the day-care centre field is continuously shaping as a result of both inner struggles and struggles with other fields. The state, the education system, and trade unions act as the dealers of professional playing cards. Struggles are fought with strategies of social closure over capitals and positions. The study aims at not only describing the object but at understanding the dynamics involved.

The concept of professionalism refers to the ideology of a professional group, according to which the group acts purposefully and in an organised manner to pursue their own interests within the rules of the game of the society. The aim of the professional group is, on the one hand, to maintain the advantages obtained and, on the other, to strengthen their position by allying themselves with the élite of the society. This project of professionalisation entails that professional groups are aiming at a professional status, distinctive from the 'ordinary work' and/or semi-professional status, in order to increase their influence in society and their expertise, and to gain better working conditions. During the process, professional groups easily enter into conflicts with various others, such as professional groups in the field, especially with the professions closest to them (e.g. day care and early childhood education). Professional status is backed up by the state and the educational system in particular. The special features of the process are: (1) the project of professionalisation takes a long time; (2) in each country the project of professionalisation has features specific to that country; and (3) the professional groups meet both supporters and opponents on the way.

RÉSUMÉ: Cet article analyse l'accueil de la petite enfance en Finlande dans un cadre de reference néo wébérien-bourduisien. L'idée conductrice est que ce champ est en constante configuration par les débats existant à l'interne comme avec d'autres champs. L'Etat, le système éducatif et les syndicats sont les négociateurs princeps dans ce jeu de cartes professionnel. Les débats se heurtent aux stratégies de fermeture sociale aux capitaux et positions. L'étude vise non seulement la description de l'objet énoncé mais encore la comprehension des dynamiques sous jacentes.

Le concept de professionnalisme se réfère à l'idéologie d'un groupe professionnel selon laquelle ce groupe agit et poursuit ses propres intérêts, de façon organisée, au sein des règles du jeu de la société. Le but du groupe professionnel est d'un côté de maintenir les avantages acquis et de l'autre de renforcer sa position en faisant alliance avec l'élite de la société. Ce projet de professionalisation exige que les groupes professionnels visent un statut professionnel, distinct du 'travail ordinaire' et/ou du statut semi professionnel, afin d'augmenter leur influence dans la société, leur expertise, et d'obtenir de meilleures conditions de travail. Au cours du processus, les groupes professionnels entrent facilement en conflit avec différentes instances, notamment les autres groupes professionnels exerçant dans le champ et en particulier les professions les plus proches (par exemple, crèche et jardin d'enfants). Le statut professionnel est grandement profilé par l'Etat et le système éducatif.

Les caractéristiques particulières du processus sont les suivantes : (1) le projet de professionnalisation se fait sur la durée, (2) dans chaque pays, ce projet présente des caractères spécifiques au pays et (3) les groupes professionnels rencontrent au passage des supporters et des opposants.

ZUSAMMENFASSUNG: Dieser Beitrag untersucht die Finnische Kindertagesstätte aus einer Neo-Weberianischen-Bourdieuschen Perspektive. Der Leitgedanke dabei ist, dass das Feld der Kindertagesstätte sich kontinuierlich als Ergebnis interner Auseinandersetzungen sowie Auseinandersetzungen mit anderen Feldern konfiguriert. Staat, Erziehungssystem und Gewerkschaften erscheinen als Akteure in einem professionellen Kartenspiel. Kämpfe werden mithilfe von Strategien Sozialer Schließung über Kapital und Positionen ausgetragen. Ziel der Untersuchung ist es, den Gegenstand nicht nur zu beschreiben, sondern die treibenden Kräfte zu verstehen.

Das zugrunde liegende Professionalitätskonzept bezieht sich auf Ideologien professioneller Gruppen, denen zufolge sie absichtsvoll und in organisierter Weise handeln, um, innerhalb der Regeln der Gesellschaft, eigene Interessen zu verfolgen. Ziel der Gruppe der Professionellen ist es, einerseits die errungenen Vorteile zu erhalten, und andererseits ihre Position durch Allianzen mit gesellschaftlichen Eliten zu stärken. Dieses Projekt der Professionalisierung bringt es mit sich, dass professionelle Gruppen einen Status anstreben, der sich sowohl von gewöhnlicher Arbeit als auch von Semi-Professionen abhebt – mit der Absicht, ihren gesellschaftlichen Einfluss und ihre Expertise zu erweitern und bessere Arbeitsbedingungen zu erreichen. In diesem Prozess geraten professionelle Gruppen leicht in Konflikt mit verschiedenen anderen Instanzen, insbesondere mit benachbarten Professionen (z.B. in Kindertagesstätte und Vorschule). Der professionelle Status wird besonders vom Staat und vom Erziehungssystem gestützt. Besondere Kennzeichen dieses Prozesses sind: (1) das Projekt der Professionalisierung erstreckt sich über einen längeren Zeitraum und zeigt (2) in jedem Land spezifische Merkmale.

RESUMEN: Este articulo examina los centros finlandeses del cuidado de niños a partir de un marco de referencia neo-Weberiano-Bourdieuano. La idea central es que el campo del cuidado de niños esta continuamente formándose como consecuencia de luchas internas y de luchas con otros campos. El estado, el sistema educacional y las organizaciones laborales actúan como repartidores de cartas en el juego de naipes. Las luchas se dan con estrategias de encierre social sobre capital y posiciones. El objetivo del estudio es no solo de describir el objeto sino de comprender las dinámicas envueltas.

El concepto de profesionalismo se refiera a la ideología de un grupo profesional, de acuerdo a la cual el grupo actúa intencionadamente y de forma organizada para resguardar sus propios intereses dentro de las reglas de juego de la sociedad. El objetivo del grupo profesional es, por una parte, mantener las ventajas obtenidas, y por otra, fortalecer su posición aliándose con la elite de la sociedad. Este proyecto de profesionalización implica que el grupo profesional ambiciona una condición profesional, diferente del 'trabajo ordinario' y/o condición semi-profesional en orden de aumentar su influencia en la sociedad, su condición de expertos , y de obtener mejores condiciones laborales. Durante el proceso, el grupo profesional entra fácilmente en conflicto con varias instancias, tales como otros grupos profesionales en el campo, especialmente con profesiones cercanas a el (por ejemplo cuidado de niños y educación pre-escolar). La condición profesional es respaldada por el estado y el sistema educacional en particular. Los aspectos especiales del proceso son: 1) el proyecto de profesionalización demora mucho tiempo y, 2) en cada país el proyecto de profesionalización muestra aspectos específicos propios del país y 3) el grupo profesional encuentra en el camino tanto aliados como adversarios.

Introduction – the short story of Finnish day-care system

Roots

The genetic history of the Finnish day-care system from the beginning of the nineteenth century to the year 1973 originates from three separate sources. These are: (1) kindergarten (educational-instructional childcare); (2) crèche, nurseries, playgrounds (social and nursing childcare); and (3) family day care, relatives, siblings, maids (traditional childcare) (Välimäki 1999). These fields and practices have functioned independently. Over time, the Frobelian kindergarten, intended for children aged three to six, became the leading form of early childhood education in Finland. It was the only early childhood institution which was (partly) funded by the state. The pedagogical importance of crèche and nurseries was marginal. Further, the family day-care institution was not systematic or wide enough to provide a real alternative for kindergartens. In urban areas in particular, its function was closer to informal neighbourhood help (Hänninen and Valli 1986; e.g. Lujala 2007.)

Finland experienced a drastic change in her economic structure in the late 1960s. Families with children moved to urban areas in southern Finland, while their relatives stayed behind. Agriculture lost its dominant position as a means of livelihood and was replaced by industry and new services. Mothers started to work outside homes, and, consequently, the labour market became increasingly dominated by women. The structural changes created a massive problem for day care, and preliminary plans for a Day Care Act were launched. Meanwhile, Finland was being remodelled into an affluent Nordic state (a 'welfare state') with a functional social services system.

State-led day-care system

The Day Care Act of 1973 introduced a state-run day-care system. The welfare state took possession of day-care centres from 1973 to the mid-1990s. This is when an actual system of day care was created, the central goal of which was to balance the demand and supply of day care. The second goal was to provide families with good care as well as a 'foster home and foster parents' while the mothers were working outside homes! In the Day Care Act, crèches and kindergartens were joined together into day-care centres. The day-care forms given were day-care centre, family day care, and supervised play centres, all of which had an equal position as the day-care system was being developed.

The day-care centre lost its symbolic status as the principal form and the 'flagship' of day care. This is partly also reflected in the fact that the traditional name 'kindergarten' ('lastentarha' in Finnish) was no longer used. It only survived in the professional title of a kindergarten teacher, 'lastentarhanopettaja'.

Pedagogical goals for the day-care institution were not formulated until the year 1980, as the report of the Pedagogical Goal Committee was published. The pedagogical goals were amended in the Day Care Act in 1983, ten years after the act was first issued. However, the emergent pedagogical development did not win full unanimity, as fears and doubts of losing the specific nature of childhood were reflected in the discussions: is the child allowed to play and live according to his or her own rhythm? Why is mathematics being taught to small children? Will the kindergarten become excessively school-like? Similarly to medicalisation, pedagogics was regarded as a threat to social services, a foreign mode of thinking completely (Kinos 2006). In addition, the supporters of the family day care and those of the day-care centres disagreed on which form of day care ought to be primarily developed (Kinos 1997).

In a relatively young urban state, people did not grow accustomed to educating young children outside the homes. Mothers in particular were burdened by a collective guilt for having to resort to a day-care system subsidized by the state and organized as paid labour in day-care centres. From this perspective, the requirement of a homely atmosphere[1] and the emphasis on nursing associated with day care are understandable and logical. The general attitudes towards day care thus largely resembled the ideology of an agrarian society even in the 1980s and the early 1990s (Kinos 2006).

The Day Care Act of 1973 was modelled by the social situation of its time. It was primarily a skeleton law with an interest for the labour policy, specifically, to enable the working and studying of mothers. The main purpose was to guarantee the quantitative growth of day care, which outshadowed the educational task. This was particularly visible in the 1980s. The organisatory needs of the adult world steered the day-care arrangements and the phrasing of questions. Defining day care as a social service spoke of adult-oriented thinking, that is, of a social task of day care that stems from the needs of adults (see e.g. OECD 2000). 'Service' was an apt word for describing the relationships between the day-care system and the parents, but not the relationships between the day-care personnel and the children (Niiranen and Kinos 2001).

The harmony and stability of the early days of organised day care were replaced by internal turmoil in the day-care centres, which resulted in a clash of working cultures formed over the preceding decades. The 1980s can further be characterised by political decision-making to support the home care of small children. This considerably affected the ways in which day care was to be organised in the future. Infant care concentrated in the homes, and a number of infant groups were discontinued at day-care centres. Meanwhile, a decision was being prepared on guaranteed and supported day care for every child before the first year of comprehensive school. The pedagogical importance of day care and its effects on educational politics were gradually clarified and specified along with the trend of preschool childhood education in the early 1990s.

Era of new explanation

From the mid-1990s, after the crisis of the welfare state and economic recession, a new period in ECE and day care was launched – the era of new explanation of the day care.

The subjective right to day care was the most essential structural change since the issuing of the Day Care Act. As of the beginning of the year 1996, all children under seven years of age have been covered by the subjective right to day care. As a result of this, the justifications for the organisation of day care were changed, since the means test originating from the early 1970s was replaced by the statutory obligation of the municipalities to guarantee day care for all children, regardless of the social or financial standing of the family. Day care became a universal institution that resembles comprehensive school, the notion of which no longer suited the ideology of social services.

The educational premises of six year olds were sealed, as a principle was written into the educational and scientific alignment in the 1999 government platform by which free preschool education was to cover the entire age group of six year olds as of 1 August, 2001. In addition, the first national binding preschool curriculum was issued in 2000, followed by the national curriculum for Grades 1 and 2 of comprehensive school as a continuum. The administrative reform of day care in municipalities was enabled in 2003. As a result of this, municipalities started to shift early childhood education (including preschool education and day care) back under educational administration after 79 years of social administration (cf. Karila's article in this volume).

The professional training and education in the field underwent a number of changes. For example, the kindergarten teacher training was permanently established at universities (1995). The key principle in the educational reform was to bring closer together the education of children of three to six and seven to eight years of age in order to create a pedagogical continuum (early childhood education – preschool education – primary education). The practical field also saw unprejudiced experiments, as so-called schools for small children emerged in Finland for children aged five to nine. Another essential change was related to the privatisation of day care and the launch of private day centres in particular.

To conclude, the Finnish day-care system has different and separate roots originating from the European kindergarten tradition, the institutes of social care and protection, and traditional family care. Over the decades, the administration has shifted between the school system and social administration. Even though social practices have been more important than school practices in administrative issues, kindergarten teachers and primary school teachers have much in common, not in the least the jointly shared roots in Germany of the 1800s. The training of early education professionals is organised as divided into various paths. In these paths, kindergarten teachers have always stood close to primary school teachers and contrary to the rest of the professionals in the field. All of these elements form a basis for different types of struggle, which can be seen in administrative practices and structures, the political debate, the educational professions, and among the professions and vocations in the field of early childhood education in Finland. These competitions and discourse among professionals are discussed in more detail in the following sections.

The theoretical main trends in the research of professions

Concepts related to professions are generally divided into two approaches. The first one, the approach called Functionalism, was dominant until the 1970s. The Functionalist tradition is founded on the ideas of Emile Durkheim; it is also inspired by the theories of the US sociologist Talcot Parsons. Gradually, dissenters encroached upon the mainstream of Functionalism. This resulted in increasing criticism towards Functionalism and eventually led to a change of paradigm, particularly launched by the ideas of Max Weber. The definition of professionalism changed, as the concept of professions as guarantors of high social morals and as altruistic appliers and interpreters of science was crushed and reversed. The service-oriented advocate of common good became a mere seeker of vested interests. In research, attention was increasingly being paid to the conservative nature of professions. The neo-Weberian approach which thus entered alongside Functionalism has since the 1980s primarily focused on the importance of the state.

Functionalism – the traits of a profession and the idea of a developing profession

Education equips professional groups with a specialised knowledge based on a systematic theory that is applied in the practice of the profession. Expertise, in turn, leads to the mastery of special skills that other professions do not possess. A professional status is based on new information obtained via research and on a professional tradition thus given a scientified (Wilensky 1964, 138; Goode 1969, 277–78). With education, professions aim at implementing their altruistic service ideal. Formal training, which is closely linked to institutional structures, qualifies a person as the guarantor of consensus. Such an ideal type is not a capitalist, a socialist, or a bureaucrat. Educated at a university, he or she is a member of a professional group (Parsons 1968, 536).

Professions are formed via certain stages. First, professions were examined as a continuum. At one end of this continuum, there are the so-called arch-professions such as doctors, priests, commissioned officers, and lawyers, professions that have succeeded in raising their qualifying education into an academic training that lasts a minimum of five years and in creating a strong trade union to defend their members. At the other end, there are the non-professional vocations; while other, professionalising groups that are also called semi-professions are located in the middle (Etzioni 1969, v). Semi-professions are half-academic professions often dominated by women, such as nursing, teaching, and social work. Such professions have failed somewhat in their attempts at professionalisation.

In Functionalism, a profession is defined as a vocation which has acquired certain distinguishing traits in its development of professionalisation (e.g. Katz 1987, 2–15). The traits, on which researchers have been unanimous (Laiho 2005, 27–29), distinguish the professions from others via a dichotomy – a vocation either is or is not a profession. A list of traits is a typical example of the interests of the Functionalist school, focusing on the development of professions towards the ideal type of a fully developed profession. Rinne and Jauhiainen (1988, 6–7) have listed the main distinctive and descriptive traits of a profession as follows:

- a high level of education;
- the intellectual status of the profession, aka the scientific basis;
- a task that is necessary for society;
- the level of professional autonomy;
- the internal control of spreading the profession – that is, control related to the education and qualification requirements;
- the organisation of practitioners into a union or association.

In Functionalism, the traits are often examined as separate phenomena and without a historical touch. Harmony is considered as the basic state of a social system. Professions are seen as static powers that establish and solidify society and follow the interests of the dominant players in society. The importance of professional organisations is emphasised, as professions act as a counterforce to forces that tear down society. To practise a profession is not solely to earn money but also to promote common good and security (Collins 1990, 11–13, 132; MacDonald 1995, 3).

The Functionalist approach included a psychological-vocational emphasis in the 1990s. This trend was called new professionalism (e.g. Hargreaves 1994; Niemi and Kohonen 1995). New professionalism refers to the profession-related requirements for knowledge, skills, and attitudes, the professional growth process, inner personal development, the mutual associations and links in the work community, and the professional's own contribution to his or her development. In this view, the opposite of a highly educated, self-developing employee is an amateur. Professionalism is a characteristic of a skilled, qualified employee.

It has been discovered that new professionalism exceeds the traditional professionalism limited to trade unions which often refers to raising the status of a profession with pay policies. New professionalism also aims at raising the status of a profession, but its fundamental motive is to improve the opportunities for personal growth and education in society and thus to contribute to social change.

The neo-Weberian movement – professional control and distinction

Max Weber emphasised power as a key incentive and driving force in society. Professions and the various social actors were now examined in their interactive process in relation to the environment. Attention was paid to the circumstances that cause certain professions to professionalise and others not. Traditional Functionalist research of professions was criticised for its lack of history and its neglect of examining the use of power in professions. Of interest now was what the practitioners of a profession in actual fact do in their work and how they maintain their special status. Researchers were no longer content with hearing what the members of a professional group said they did or what they were generally supposed to be doing, following some ideology or another. The changes in the research of professions were not caused by the internal reorientation of science, but rather also by the changes in the social reality.

The professional system to be examined as a whole – an antithesis for Functionalism

Society and its structures became the new foci of research. The traits and emblems of professions were incorporated into the invigorating examination of macro-structures. The main concepts of the Functionalist theory were soon utilised in recognising phenomena and charting them in a historical perspective. Using traits was a research technical method, not a research task in itself. The historical development of an individual profession was linked to the closely knit professions and to the professional system – that is, to the whole formed by the professions outlined from the perspective of the particular nature of the respective era. This holistic view (cf. Bourdieu's concept of fields later) provided a basis for examining the mutual statuses of professions as well as for recognising and organising the 'front lines' in the field of professions. The key principle is to emphasise the varying characteristics of the formation of a professional system that depend on the society to be examined and its respective history (Collins, 1990, 13–15; Torstendahl 1990, 4–5; Konttinen 1991, 1993, 9–10).

The neo-Weberian movement reversed the interpretation of a number of traits of Functionalism. High-level specialisation was considered to acquire forms that would result in neglecting the holistic view that aimed at common good and focusing instead on the narrow partial view based on the interest of an individual profession (Konttinen 1993, 8). It was stated that, for example, lawyers are increasingly advocating business interests rather than serving the public, which has guaranteed a sound income for lawyers (Scott 1989). Antiprofessionalism is explained by the general public scepticism against professional groups. The scepticism was based on the fact that professionals were no longer considered altruistic, neutral practitioners of trade with no financial interests (Menand 1995). Freidson (1994) went so far as to call professionalism 'an Anglo-American illness'.

Professionalism was now interpreted as a social or political ideology that formed a basis for the occupational groups to act in a conscious and organised manner for its interests. The changes in the attitudes reflect the conflict between reality and the traditional professional ideal.

According to the neo-Weberian definition of a profession, professionalism is a strategy for controlling the rise and/or maintenance of one's social status. The control extends to, for example, the entrance into a profession, the professional qualifications, and professional education. Professionalism as an ideology is based on the belief of public justification of work. The strategic task of this ideology is to distinguish the various professions. Primarily, it is a question of establishing a monopoly of professionals and experts in a certain territory. The underlying logic is the competition between occupational groups for respect, power, and income. In this process, the state (and education) plays a crucial role. A profession is defined as a result of the successful control and closure measures carried out by the trade unions. A profession is an occupational group that has managed to exclude rivalling occupational groups from its area of operations by monopolising its professional tradition and rendering it more scientific (Hoyle 1980, 43; Weber 1980, 7–12).

The basic logic behind the relations of occupational groups – continuous tension, social closure, and usurpation

It is thus characteristic to neo-Weberian thinking that the operations of occupational groups are examined from the point of view of conflicts and power. The concept of social closure, launched by Max Weber, refers to exclusion and a monopoly that one occupational group has managed to create when attempting to guarantee the scanty privileges to its own members (MacDonald 1995, 27).

Tangible tools of social closure include statutory professional qualifications, proficiency requirements, educational degrees and diplomas, as well as the ability and the willingness of the groups higher up in the hierarchy to distinguish themselves from the others. Occupational groups seek to affect the proficiency requirements and to limit the operations in certain tasks for holders of a certificate of qualification only. The winners have thus succeeded in pushing the rivalling groups, the closely knit professions in particular, out of the field of qualification. Social closure thus inevitably leads to continuous tension and conflicts between closely knit occupations on the same field, as these will become the object of sidelining measures. According to the professional ideology, the groups that remain low in status organise themselves for the struggle to raise their status by imitating the traditions and practices of the higher, academically educated groups. Reaching upwards refers to one occupational group aiming to rise to the territory of a privileged profession. The purpose then is to usurp and allocate a maximal amount of the 'limited resources' occupied by the privileged occupational group (Weber 1980, 201–03; Murphy 1984, 555–56; Freidson 1986, 42–43).

An occupational group needs to struggle to maintain and widen the acquired scope and status. There are always new occupational groups aiming to enter the field along with the existing ones. Continuous struggle also exists due to the regular re-evaluation of work, tasks, and statuses, as the boundaries between professions are seldom static and distinct. New tasks can be generated; old ones can be discontinued or reshaped. Losing in such a struggle leads to the deprofessionalisation of the occupational group (Abbot 1988, 33–34, 91; MacDonald 1995, 32–35). Along with professionalisation, therefore, deprofessionalisation and proletarianisation may take place. For example, a profession may lose its relatively independent status acquired by education over the course of a long historical process and become the subject of the increasing control of the state and/or the market (Murphy 1990, 72–75).

The professional tradition, shared tasks, and the working culture form the context (the field) in which the struggle for privileges between closely knit professions takes place and in which the interest of the professional collective is incarnated. In this supervision of interests, a long professional tradition, a clear professional identity, and a dynamic working culture are powerful weapons for the occupational groups (Collins 1979, 47–48, 172–73). When examining a professional system, therefore, we must not overlook the individual operations of occupational groups. Occupational groups everywhere strive to seek their vested interest, to develop strategies and tactics in order to promote their goals and reinforce their status. The contribution of occupational groups and opportunities thereof are often examined in proportion to their social environment.

Struggle in the field is rarely open, as people do not admit its existence

A field only exists when actors and their capital man the dominant positions and when these manners (individuals, groups, institutions) struggle for something that is shared. A field emerges where people struggle for their existence, their positions and capitals. A field is formed with the concept of capital. The relative strength and position of the actors depend on the volume and the structure of the capitals. The actors struggle to reinforce their capital – that is, to increase the qualities that are most valued in the field. The struggle aims to make the field function according to the personal interest of the actors. Therefore, the struggle in the field is primarily a classification struggle: what is labelled good and what bad. The essential thing is that the struggle is rarely overt – people are either not aware of their profit-seeking or do not admit it (Bourdieu 1986; 1989, 5–9; Broady 1989, 2–3; Bourdieu and Wacquant 1995, 123–27, 134–37; cf. Larson 1977).

Each field has its own élite (the makers of the rules) which consists of people in the dominant positions of the field. It may be difficult to outline the élite, however, as the dominant group often remains undefined and nameless. An academic élite consists of professors, as academic and scientific power is mostly distributed to professors of the respective field. Key institutional actors in the national field and the joined administrative fields include offices, committees, working groups, and civil servants. Within this entity, the actors struggle for the form of authority typical to the specific field – that is, for the power to control with various laws, regulations, and administrative provisions. This national capital in turn provides power over various types of capital and repetitions thereof, particularly via the educational system (Bourdieu and Wacquant 1995, 140–42, 144).

To summarise, we can state that despite the idea of a developing profession already included in Functionalism, it was not until the neo-Weberian movement and its emphasis on history and society that an aspect of genuine change was introduced. Pierre Bourdieu's field theory, in turn, directs the analysis towards identifying the real subjects of action and the dynamics and effects of their interaction on the whole. Thus, from the neo-Weberian-Bourdieuan perspective, we can join the micro-level (jobs, institutions, the relations between the occupational groups, the mutual statuses, hierarchies, and the internal tension within occupations) and macro-level (the state, education, trade unions) views and study the professional system, the field, as an entity. Only the neo-Weberian approach and the field theory together were able to form a dynamic interpretative framework to provide tools for empirical analysis in a constantly and rapidly changing globalised world in which today's kindergarten professionals work.

The day-care system under construction – day-care centre professionals lose their status and face each other in struggle

In this section, I will examine changes in the day-care centre field and progress in professionalisation from the late 1960s to the mid-1990s.[2] The key idea is that the field of day-care centres is continuously shaping as a result of both inner struggles (within the day-care centres) and struggles with other fields. The state, education, and trade unions are the dealers of professional playing cards. Struggles are fought with strategies of social closure over capitals and positions. The aim is to describe the field of day-care centres in such a way as to cover the connections of the day-care centre to its environment as extensively as possible. Because of this point of view, the day-care centre cannot be examined as an island on its own. The history of day-care centres is always also history of the whole day-care system (Figure 1) as well as of the professional system.

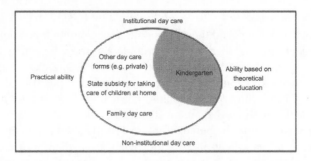

Figure 1.   Day-care field of the children under school age in Finland.

The increase and excess of state intervention

The construction of the public day-care system, related to the vigorous change in societal structures in the late 1960s, culminates in 1973 as the Day Care Act introduces a state-run system of day care. The welfare state takes possession of day care from 1973 to the mid-1990s.

State intervention covers all central areas of day care. In general terms, it can be said that intervention holds day care in its grip during the entire period. The administrative sectors of the forming Finnish welfare state were planning themselves and distributing their territories. Day care was one card in this game, because social capital (social services) demands its field. A day-care system becomes the most central guarantee for the existence of this field, as the day-care personnel increases rapidly in number to form approximately 50% of the entire social services personnel by the late 1980s. It is possible that the social services system could not have been built without day care. Day care lends a positive image to social services which, at the time, is struggling with the social problems of marginal groups. Consequently, it guarantees political support from the middle class in particular to construct the social services system (cf. Heikkilä and Haverinen 2007). The welfare administration thus receives day care, while the educational administration takes care of the reformed school education in the form of the new comprehensive school emerging in the early 1970s – something for everyone!

The specific dynamics in the field stem from the conflicts often created by the autocratic National Board of Social Affairs. It is interesting that the board also attempted to solve some of the conflicts created. For example, amidst the problems related to job descriptions generated by the new personnel structure (cf. Karila's article in this volume) issued by the board in 1980, it recommends a new hierarchisation of the jobs – thus alternating between the roles of a midwife and a judge!

The professional groups have played the kindergarten game largely by the rules of the National Board of Social Affairs,[3] and they have mainly played the role of marionettes. The authority of the professional groups was not sufficient in the struggle. The representatives of the trade unions have, naturally, been included in the main planning committees and workshops, but they have been 'quietly accepting' the authority-centred day-care policy. Professional groups are partly themselves 'guilty' for their losses in the struggle for the field.

Incomplete professionalisation – is professionalisation even possible in a female-dominated field?

According to one view, it is not until the field is completely monopolized by one professional group that the term 'professional form' is justified. The closure ought to cover professional activities and be based on the existence of formal degrees and other professionals' traits. In the day-care centre work, no profession (or professional group) has been able to monopolise the field in order to secure for themselves the most esteemed positions. The recent history of the day-care centre is rather an example of how, as a result of continuous struggle in varying conditions and conjunctures, the professional groups have on one hand moved upwards and on the other hand moved in the opposite direction – downwards.

One explanation may be that traditional professionalisation in day-care centre work (and in day-care work in general) is nearly impossible as the border between practical ability and ability based on theoretical education is shifting and obscure. Working in a day-care centre always includes to a great extent very general humane knowledge and skills. Examining the knowledge base in a female-dominated field has been difficult: does the knowledge base in actual fact differ from the requirements of traditional education and nursing at homes or in family day care? What is the nature of qualifications and skills acquired via theoretical training? On the other hand, it has been discovered that making the nursing and education of very young children more 'motherly', as promoted by, for example, family day care, may lead to increasing attempts at teacher professionalisation in order to raise the status and the wages. Poor wages may even as such increase professionalisation in female-dominated fields (Tallberg Broman 1994a, 29, 121; 1994b, 5; cf. also Laiho 2005, 30).

No single form of day care (see Figure 1) has obtained the position of monopoly. In fact, the field of day care changed since the mid-1980s to the opposite direction, at which point the competitive setting for the various forms of day care was created. The day-care centre entered a situation where it had to increasingly struggle for its position with other day-care solutions. In the early 1990s, the competition expanded between various service sectors (e.g. hospital, old people's home, children's home, care of the disabled, care of the alcoholics, day care) as the state in its fiscal crisis was trying to discard its role as the monopoly buyer of welfare services.

Defending the status of day-care centres was at times the sole uniting factor between the professions in the 1980s and 1990s. This was logical, as the various professions had a mutual interest in safeguarding the existence of the field and maintaining the jobs in it.

Habitus was not exactly a fish in water – rejecting the day-care centre

The rejection phenomenon is connected to the kindergarten field. The professional habituses (cf. Urban in this volume) of the professional groups were not compatible with the kindergarten field. In fact, they have not wished to be part of a field defined in the Day Care Act and nurtured by the National Board of Social Welfare.

Kindergarten teachers have mainly wanted to be part of the field of education, and kindergarten nurses part of the field of health care, whereas social-pedagogical child care and child protection was the very own area of social pedagogues. In a field that emphasises pedagogics, the habitus of a nursery nurse with a healthcare education was not one of a fish in water. Similarly, the habitus of a kindergarten teacher did not function without friction in a professional field emphasising care and nurturing. In such a situation, the habitus and the objective circumstances did not correspond, which led to a struggle to reshape the day-care centre field as corresponding to the habitus of each professional group.

The rejection phenomenon connected with the inertia of professional habitus can be explained by the contradictory situation: although the day-care field has existed as a uniform field in an administrative and juridical sense since 1973, there have been, in practice, no uniform day-care personnel operating in it. The inertia of the habitus is related to situations in which there is a conflict between the habitus and the field. In some historical events, the objective structures change at such a rapid pace that individual professions cannot follow. The result is that people and the professions they represent adopt a conservative view and start to operate in opposing and resistant ways, regardless of the era (Bourdieu and Wacquant 1995, 161–62). The professional traditions formed over the decades, the types of cultural capital produced by education, and the resulting professional identities do not make it in time to adapt themselves to the requirements of the new institution.

There is another paradox related to the field of day-care centres. As the types of capital are valuable and they only function in relation to the field, in this case, the day-care centre (Bourdieu and Wacquant 1995, 156–60), the necessary capital can only be defined within the day-care centre. We may thus assume that playing the cello, for example, would not be as highly valued capital in the day-care centre as it is in a symphony orchestra. How, then, could we have defined the capitals of kindergarten teachers, knowing that the quality of being a teacher in a day-care centre, as defined by the National Board of Social Welfare, did not exist the way it exists in a comprehensive school?

Unclearness of ability and the inflation of expertise

It is very difficult to answer the question as to what the most durable and valid form of cultural capital was in the state-led day care system of kindergarten. There may not necessarily be one to be found. On the other hand, the only valid currency was the day-care capital – that is, nursing and education itself (Figure 2). However, the professional groups did not commit themselves to this form of capital. Theoretical education of kindergarten professionals has not, in spite of the attempts made, been able to explicitly produce this kind of ability.[4] The state-led, centralized system wanted nursing and education, the education system was producing something else, and the professional groups held on to and counted on their traditions.

The state-guaranteed and -originated definition of cultural capital was not valid currency in the customer work of day-care centres. No professional group had the power to define the capitals and thus obtain an autonomous position in the field. Definition power was strictly in the hands of the bureaucratic élite. The monopoly of definition can partly be explained by the fact that the bureaucratic élite of the social sector had no opposing force that would have been strong enough to make their own definitions. The professional groups had no allies to be reckoned with. The academic (professorial) élite of the day-care field started to form as late as at the end of the 1990s (Husa and Kinos 2005). As we stated earlier, trade unions operated as marionettes pulled by the bureaucratic élite.

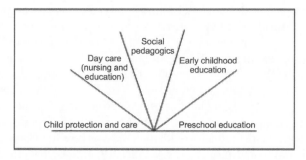

Figure 2.   A main subdivision of the cultural capital (know-how) of day-care centres in an era of a state-led day-care system in Finland.

As a result of the economic recession in the early 1990s, the state economy was balanced. The partial dismantling of the system of social services led to reductions in the supply of day-care services. On the ideological level, too, attitudes towards day care were changed. Reforms in the day-care field (home-care subsidy, the right to tax deductions for hiring domestic help, employment subsidy) were justified by cost savings and the ensuing freedom of choice. Critique aimed at expertise also resulted in justifying less professional day care. The relative significance of ability based on theoretical education had been gradually decreasing since the mid-1980s.

The educational system and social closure

As mentioned before, the educational status of kindergarten teachers, social pedagogues, and nursery nurses was high and clear before the Day Care Act. The position of the professionals then became contradictory. Their education was caught in the cross-fire of different fields of education and service sectors of the welfare state. The professions were left drifting in the educational system. Day care, a new 'service', was another underdog in the struggle with such established service forms as the hospital, the school, and the social services. In this situation, kindergarten teachers, social pedagogues, and nursery nurses representing different circles of interest became opposite parties in matters of professional issues.

The great reforms of the educational system turned into strategies of social closure in day care. An 'upper class' of the specially trained professionals and poorly educated 'pariah class' were formed. A pariah was deprived of the protection of their degree title produced by education, special know-how, and qualification requirements. Even the principle of continuous education turned into a tool for social closure as the degrees now came in successive order and the required qualifications made the system rigid. In the professional new deal, some professions fell, some were elevated, and some were altogether abolished.

The reforms of the educational system became servants of the professional interests. From the viewpoint of professional fields, the hierarchisation of degrees referred to an internal struggle for status between the various professional groups within one professional field. For example, it was in the interest of the social workers to deprofessionalise social pedagogues – that is, to shift their education towards the reformed secondary-level education of the social sector. This eliminated the social worker's fear of an inflationary development of the status of their own university-level degree. The exclusion also had a counter-trend, as the emergence of the new secondary-level education attracted professional groups to enable its formation. The importance of kindergarten teachers for the field of education was in turn emphasised at the end of the decade, as the establishing of university-level kindergarten teacher training in 1995 and the formation of the academic field of early childhood education in the late 1990s were measures to prevent the other teacher training (that of comprehensive school teachers in particular) from being shifted down to polytechnics (Husa and Kinos 2005).

Expertise and the monopoly of knowledge are difficult to identify. This is partly due to the semi-professional nature of the professions and partly to the rejection phenomenon directed to the field of day-care centres. Pre-school education was maybe the only clear area of tasks, where attempts were made to create such a monopoly. Neither has any field of science been able to offer protection to the day-care professions. Science of education was involved with the status of comprehensive school teachers, social politics with the status of social workers, and nursing science with that of the healthcare professions, such as hospital nurses.

External closure was a consequence of such state intervention factors as the educational system, legislation, and qualification requirements. As a result of this, the status of the professions examined decreased in the era of state-led day care. The training of personnel was altogether left 'open', in the same way as at the end of the 1960s.

Internal closure is a consequence of the activity of the profession itself, the trade union organisation. As a consequence, a hierarchy is wanted within the field. Internal closure leads to a pecking order therein. The same thing happened to kindergarten teachers as to the other professional groups in this study. They were barred from their traditional qualification fields. Kindergarten teachers were barred from the teaching profession and social pedagogues from social work. The history of the social pedagogues is in this respect clearer than that of kindergarten teachers. Barring social pedagogues from social work was the result of logical and meditated action of the trade union for social work. Kindergarten teachers' organisational and functional integration into the teaching profession was slack at the time, which makes it difficult to point out actual internal closure in the field. On the contrary, at the end of the period, cohesion within the teaching profession increased along with its contacts with the professional tradition.

Similar features exist in the history of kindergarten nurses. Kindergarten nurses were 'eliminated' partly as a result of the action of the trade union for health care. The price paid for the closing down of the kindergarten nurse training in 1995 was a development promoted by the healthcare élite: a classic example of getting bitten by our own dogs.

The struggle goes on

Motto: Knowledge is the currency of competition (Abbot 1988)

The education of kindergarten professionals started early – kindergartens teachers in 1892, nursery nurses in 1910, and social pedagogues in 1918. Over the past 30 years, their work has been a field of constant conflicts and struggles. Over that time, the field has experienced discourse both undervaluing the work and emphasising its importance.

The struggles in the field change and acquire various shades of meaning over time. In retrospect, the key historical milestones in the near history of the Finnish kindergarten/day-care centre that have controlled the day-care system and the training of kindergarten professionals and thus had an influence on both their work and their mutual relations include:

- The Day Care Act in 1973: created the basis for building the national day-care system.
- The Child Home Care Allowance Act in 1985: the day-care centre lost its status and position as the principal form of day care.
- Kindergarten teacher training established at universities in 1995: the formation of the academic infrastructure of early childhood education.
- The entitlement to day care in 1996: guaranteed a day-care place for all children under seven years of age and changed the social service–oriented nature of day care.
- The Act to amend the Education Act in 1999: launched statutory preschool education and joined it as part of the educational system.
- The Act to amend the Day Care Act in 2003: tore down the organisatory monopoly of the social administration in day-care affairs.

Kindergarten teacher training was established as permanent in universities, and now led to a lower university degree (BA, Bachelor of Education). Concurrently, professorships and other research posts in early childhood education were launched in all universities. The academic infrastructure of early childhood education acquired its current form in 1995–2003, at which time degree studies of Masters of Early Childhood Education (MA) also emerged in all universities. The semi-professional status of kindergarten teachers has thus been continuously raised upwards. The training of social pedagogues was also established at higher education. The training of social pedagogues was transferred to the new polytechnics (nowadays, universities of applied sciences) in the late 1990s. At that point, the degree was renamed 'socionomist' (Bachelor of Social Sciences).

With the other two professional groups, the development has been quite the opposite. A joint basic degree for the field of social services and health was launched in 1995 to replace the nursery nurse and day-care nurse training. In the new practical nurse training, the contents of social services and healthcare had overshadowed day care and early childhood education.

New reasons exist for the struggle between kindergarten teachers (Bachelors of Education) and socionomists (Bachelors of Social Sciences). The trade union of socionomists is eagerly pushing a preschool teacher qualification for its members – along with statutory preschool education, only kindergarten teachers and comprehensive school teachers would be qualified for this. On the other hand, the trade union in question, together with the bureaucratic élite of the social administration, aims at introducing a new subtype of cultural capital alongside the current types of early childhood education and preschool education in the field. They attempt to define the function of day-care centres as part of family work! Thus, socionomists aim to sit on two stools to reinforce their status (e.g. Heikkilä and Haverinen 2007; Mehtonen 2007).

There is sometimes harmony and sometimes distinct tension between the points of the state–professional triangle (Figure 3). The role of the state changed, which has been reflected in the cancellation of the role of the state as an instance that creates the norms for day-care centre practices. This is visible, for example, in the loosening of qualification requirements and the minimization of the control for the group sizes in day-care forms. Day care has also been allowed to develop into a system resembling a partial market in which the service coupon, service money, competitive bidding, and privatisation provide new dynamics for the kindergarten field.

The present and the future of day care are influenced by many other instances than those contained in the professional triangle (Rinne and Jauhiainen 1988, 46). The triangle has turned into a hexagon, at the least. This direction of development means increasing pluralism and more flexible day-care arrangements.

The relationship between professional groups (trade unions) and the state has been reciprocal also in Finland, a clearly state-oriented society. Even though professions have been subject to various forms of constitutional control, it has nevertheless been in the interest of the professions to have 'special relations' with the state, the networks of power. The

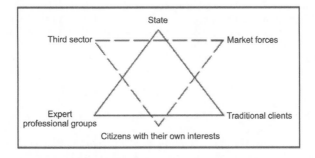

Figure 3.   Central organisers of present day care of children under school age in the New Era of Explanation in Finland.

union with the state has provided, and still provides, customers for the professional groups particularly after the professional groups have managed to confirm the state of their unique ability to provide the services.

The rejection phenomenon is also ongoing. The shortage of kindergarten teachers has radically increased over the past decade. The proportion of kindergarten teachers has decreased in day-care centres, and socionomists have been hired to carry out their tasks. The reason for this is the fact that the Ministry of Social Affairs and Health has not carried out the necessary charting of estimated needs for kindergarten teachers, only for the 'traditional' professional groups in social services, such as social workers. Neither have the tasks of the Ministry of Education included the quantitative estimation of needs in the professional education of day-care personnel. The administrative organs have thus carried on with the division for territories agreed upon 30 years ago (e.g. Kinos and Laakkonen 2006)!

The research of professions has traditionally had two parallel lines. In Great Britain and the United States, professional groups have struggled in the service market without a radical intervention by the state. In these countries, the development of professions can be characterised by bottom-to-top professionalisation. By contrast, in continental Europe (for example, France, Germany, and the Nordic countries), the development has been state-controlled and state-oriented. The state has not only controlled and legitimised the operations of professional groups, but also centrally organised education and standardised degrees. The continental tradition is thus characterised by a top-to-bottom process.

European integration, globalisation, the ideology of the Anglo-American New Right, and the European neo-liberalism have, nevertheless, had an impact on the increasing homogeneity of societies. In the Finnish day care of children this is visible in the reduced control by the state, increased day-care entrepreneurship, market-orientation, competitive bidding, and privatisation. This homogenisation has made the dominant Anglo-American sociology of professions increasingly more suitable for examining professional groups in Europe as well. In an altered situation, the integration of differing views and theories assists in understanding, explaining, and interpreting the professional system as a whole.

Notes

1. Attitudes are in a way reflected also in the name of the institution: A direct translation of 'day-care centre' ('päiväkoti' in Finnish) is 'daytime home' or 'day home'.
2. The empirical observations in this chapter are based on the PhD dissertation 'Kindergarten as a Field for Struggle for Professional Groups' (Kinos 1997). The results of this research have also been introduced in two articles (Kinos 1998; Kinos, Laiho, and Palonen 1998). The documentary material of the research consists of laws and regulations, reports and memoranda of the public administration, official decisions, and professional journals and trade papers.
3. Later, National Research and Development Centre for Welfare and Health (Stakes).
4. From the point of view of the day-care interest, day-care nurses who had their degree in 1985–1995 were the only educated professional group. They were trained to replace nursery nurses in day-care centres. The group of day-care nurses, however, remained very small in number.

References

Abbot, A. 1988. *The system of professions: An essay on the division of expert labour.* Chicago: University of Chicago Press.
Bourdieu, P. 1986. The forms of Capital. In *Handbook of theory and research for the sociology of education,* ed. J.G. Richardson, 241–58. New York: Greenwood Press.
———. 1989. An interview with Pierre Bourdieu. For socio-analysis of intellectuals: On Homo Academicus. *Berkeley Journal of Sociology* 34: 1–29.

Bourdieu, P., and L.J.D. Wacquant. 1995. *Refleksiiviseen sosiologiaan. Tutkimus, käytäntö ja yhteiskunta.* [An invitation to reflexive sociology: Research, practise and society]. Joensuu: Joensuu University Press.

Broady, D. 1989. *Kapital, habitus, fält: Några nyckelbegrepp i Pierre Bourdieus sociologi.* [Capital, habitus, field: The few key concepts in the sociology of Pierre Bourdieu]; Stockholm: UHÅ.

Collins, R. 1979. *The credential society: A historical sociology of education and stratification.* New York: Academic Press.

———. 1990. Changing conceptions in the sociology of the professions. In *The formation of professions. Knowledge, state and strategy,* ed. R. Torstendahl and M. Burrage, 11–23. London: Sage.

Etzioni, A., ed. 1969. *The semi-professions and their organization: Teachers, nurses, social workers.* New York: The Free Press.

Freidson, E. 1986. *Professional powers: A study of the institutionalization of formal knowledge.* Chicago: University of Chicago Press.

———. 1994. *Professionalism reborn: Theory, prophecy and policy.* Cambridge: Polity Press.

Goode, W. 1969. The theoretical limits of professionalization. In *The semi-professions and their organization: Teachers, nurses, social workers,* ed. A. Etzioni, 266–313. New York: The Free Press.

Hänninen, S.-L., and S. Valli. 1986. *Suomen lastentarhatyön ja varhaiskasvatuksen historia.* [The history of Finnish kindergarten and early childhood education]. Keuruu: Otava.

Hargreaves, D.H. 1994. The new professionalism: The synthesis of professional and institutional development. *Teaching & Teacher Education* 10, no. 4: 423–38.

Heikkilä, M., and R. Haverinen. 2007. Liudentuuko sosiaalinen näkökulma? [Does the social point of view become obscure?] *Premissi. Terveys- ja sosiaalialan johtamisen erikoisjulkaisu* 2, no. 6: 13–17.

Hoyle, E. 1980. Professionalization and deprofessionalization in education. In *World yearbook of education,* ed. E. Hoyle and J. Megarry, Professional development of teachers, 42–53. London: Kogan Page.

Hughes, E. 1966. The social significance of professionalisation. In *Professionalisation,* ed. H. Vollmer and D. Mills, 62–71. Englewood Cliffs, NJ: Prentice Hall.

Husa, S., and J. Kinos. 2005. Academisation of early childhood education. *Scandinavian Journal of Educational Research* 49, no. 2: 133–51.

Katz, L. 1987. *Current topics in early childhood education 7: The Nature of Professions. Where is Early Childhood Education?* Norwood: Ablex.

Kinos, J. 1997. *Päiväkoti ammattikuntien kamppailujen kenttänä.* [Kindergarten as a field for struggle for professional groups]. Sarja C: 133. Turku: Turun yliopiston julkaisuja.

———. 1998. Päiväkoti – kolmikymmenvuotinen kiistakapula ja taistelutanner. [Kindergarten – The bone of contention and battlefield lasting 30 years] *Kasvatus* 30, no. 5: 524–34.

———. 2006. Varhaiskasvatuksen keskeiset kehittämishaasteet ja -kohteet. *Puheenvuoroja varhaiskasvatuksen kehittämisestä.* [The central developmental challenges of early childhood education. Essays on developing the early childhood education], 13–17. Helsinki: Opetusalan Ammattijärjestö.

Kinos, J., and E. Laakkonen. 2006. *Pienten lasten opettajat Varsinais-Suomessa. Selvitys lastentarhanopettajatilanteesta Varsinais-Suomen maakunnassa.* [The teachers of little children in southwest Finland. Research of the situation of kindergarten teachers in the province of Varsinais-Suomi]. Turun yliopisto. Turku: Kasvatustieteiden tiedekunta.

Kinos, J., I. Laiho, and T. Palonen. 1998. Kuka päättää, ketä kuullaan päivähoidossa. *Lastentarha.* [Who are deciding, who are the consulting experts in day care?] 61, no. 4: 56–58.

Konttinen, E. 1991. *Perinteisesti moderniin. Professioiden yhteiskunnallinen synty Suomessa.* [The traditional way to the modernity. The birth of the professions in Finland]. Tampere: Vastapaino.

———. 1993. Professionäkökulman lupaus. In *Ammattikunnat, yhteiskunta ja valtio. Suomalaisten professioiden kehityskuvia.* [The promise of the professionalism. In Professions, society and state. The development of the Finnish professions], ed. E. Konttinen, Julkaisuja 55: 7–13. Jyväskylä: Jyväskylän yliopiston sosiologian laitos.

Laiho, A. 2005. *"Sisar tieteen saloissa" – sairaanhoitajien akatemisoitumisprojekti Pohjoismaissa 1900-luvulla.* [Sisters and science – the project of academicising nurses in the Nordic Countries in the 1900s]. Turun yliopisto. Sarja C 232. Turku: Turun yliopiston julkaisuja.

Larson, M. 1977. *The rise of professionalism: A sociological analysis.* Berkeley: University of California Press.

Lujala, E. 2007. *Lastentarhatyö, kansanopetuksen osa ja kotikasvatuksen tukitoiminnan päämäärät ja toteutuminen Pohjois-Suomessa 1800-luvun lopulta vuoteen 1938.* [Kindergarten work as a part of popular education and in support of home education – goals and fulfilment of activities in Northen Finland from the late 19th century to 1938]. Kasvatustieteiden ja opettajankoulutuksen yksikkö. Oulun yliopisto E 89. Oulu: Kasvatustieteiden tiedekunta.

MacDonald, K.M. 1995. *The sociology of the professions.* London: Sage.

Mehtonen, M. 2007. *Sosiaalipedagogiikka-projekti. Sosionomien (AMK) varhaiskasvatuksen ja sosiaalipedagogiikan osaaminen.* [The project of social pedagogy. The cultural capital and ability of the socionomists in the fields of early childhood education and social pedagogy]. Helsinki: Sosiaalipedagogit Talentia.

Menand, L. 1995. The trashing of professionalism. *Academe* 81 (May/June): 16–19.

Murphy, R. 1984. The structure of closure: A critique and development of the theories of Weber, Collins and Parkin. *British Journal of Sociology* 35, no. 4: 547–65.

————. 1990. Proletarianization or bureaucratization: the fall of the professional. In *The formation of professions: Knowledge, state and strategy,* ed. R. Torstendahl and M. Burrage, 71–96. London: Sage.

Niemi, H., and V. Kohonen. 1995. *Towards new professionalism and active learning in teacher development: Empirical findings on teacher education and induction.* Reports from the Department of Teacher Education A 2. Tampere: University of Tampere.

Niiranen, P., and J. Kinos. 2001. Suomen lastentarha- ja päiväkotipedagogiikan jäljillä. In *Varhaiskasvatuksen teoriasuuntauksia* [Following the tracks of Finnish kindergarten and day care centre pedagogies]. In *The trends of the theories in early childhood education,* ed. K. Karila, J. Kinos, and J. Virtanen, 58–85. Juva: PS-Kustannus.

Organisation for Economic Co-operation and Development (OECD). 2000. Early childhood education and care policy in Finland. Helsinki: Ministry of Social Affairs and Health 21.

Parsons, T. 1968. Professions. In *International encyclopaedia of the social sciences,* vol. 12, ed. E. Shils, 536–46. New York: Macmillan.

Rinne, R., and A. Jauhiainen. 1988. *Koulutus, professionaalistuminen ja valtio. Julkisen sektorin koulutettujen reproduktioammattikuntien muotoutuminen Suomessa.* [Education, professionalization and state. The developing of the reproduction occupations in public services in Finland]. Kasvatustieteiden tiedekunta. Julkaisusarja A: 128. Turku: Turun yliopisto.

Scott, P.M. 1989. Professionalism: Has the meaning changed? *Trial* 25 (June): 87–88.

Tallberg Broman, L. 1994a. *"För barnets skull." En studie av förskolan som ett kvinnligt professionaliseringsprojekt.* [For the sake of children. Research of kindergarten as a female project of professionalization]. Lunds universitet. Lörarhögskolan. Institutionen för pedagogik och specialmetodik 594. Malmö.

————. 1994b. Lärarutbildning, kön och professionalisering. Med förskollärarutbildningen som ett historisk exempel. [Teacher education, gender and professionalization. Kindergarten teacher education as a historical example]. Lunds universitet. Lärarhögskolan. Institutionen för pedagogik och specialmetodik 804. Malmö.

Torstendahl, R. 1990. Introduction: Promotion and strategies of knowledge based groups. In *The formation of professions: Knowledge, state and strategy,* ed. R. Torstendahl and M. Burrage, 1–10. London: Sage.

Välimäki, A.-L. 1999. *Lasten hoitopuu. Lasten päivähoitojärjestelmä Suomessa 1800- ja 1900 – luvuilla. Suomen Kuntaliitto.* [The tree of day care. The day care system in Finland in 19th and 20th centuries]. Helsinki: Kuntaliiton painatuskeskus.

VN. 1999. Paavo Lipposen II hallituksen ohjelma. [The programme of the second government of Paavo Lipponen]. Valtioneuvosto. 18 April. http://www.vn.fi/vn/suomi/tiedote/99xx_ohjelma.htm.

Weber, M. 1980. Protestanttinen etiikka ja kapitalismin henki. [Protestant ethics and the spirit of capitalism]. Porvoo: WSOY.

Wilensky, H. 1964. Professionalisation for everyone? *American Journal of Sociology* 70, no. 2: 137–58.

Nannies, nursery nurses and early years professionals: constructions of professional identity in the early years workforce in England

Gill McGillivray

Newman University College, Birmingham, UK

ABSTRACT: Recent policy in England has created a new status of 'Early Years Professional', thus imposing professionalisation of the early years workforce. There has been an increase in policy focus on those working with young children, and such a focus raises questions about practitioners' own responses to the debate about their training, education, qualifications and work. How early years practitioners see themselves, their collective or individual identity, or both, may be unsettled by being the centre of discussion and reform.

This research aimed to investigate historical and recent texts using discourse analysis to expose discourse that may have shaped and contributed to the workforce's construction of their professional identity. A theoretical framework of professional identity, proposed by Tucker, is useful in its recognition of how prevailing and contemporary discourses contribute to the construction of professional identity.

Findings suggest that constructs may exacerbate uncertainty, change and struggle for the workforce, and that there are complex and enduring aspects of professional identity that may influence perceptions. Imposed changes in training, assessment and qualifications, long-held beliefs evident in discourse, ideology and day-to-day practices also contribute to constructs of professional identity.

The implications for practice are a need to recognise the complexity of professional identity and therefore the needs of some members of workforce as they move towards professionalisation. It is also argued that the voice of the workforce has been absent historically, and that current reform provides an opportunity for listening and responding.

RÉSUMÉ: Une politique récente a créé en Angleterre un nouveau statut pour les 'professionnels de la petite enfance' qui impose ainsi une professionnalisation des personnels de la petite enfance. Il y a eu un intérêt grandissant pour ceux qui travaillent auprès de jeunes enfants et un tel intérêt soulève la question des réponses que les praticiens, eux-mêmes, apportent au débat relatif à leurs formation, éducation, qualifications et travail. La façon dont les praticiens de la petite enfance se voient, leur identité collective ou individuelle ou les deux, peut être perturbée pr le fait d'être au centre des discussions et des réformes.

Cette recherche, qui avait pour but d'étudier les textes anciens et récents à l'aide d'une analyse de contenu, présente des discours qui ont pu modeler et contribuer à la construction de l'identité professionnelle de ces personnels. Le cadre théorique de l'identité professionnelle, proposé par Tucker est utile de par la reconnaissance de la façon dont les discours contemporains dominants contribuent à la construction de l'identité professionnelle.

Les résultats suggèrent que ces constructions peuvent exacerber incertitude, changement et difficultés chez le personnel et qu'il y a des aspects de l'identité professionnelle, complexes et durables, qui peuvent influencer les perceptions. Les changements imposés dans la formation, l'évaluation, les qualifications, les croyances anciennes, évidentes dans les discours, les idéologies et les pratiques quotidiennes contribuent aussi à la construction de l'identité professionnelle.

Les implications pour la pratique consistent en un besoin de reconnaître la complexité de l'identité professionnelle et donc les besoins de certains personnels lorsqu'ils sont amenés à se professionnaliser. Il est aussi soutenu que la voix des personnel a été absente historiquement et que les réformes actuelles donnent une occasion pour l'entendre et lui répondre.

ZUSAMMENFASSUNG: In England wurde von der Politik kürzlich der neue Status des 'Early Years Professional' geschaffen; 'Professionalisierung' den im Feld Tätigen dadurch aufgedrängt. Die politische Aufmerksamkeit für diejenigen, die mit jungen Kindern arbeiten, wächst. Dieses neue Interesse wirft Fragen auf; etwa über die Sichtweise der Praktikerinnen selbst, wenn es um ihre Aus- und Weiterbildung, formale Qualifikation und Arbeit geht. Im Zentrum von Reformen und öffentlicher Diskussion zu stehen, kann das Bild, das Frühpädagoginnen von sich selbst haben – ihre kollektive und individuelle Identität – durchaus erschüttern.

Die vorliegende Studie untersucht mithilfe eines diskursanalytischen Ansatzes historische und aktuelle Texte, um Diskurse herauszustellen, die möglicherweise zur Konstruktion professioneller Selbstbilder beigetragen haben. Der von Tucker vorgeschlagene theoretische Rahmen professioneller Identität ist dazu hilfreich in seiner Anerkennung der Beiträge vorherrschender zeitgenössischer Diskurse zur Konstruktion professioneller Identität.

Die Ergebnisse legen nahe, dass die so entstehenden Bilder Unsicherheit, Veränderung und Belastung für die Beschäftigten verstärken, dass es aber auch komplexe und dauerhaft wirkende Aspekte professioneller Identität gibt, die die Wahrnehmung beeinflussen. Verordnete Veränderungen von Ausbildung, Beurteilung und Qualifikation tragen dabei ebenso zu den Konstrukten professioneller Identität bei wie Überzeugungen, die sich in den Diskursen dauerhaft halten, Ideologien und tägliche Praxis.

Für die Praxis ergibt sich daraus die Notwendigkeit, die Komplexität professioneller Identitäten anzuerkennen, und damit verbunden auch die Bedürfnisse einiger Beschäftigter auf dem Weg zu ihrer Professionalisierung. Es wird argumentiert, dass die Stimmen der Praktiker in der Vergangenheit nicht präsent waren, dass aber die aktuelle Reform eine Gelegenheit bietet, dies zu ändern.

RESUMEN: Políticas recientes en Inglaterra han creado la nueva condición de 'Profesional pre-escolar', imponiendo así la profesionalización de la fuerza de trabajo pre-escolar. El aumento del interés político en quienes trabajan con niños, hace preguntarse cuales son las respuestas de los prácticos al debate acerca de su preparación, educación, calificaciones y trabajo. Como se perciben los prácticos pre-escolares a si mismos, sus identidades individuales o colectivas, puede estar al centro de la discusión y la reforma.

Esta investigación tiene como objetivo estudiar textos históricos y recientes, usando análisis de discursos, para poner al descubierto los discursos que pueden haber formado y contribuido a la construcción de las identidades profesionales de la fuerza de trabajo. Un marco teórico de identidad profesional propuesto por Tucker es útil para reconocer como discursos contemporáneos y prevalecientes contribuyen a la construcción de identidades profesionales.

Resultados sugieren que las construcciones pueden exacerbar la incertidumbre, el cambio y la lucha para la fuerza de trabajo, y que hay aspectos complejos y duraderos de la identidad profesional que pueden influir en las percepciones. Cambios impuestos en la capacitación, evaluación y calificaciones, creencias evidentes en los discursos, ideologías y práctica diaria también contribuyen a construir identidad profesional.

Las implicaciones para la práctica son una necesidad de reconocer la complejidad de la identidad profesional y por ello las necesidades de algunos miembros de la fuerza de trabajo que se están moviendo hacia la profesionalización. Se argumenta además que la voz de la fuerza de trabajo ha estado históricamente ausente, y que la actual reforma implica una oportunidad para escuchar y responder.

Introduction

How do members of the early years care and education workforce in England perceive their identity as a 'professional'? The need to ask such a question has been exacerbated by recent government policy development of children's services in England with the introduction of the status of Early Years Professional in 2006 (DfES, 2006; see also Moss 2003, 2006; Osgood 2006). The vision to reform and develop the early years workforce in England provides an opportunity to reflect on past discourse and how it may have shaped the sector workforce as it is today.

Terminology that identifies those who are the early years workforce is confusing (practitioner, nursery worker, nanny, child-carer, nursery nurse), so a multiplicity of titles may have contributed to confusion about identity, creating uncertainty as to what the various titles, roles and responsibilities mean. The research reported here intends to provide the backdrop for continuing research with early years practitioners to investigate their own constructions of professional identity.

The desire to conduct research into professional identity within the early years workforce was born out of frequent and numerous conversations with both students undertaking early years qualifications in colleges of further and higher education and others more peripheral to the workforce (such as advisers and careers teachers). Some students had many years of experience, others were moving from compulsory education into training at sixteen years of age. Conversations suggested that there are variations in constructs of professional identity within and beyond the workforce, and discourse analysis was intended to begin a process of exploration of constructs. Debate on what constitutes professional identity will be considered as part of the review of literature that follows. The aim of the research was thus to begin the process of deconstruction of professional identity by exploring historical documents containing discourse relating to the early years workforce.

A brief context

The development of the early years workforce in England has been influenced by the historical separation of those who care for babies and young children and those who educate them (Sylva and Pugh 2005). The history of childhood provides insight into past perceptions of children as small adults, in need of training in order to take their place in the world of 'grown ups', for example (Aries 1962). Other images and constructs may enhance an understanding of how those who cared for children were seen as minders, a low-status role that mirrored the low status of children in society (Cohen et al. 2004). Constructs of children and childhood and those who work with children are woven together from cultural and economic strands within society. Texts that explore childhood in western societies include James and Prout (1990), Kehily (2004), and Jenks (2004). An analysis of images and constructs of teachers in the USA and the United Kingdom (Weber and Mitchell 1995), and the role of the Victorian governess (Hughes 1993), provide insight into the struggles arising from stereotypical images, conflicting demands and expectations experienced by both groups.

In the late 1990s, as part of the National Childcare Strategy in England (DfEE 1998), which set out the newly elected Labour government's vision for families and childcare, the amalgamation of care-based services with education posed several challenges. For example, pay, status and conditions for employees in care services were inferior compared with those in the education sector who generally had higher pay, longer holidays and a shorter working day. Key events such as the Second World War and the Laming Report (2003) have also had significant impact on demand for and provision of childcare and education services, resulting in unification and reconfiguration. Such events inevitably impact on the workforce too, as fundamental ways of working are challenged and can lead to problematisation. The language of 'reform' suggests a need for change and improvement; that what had gone before was not 'good enough'.

Tucker (1999) argues that problematisation arises from historical influences, and this includes media, research and policy portrayal. In the field of early years, current discourse relates to affordable childcare, reform of the early years workforce, children who achieve the five outcomes stated within Every Child Matters (DfES 2003), meeting the needs of working parents (HM Treasury 2004) and the effects (both beneficial and damaging) of childcare. Such discourse reinforces perceptions of the need for a workforce that is redemptive and offers the children it works with protection and safety (Cohen et al. 2004). Social perceptions of children and childhood that have created problematisation for the early years workforce include early years care as 'women's work' (Moss 2003), along with structural and theoretical constraints (Dahlberg, Moss, and Pence 2007). A tension arises from the dichotomy between a workforce that is construed as caring, maternal and gendered, as opposed to professional, degree educated and highly trained.

Tucker (2004, 84) proposes that any framework that examines professional identity should be able to assist analysis of those forms of discourse that are used to define particular forms of work; show how ideas are struggled over and contested at various levels of experience; and demonstrate how such matters directly impact upon the professional identities which individuals and groups adopt in their everyday work.

Tucker (2004) also offers a framework for analysis that identifies factors involved in the construction of professional identity (see Figure 1). Such factors are helpful in beginning to develop lines of enquiry for this research, and the themes of training, expectations and ideologies recur in Ellis and Whittington (1988) and Eraut (1994).

What is understood by the term professional identity is enhanced by research undertaken into the professional selves of teachers in England by Day et al. (2006). They considered past research and aimed to draw together 'the relationships between social structures and individual agency; between notions of a socially constructed, and therefore contingent and ever-remade "self", and a "self" with dispositions, attitudes and and behavioural responses which are durable and relatively stable; and between cognitive and emotional identities' (Day et al. 2006, 601). These notions are also helpful, reflecting how the fluidity of identity is influenced by notions of self, emotional identities, dispositions and attitudes. Such themes are similar to those proposed by Britzman (1992, 42), who states 'the taking up of an identity is a constant social negotiation that can never be permanently settled or fixed, occurring

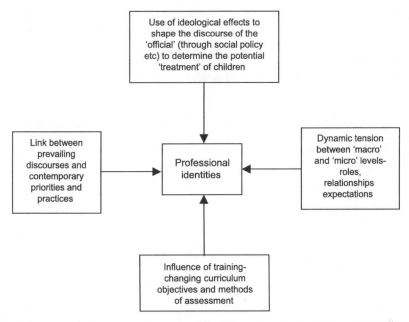

Figure 1.   Factors involved in the construction of professional identity (Tucker 2004, 88).

as it necessarily does within the irreconcilable contradictions of situational and historical constraints'.

The literature thus informs us that professional identity is construed on shifting but simultaneously enduring perceptions, influenced by history, society, ideologies and discourse. Individual dispositions and emotions, day-to-day lives and relationships, training and education are also influential in creating or sustaining professional identity. Problematisation and an unsettling of the workforce are implicitly written into the dominant discourse of current early years care and education policy as change is initiated through the implementation of the Children's Workforce Reform (DfES 2005).

Discourse analysis

Discourse analysis offers potential as a research method to explore text through the themes identified in literature. Seeking prevailing discourses at different points in time, thus identifying historical influences on constructs of the early years workforce, could provide a backdrop for further research into the views of practitioners themselves. Fealy (2004) undertook discourse analysis relating to nurses in Ireland, and revealed how the public discourse was influenced by culture and socio-political influences, from his analysis of nursing periodicals from the 1920s to the 1980s. Fealy (2004, 649) sought text relating to 'what nurses were doing and saying, including evidence of professional debate'.

Similarly, representations and constructs of young people through society and the media have been documented by Gillis (1981) and Griffin (1993). Both authors consider the impact of social history on young people, and this research, although on a significantly smaller scale, attempts to explore texts that may reflect societal changes in need and demand for childcare and education and any resultant impact on what is written about the workforce that provides the care and education. Thus, discourse analysis seems to offer a line of enquiry in the search for equivalent discourse relating to early years professionals.

Osgood (2006) has presented a deconstruction of discourse related to current (as opposed to historical) policy on early years workforce reform, and sought to expose how the discourse used in policy documents reinforces 'certain discursive truths, in this instance around what it means to be a professional in early childhood education and care' (Osgood 2006, 7). Truth as well as knowledge and power are critical in the debate, as reinforced by Swingewood:

> Discourse is a form of power exercised by particular social groups; discourse decides 'who' speaks and what they say, for no one has the right to say anything. ... Hence power and knowledge are joined. As social practices put knowledge to work, it is the discourses that produce truth. (Swingewood 2000, 197)

What was written about the workforce, by whom and for whom, and indeed what has not been written, therefore warrants exploration. Constructs of those who work with young children can be contested, once we examine what we may have accepted previously as what we know: making the familiar strange (Delamont 2002). The research is not intended to emancipate or liberate the workforce from the constraints of dominant discourse. Instead, it is hoped that some reproduction of texts might create opportunities for deconstruction and consideration of recurring themes, commonality and contradiction.

Initial research determined the two parameters that made the tasks of seeking texts manageable and focused. First, texts would relate to the early years care and education workforce in England (as there are differences across the United Kingdom; current workforce reform policy relates to England only). Second, the dates between 1940 and the current date were selected, in order to focus on comparatively recent research, changes and developments that have occurred since World War II. Initial scrutiny also revealed the range of nomenclature by which the workforce was called – hence the inclusion of the first research question below.

Sources that provided historical documentary evidence of discourse pertinent to the early years workforce were selected with reference to university library catalogues, specialist magazines for early years practitioners, academic journal articles and their reference lists, government policy documents and reports, electronic bibliographic databases and *Hansard* (the record of parliamentary debate at Westminster).

The following three questions were designed to elicit information from the documents that would highlight vocabulary, terminology and themes that seemed to be related to the issues revealed in the review of literature. The research required the identification of pages or sections of texts that offered some relevance or response to them.

(1) What terms are used to identify members of the early years workforce (who are not teachers)?
(2) What levels of training, qualifications, type of employment, knowledge, understanding and skills and personal qualities are explicit or implicit within the documents?
(3) What discourse relates to status and gender?

The examination of texts has assumed transparency in content, and is thus open to critique. Texts are 'socially produced' and 'documents must be skeptically read and examined in their social context' (Delamont 2002, 123). It is also acknowledged that the researcher cannot be without bias and position in the selection of sources and sections of text for consideration, but, as Delamont (2002, 125) suggests, 'It is important not to despise any documentary source, because however "edited", "censored" or "trivial", it can lead to fresh questions for the researcher,' providing some justification for methodological decisions.

Terminology

It became apparent that the sources located for the earlier decades, from the 1940s through to the 1960s, had scant mention of the early years workforce, other than teachers or nannies. Such a paucity of mention suggests invisibility of those providing care and education in settings other than schools or private homes, and that the children who were receiving care and education did so from an anonymous workforce. This has implications for the identity of those working to support children's learning in care-based settings and pre-schools, for example. Table 1 below shows terms used to identify the workforce in texts such as *Nursery World* magazine, textbooks, government policy and academic journals.

The range of terms presented in Table 1 suggests change arising from linguistic trends (the change from nannie to nanny from the 1980s to the 1990s, for example), ambiguity (vague titles such as 'speaking adults' and 'adults' or 'other adult staff') and uncertainty (as to what the term 'pedagogue' means, or just 'workforce') as terms differ from one decade to another and lack consistency (other than including the word 'nursery'). Change may also be a reflection of key policy developments. The expansion of nursery education in the 1970s followed by the National Childcare Strategy at the end of the 1990s has been significant in the impact on provision in England. The term 'nursery nurse' seemed to become unfashionable after the 1980s, possibly due to the connotations of a role that demanded no more than an ability to 'wash paint pots'. The terms in Table 1 were from texts written by authors who were academics, researchers and policy writers – thus people who were not members of the early years workforce. It could be argued that the writers did not have a shared and universal discourse on nomenclature, and so resorted to generic terminology (workers, adults) so as not to offend or exclude those who did not fit the specific title of nursery nurse, for example.

In the 1970s, there was increased availability of childcare and different types of places where early years practitioners worked. In the 1990s, terms may be more varied, general and generic to encompass those members of the workforce who may be working in a voluntary or unqualified capacity. The number of people working in a voluntary capacity with young children is uncertain, and their role, status and membership of the early years workforce adds to the complexity of knowing who the workforce is and how they should be known. Cameron (2004, 17) makes a plea that 'There is a strong case for developing a unifying title to refer to these "children's workers" and for a new language to reflect an emphasis on an integrated pedagogical approach.'

Breadth in nomenclature in an attempt to be inclusive could therefore add to the uncertainty for members of the workforce, avoiding the identification of a clear title or name. Despite attempts to rectify this situation when the Children's Workforce consultation

Table 1.　Terms used to describe the workforce.

Decade	Terminology
1950s	Nursery school helper
1960s	Nursery assistants
1970s	Nursery matron, childminders, qualified nursery nurses, NNEB trained personnel, nursery nurses
1980s	Adults, other adult staff, nannie
1990s	Those working with young children, workers, professionals, nursery staff, staff, other adults, those working with under fives, nanny
2000s	Speaking adults, practitioners, nursery nurses, day nursery workers, workforce, workers, early years workforce, early years professionals, pedagogues, 'new' teachers

(DfES 2005) sought views on 'pedagogue' or 'new teacher' models, the title Early Years Professional was the outcome, rejecting both. More recent terms suggest that professionalism was not apparent in earlier decades; 'practitioners', 'professionals' and 'new teachers' have been introduced, but not without debate (cf. Adams in this issue).

Becoming an early years practitioner: training, education, qualifications, personal qualities, status and gender

Selected texts on issues related to becoming an early years practitioner (training, qualifications, education, status, personal and professional qualities, gender) were intended to provide insight into how others construed aspects of the workforce, who they should be and what they did. Table 2 indicates discourse articulated by academics, researchers, policy writers and others on such issues, selected for exploration in response to questions 2 and 3 above.

Table 2.   Discourse on issues related to becoming an early years practitioner: training, education, qualifications, personal qualities, status and gender.

Decade	Text
1940s	'Women were carefully chosen for their personal and practical experience of the mothering of young children. Where possible they were womenfolk who had had children of their own, and whose children were growing up' (Stross 1946, 701).
1960s	'The status and salary for aides and nursery assistants would be superior to that of welfare and meals assistants' (Plowden 1967, 331).
1970s	'You are responsible and practical, with a sense of humour and a real liking for children – the naughty ones as well as the sweeties' and 'It is a student's temperament that counts, along with good sense' (Elias 1972, 14). 'They are not grasping money (no-one gets prosperous on illegal minding); ... they are providing a sadly necessary but very low-grade service' (Jackson 1973, 523). 'some concern has been felt about the adequacy of existing courses for work which call for maturity, special skills and more than a little knowledge of child development and family relationships' (Kellmer Pringle and Naidoo 1975, 132).
1980s	'Are you kind, loving, sympathetic and yet firm with young children?' (Turnor 1984, 9) 'Too often the nursery nurse issue is swept under the carpet ... Nursery nurses host a cluster of grievances, both real and imagined, and imposed and self-inflicted' (Heaslip 1987, 34). 'we cannot ignore the importance of training as a source of information and ideas about child development and pedagogic techniques appropriate for children aged under five' (Osborn and Millbank 1987, 45). 'she must be warm and outgoing and sensitive to the needs of others. Coexisting with her maturity there must be a childlike relish for the joy of playing' (Henderson and Lucas 1989, 96).
1990s	'The standards of training and qualifications should remain high at each stage. Working with young children is a complex and demanding task – it requires a team of professionals who are appropriately trained to adopt a variety of roles and responsibilities' (Ball 1994, 58). 'a view exacerbated by differences in pay and conditions of employment between qualified teachers and permanent day nursery staff' (Audit Commission 1996, 69).
2000s	'We need to do more to ensure that working with children is seen as an attractive career, and improve skills and inter-professional relationships. Many of those who work with children ... feel undervalued, and in some cases under siege' (DfES 2003, 22). 'Working with pre-school children should have as much status as a profession as teaching children in schools' (HM Treasury 2004, 4).

Repeated demand for improved training and qualifications structure since the 1970s is apparent (Plowden 1967; Osborn and Milbank 1987; Ball 1994; Audit Commission 1996), and
reinforces a sense of lack of action and strategy in addressing the need to improve training,
education, qualifications and career structure for the early years workforce over past decades.
The Children's Workforce Reform (DfES 2005) is the most recent political response to bring
about such change, and the development of an integrated qualifications framework (IQF)
may address accessibility and progression in the future, but questions remain as to what the
views of practitioners are in terms of how reform is meeting their individual or collective
needs. Tensions may arise if members of the workforce sense an imposition of training and
qualifications requirements, where their own preference is to remain unqualified and enjoy
the challenges of their job without the pressure of study and training. Further research could
seek to discover whether such tensions exist. The language presented in the examples in
Table 2 is of what is *needed*, what *should* be done, what *cannot be ignored,* in terms of training and qualifications. It is the language of rhetoric; the reality is yet to be achieved as reform
aims to create a graduate workforce. If there is a continuing need to recruit more into the
early years workforce in England to staff the increasing numbers of children whose parents
work or require childcare, but at the same time staff are leaving for reasons such as low pay
and poor conditions (Bertram and Pascal 2001; Cameron et al. 2001), the challenge is to
create a model that accommodates a workforce that becomes attractive to all.

Gender is inextricably tied into the early years workforce: if the workforce is largely
made up of women, some of whom will be mothers, is there inherent tension between the
role of caregiver to a child whose mother has left to go to work, and the role of mother who
should be at home to bring up her children (Cohen et al. 2004; Eckert 2004)? It could be
concluded that prior to recent times, assumptions were made that it was only necessary to
be a mother to become a member of the workforce (Stross 1946) and not to be able to meet
any other prerequisites (Fealy 2004). Thus stereotypes that caring for young children is an
easy job and can be done by anyone with the desired prerequisites are perpetuated
(frequently recounted anecdotally, but also reinforced by Liddle 2006). Similar stereotypes
of female teachers of young children (amongst others) are examined in images, film and text
by Weber and Mitchell (1995). Being maternal, being a mother, a liking for children, having
good sense, being kind and loving, being warm and sensitive: such is the discourse of what
is desirable when working with young children. The authors again are predominantly
researchers, academics and policy writers, but there are also voices of experts included here;
those who wrote articles in *Nursery World*, for example.

What impact can such discourse have on those who read the articles and magazines where
they are located? Fairclough (2003, 206) suggests there are three ways in which discourse
figures in social practices: first, language used in our job role; second, representations in text,
social discourse and images that we incorporate into what we say and do (a recontextuali-
sation); and third, discourse 'in the constitution of identities'. It is the constitution of identities within the discourse of dispositions and qualities, such as being maternal, kind and
loving, that has created the role of what it means to be an early years practitioner, and it has
consequently been acted out by the workforce since the 1940s and 1950s. Fairclough (2003,
207) reinforces the role of discourse in representing 'How things are and have been.' He
continues, suggesting that imaginaries in discourse can materialise, and people can come 'to
"own" discourses, to position themselves inside them, to act and think and talk and see themselves in terms of new discourses' (Fairclough 2003, 208). Thus constructs of what it means
to be an early years practitioner may influence career choices made by those becoming an
early years practitioner. Decisions may be made because individuals consider themselves to
possess the desired qualities, or they aspire to possess such qualities.

Discourse relating to other prerequisites includes to be knowledgeable (Kellmer Pringle and Naidoo 1975), particularly to know about child development, to have an inherent 'talent' and almost to have childlike qualities themselves (Henderson and Lucas 1989) in order to be an effective worker. The discourse in Table 2 reinforces the perception of a workforce that is childlike in itself, has an ability to play, has a certain temperament (that is not articulated) and has an ability to like all children. Changes in the prerequisites to be an early years practitioner could arise from the discourse in policy, a reflection of societal changes of childhood and the needs of children (Gittins 2004; Jenks 2004), as well as the emerging co-construction of the role of childhood professionals as 'a vital one, a valued one, and as one of social, cultural, educational and political importance' (Oberhuemer 2005, 14).

The interface between new discourses and historical influences are acknowledged by Wenger (1998, 47), who states that practice when done 'in a historical and social context gives structure and meaning to what we do'. It could be argued that tensions may exist between early years practitioners who made career choices to join a workforce whose prerequisites were maternal and caring personal qualities (the discourse dominant in the 1940s through to the 1970s), and those who more recently have aspirations of career possibilities into management and leadership instead, articulated through new discourses (in the 1980s to 2000s). Struggles for the workforce emerge here, accompanied by the issue of status.

Discourse relating to rates of pay and status reinforce a low position in a hierarchy, often in comparison to teachers (Cameron et al. 2001; Cameron, Owen, and Moss 2001). Authors talk of being *under siege* and *under-valued*: a language of inferiority and conflict. Resentment and struggles to maintain a low-paid job have been articulated by childcare students: 'Childcare work was being seen, they felt, as a "vehicle" for delivery of labour market objectives, and not as a valuable career in its own right' (Cameron et al. 2001, 20). Students had also recognised that 'low pay was part of the low valuation, but other indicators of low value were feeling "taken for granted" or even "unimportant" by some parents, employers and wider society' (Cameron et al. 2001, 20).

It is useful to return to the discourse analysis of workforce reform policy undertaken by Osgood, as she echoes a similar call by Siraj-Blatchford (1993, 393), for a 'less reverential attitude to government proposals' in the context of professional identity of early years teachers. Osgood concluded that 'Practitioners have at their disposal an opportunity to subvert and resist prevailing and dominant understandings of their professionalism' (2006, 12) as the present workforce reform in England may provide openings for challenge and change.

Conclusion

What has discourse revealed in terms of insight into the professional identity of the early years workforce, specifically in terms of nomenclature, training, education, personal qualities, status and gender? The definition of what a professional is suggests that it requires a high level of training and education (Ellis and Whittington 1988; Eraut 1994). This is an aspiration that is only now becoming within the grasp of the early years workforce. The unheeded demand articulated within the discourse for improved status and training, however, suggests past voices went unheard. At the time of writing, the Children's Workforce Development Council (CWDC) are investigating whether early years practitioners who have achieved Early Years Professional Status (EYPS) are earning more than those without; so longer term outcomes may reveal whether increased status has any impact on pay.

Uncertainty and ambiguity are inherent in the daily lives of early years practitioners, not least resulting from a rapid pace of government-imposed change, but also arising from discourse that revealed the absence of an established job title that identifies who they are. There seems to be no other profession where such uncertainty has existed: job titles such as nurse, teacher, social worker, probation officer, youth worker are well established and understood by society. Early years practitioners currently struggle with a range of vague and ambiguous titles.

Invisibility may also be sustained through lack of voice and presence in policy and discussion. Changes over time reveal discourse that ranges from subversion (illegal minding) to resentment (having grievances about relative status compared with teachers, for example). There is a risk of workforce reform policy being imposed on the workforce without their approval or agreement (despite opportunities for consultation) and for ideologies (those of the policy writers and implementers, compared with the workforce themselves) as to what kind of a workforce is needed to be in conflict with each other.

Recurring themes of being expected to have a liking for children and play in order to become a practitioner and low status have also been revealed in discourse. Siraj-Blatchford (1993) cites the vulnerability of women, the influence of media and modern misconceptions as exacerbating factors in the lack of status of early years work. Issues of status and gender are deeply embedded culturally and sociologically. Some (such as Liddle 2006) believe that being an early years practitioner is the same as being a parent, and are dismissive of the need to promote the status and training of the workforce. A struggle is emerging and the power to bring about change lies with the workforce and its supporters.

However, it is acknowledged that what is presented here is a small, subjective sample of a much wider range of literature. Questions of audience, position and prejudices, power and postmodern perspectives have not been addressed. Future research will seek the views of practitioners themselves in order to explore the complexity of factors that contribute to professional identity. What has emerged from the scrutiny of past and current discourses relating to the early years workforce in England is how embedded constructs are, and that for change to be initiated (if the workforce itself desires change) there may need to be a period of introspection and reflection, in order to create a model of a workforce that belongs to the workforce itself, with constructs of professional identity informed by a shared vision and understanding.

References

Adams, K. 2005. What's in a name? University of Strathclyde. Paper presented at the EECERA Conference, September 1-3, in Dublin, Ireland.

Aries, P. 1962. *Centuries of childhood.* London: Cape Publishing.

Audit Commission. 1996. *Under fives count. Management handbook.* London: The Audit Commission.

Ball, C. 1994. *Start right. The importance of early learning.* London: Royal Society for the Encouragement of Arts, Manufactures and Commerce.

Bertram, T., and C. Pascal. 2001. The OECD thematic review of early childhood education and care: Background report for the UK. http://www.oecd.org/.

Britzman, D.P. 1992. The terrible problem of knowing thyself: Toward a post-structural account of teacher identity. *Journal of Curriculum Theorizing* 9, no. 3: 23–46.

Cameron, C. 2004. Building an integrated workforce for a long-term vision of universal early education and care. London: Daycare Trust Policy Paper No 3.

Cameron, C., A. Mooney, C. Owen, and P. Moss. 2001. Childcare students and nursery workers: Follow up surveys and in-depth interviews. London: Thomas Coram Research Unit, DfES Research Report No 322.

Cameron, C., C. Owen, and P. Moss. 2001. Entry, retention and loss: A study of childcare students and workers. London: Thomas Coram Research Unit, DfES Research Brief No. 275.

Cohen, B., P. Moss, P. Petrie, and J. Wallace. 2004. *A new deal for children?* Bristol: The Policy Press.

Dahlberg, G., P. Moss, and A. Pence. 2007. *Beyond quality in early childhood education and care.* Abingdon: Routledge.

Day, C., A. Kington, G. Stobart, and P. Sammons. 2006. The personal and professional selves of teachers: Stable and unstable identities. *British Educational Research Journal* 32, no. 4, August: 601–16.

Delamont, S. 2002. *Fieldwork in educational settings.* London: Routledge.

Department for Education and Employment (DfEE). 1998. *Meeting the childcare challenge.* London: The Stationery Office.

Department for Education and Skills (DfES). 2003. *Every child matters.* London: DfES/SureStart.

———. 2005. *Children's workforce strategy.* London: DfES.

———. 2006. *Children's workforce strategy: The government's response to the consultation.* London: DfES.

Eckert, P. 2004. The good woman. In *Language and women's place,* ed. M. Bucholtz. Oxford: Oxford University Press.

Elias, E. 1972. So you want to work with children. *Nursery World,* 13 January.

Ellis, R., and D. Whittington. 1988. Social skills, competence and quality. In *Professional competence and quality assurance in the caring professions.* Chapter 10. ed. R. Ellis. London: Chapman and Hall.

Eraut, M. 1994. *Developing professional knowledge and competence.* London: RoutledgeFalmer.

Fairclough, N. 2003. *Analysing discourse.* Abingdon: Routledge.

Fealy, G.M. 2004. "The good nurse": Visions and values in images of the nurse. *Journal of Advanced Nursing* 46, no. 6: 649–56.

Gillis, J.R. 1981. *Youth and history.* London: Academic Press.

Gittins, D. 2004. The historical construction of childhood. In *An introduction to childhood studies,* ed. M.J. Kehily. Maidenhead: Open University Press.

Griffin, C. 1993. *Representations of youth.* Cambridge: Polity Press.

Heaslip, P. 1987. Does the glass slipper fit Cinderella? Nursery teachers and their training. In *Roles, responsibilities and relationships in the education of young children,* ed. M.M. Clark. Occasional Publication Number 13, Educational Review. Birmingham: University of Birmingham, Faculty of Education.

Henderson, A., and J. Lucas. 1989. *Pre-school playgroups: The handbook.* London: Unwin.

HM Treasury. 2004. *Choice for parents, the best start for children: A ten- year strategy for children.* London: HM Treasury.

Hughes, K. 1993. *The Victorian governess.* London: The Hambledon Press.

Jackson, B. 1973. The childminders. *New Society,* 29 November.

James, C. 2005. *Childhood,* 2nd ed. London: Routledge.

James, C., and A. Prout, eds. 1990. *Constructing and reconstructing childhood.* Basingstoke: Falmer.

Jenks, C. 2004. Constructing childhood sociologically. In *An Introduction to Childhood Studies,* ed. M.J. Kehily. Maidenhead: Open University Press.

Kehily, M.J., ed. 2004. *An introduction to childhood studies.* Maidenhead: Open University Press.

Kellmer Pringle, M., and S. Naidoo. 1975. *Early child care in Britain.* London: Gordon and Breach.

Laming Report. 2003. *The Victoria Climbie Inquiry: Report of an inquiry by Lord Laming* (Cm 5730). London: The Stationery Office.

Liddle, R. 2006. Stupidity has its place. *The Sunday Times,* 6 August.

Moss, P. 2003. Beyond caring: The case for reforming the childcare and early years workforce. Facing the Future Policy Paper No 5. London: Daycare Trust.

———. 2006. Structures, understandings and discourses: Possibilities for re-envisioning the early childhood worker. *Contemporary Issues in Early Childhood* 7, no. 1: 30–41.

Oberhuemer, P. 2005. Conceptualising the early childhood pedagogue: Policy approaches and issues of professionalism. *European Early Childhood Research Journal* 13, no. 1: 5–16.

Osborn, A.F., and J.E. Millbank. 1987. *The effects of early education.* Oxford: Clarendon Press.

Osgood, J. 2006. Deconstructing professionalism in early childhood education: Resisting the regulatory gaze. *Contemporary Issues in Early Childhood* 7, no. 1: 5–14.

Plowden, B. 1967. *Children and their primary schools.* London: HMSO.

Siraj-Blatchford, I. 1993. Educational research and reform: Some implications for the professional identity of early years teachers. *British Journal of Educational Studies* 41, no. 4: 393–408.

Stross, B. 1946. Young children (care and education). Parliamentary debates, 6 December. *Hansard* 5th ser., vol. 431.

Swingewood, A. 2000. *A short history of sociological thought.* Basingstoke: Palgrave.

Sylva, K., and G. Pugh. 2005. Transforming the early years in England. *Oxford Review of Education* 31, no. 1: 11–27

Tucker, S. 1999. Making the link: Dual 'problematisation', discourse and work with young people. *Journal of Youth Studies* 2, no. 3: 283–95.

———. 2004. Youth working: Professional identities given, received or contested? In *Youth in society,* 2nd ed., ed. J. Roche, S. Tucker, R. Thomson, and R. Flynn. London: Sage Publications.

Turnor, M. 1984. So you want to be a nannie? *Nursery World,* 24 May.

Weber, S., and C. Mitchell. 1995. *"That's funny, you don't look like a teacher".* London: Falmer Press.

Wenger, E. 1998. *Communities of practice.* Cambridge: Cambridge University Press.

Developing professionalism within a regulatory framework in England: challenges and possibilities[1]

Linda Miller

The Open University, Milton Keynes, UK

ABSTRACT: Early Childhood Education and Care (ECEC) is now firmly on government agendas in many countries, including England, and the need to develop a professional workforce is generally agreed. The reform of the children's workforce in England acknowledges that increasing the skills and competence of this workforce is critical to its success. Two new professional roles, as routes to creating a more professional workforce, are discussed in this article: the Senior Practitioner and the more recent Early Years Professional role. The article provides a critical review of policy developments leading to the creation of these roles and discusses the tensions and challenges of developing new professional roles within the context of meeting externally prescribed requirements and standards. The article questions whether such standards and requirements help to create this new professionalism or whether, as some critics have argued, they inhibit professional autonomy and promote a model of technical practice. The article draws on a broader international study of professionalism in ECEC and uses data from the English part of this project to illustrate that practitioners working in this English context can and do develop a sense of professional identity and engage in practices which can be described as 'professional'.

RÉSUMÉ: L'accueil et l'éducation de la petite enfance (ECEC) est maintenant fermement inscrite dans les programmes des gouvernements de nombreux pays, dont l'Angleterre, et le besoin de développer une main d'œuvre professionnelle est généralement reconnu. La réforme des professions de l'enfance en Angleterre reconnaît que l'accroissement des savoirs faire et des compétences de cette main d'œuvre est décisif pour son succès. Deux nouveaux rôles professionnels conçus comme des voies permettant de créer une main d'œuvre plus professionnelle sont discutés dans cet article: le praticien senior et, plus récemment, le professionnel petite enfance. L'article propose une revue critique des décisions politiques qui ont conduit à la création de ces nouveaux rôles professionnels et discute les tensions et les défis qui existent dans le développement de ces rôles dans un contexte présentant des exigences et normes prescrites de l'extérieur. Il s'agit de savoir si de telles normes et exigences aident à créer ce nouveau professionnalisme ou si, comme certaines critiques le soutiennent, elles inhibent l'autonomie des professionnels et favorisent un modèle de pratique technique. L'article s'appuie sur une étude internationale, plus large, du professionnalisme dans l'éducation préscolaire et utilise les données de la partie anglaise de ce projet pour montrer que les praticiens qui étudient et travaillent au sein d'un environnement hautement réglementé peuvent développer un sens, très clair, de leur identité professionnelle.

ZUSAMMENFASSUNG: Frühpädagogik (ECEC) hat heute in England, wie in vielen Ländern, einen festen Platz auf der Tagesordnung der Regierung und es gibt einen generellen Konsens darüber, dass es notwendig ist, Professionalität im Feld zu entwickeln. Es wird anerkannt, dass ein Zugewinn an Fachwissen und Kompetenz der

Schlüssel zum Erfolg der Reform ist. Zwei neue Berufsbilder, geschaffen als Wege zur Professionalisierung der Frühpädagogik, werden in diesem Beitrag diskutiert: das des "Senior Practitioner' und das des kürzlich hinzugekommenen" Early Years Professional'. Der Beitrag liefert eine kritische Erörterung der politischen Prozesse, die zu Herausbildung dieser neuen Berufsbilder geführt haben und diskutiert die Spannungen und Herausforderungen die entstehen, wenn ein neues Professionsbild im Kontext extern bestimmter Standards und Anforderungen entwickelt wird. Der Artikel hinterfragt kritisch, ob solche Standards und Anforderungen hilfreich sind um Professionalität zu fördern, oder ob sie, wie Kritiker argumentieren, professionelle Autonomie hemmen und stattdessen ein unterkomplexes, technisches Verständnis von pädagogischer Praxis hervorbringen. Der Beitrag bezieht sich auf ein breiter angelegtes internationales Forschungsprojekt zur Professionalität in der Frühpädagogik und verwendet Daten aus dem Englischen Teilprojekt um zu zeigen, dass Praktikerinnen, die in einem hoch-regulierten Kontext lernen und arbeiten, eine klare professionelle Identität entwickeln können.

RESUMEN: La educación pre-escolar esta hoy en día en las agendas de gobiernos de muchos países, inclusivo Inglaterra, y existe un consenso general acerca de la necesidad de un desarrollo profesional de la fuerza de trabajo. La reforma de la fuerza de trabajo parvularia en Inglaterra reconoce que el mejoramiento de las habilidades y competencia de la fuerza de trabajo es clave para obtener éxito. Dos roles profesionales nuevos, como medios para crear una fuerza de trabajo más profesional, son discutidos en este artículo: el Práctico Superior (Senior Practitioner) y el más reciento rol de Profesional Parvulario. El articulo presenta una revisión critica de las políticas de desarrollo que llevan a la creación de esos roles y discute las tensiones y desafíos que significa desarrollar nuevos roles profesionales en un contexto que enfrenta presiones y estándares externos. El articulo cuestiona si esas presiones y estándares ayudan a crear un nuevo profesionalismo o si, como algunos críticos argumentan, inhiben la autonomía profesional y promueven un modelo de práctica tecnocrático. El artículo hace uso de un amplio estudio internacional del profesionalismo en la educación pre-escolar y usa datos de la parte inglesa del proyecto, para ilustrar que prácticos estudiando y trabajando en un medio altamente reglamentado pueden desarrollar un claro sentido de identidad profesional.

Introduction

The *Starting Strong II* Report (OECD 2006) cites England as having made most progress of all countries in children's services since the first Organisation for Economic Co-operation and Development (OECD) review in 1999, although it could be argued that this was from a low baseline. In England the generic term 'early years' has been widely adopted because of a long-standing campaign to eliminate the split between care and education services. In this article it is used interchangeably with the term 'early childhood education and care', which is more commonly used in Europe and beyond (OECD 2006).

The government in England has committed to the reform of the children's workforce through 'a transformational reform agenda designed to improve life chances for all and reduce inequalities in our society' (DfES 2006, 2); it acknowledges that increasing the skills and competence of the workforce is critical to the success of this agenda which is enabled by 'transformation' funding. One recent outcome of the transformation funding has been the development of a new Early Years Professional (EYP) role. The EYP role is intended to achieve graduate leadership across early years services in the private, voluntary and independent (PVI) sector, and, as part of the overall process of workforce reform, this new role will contribute to a new professional identity for the early years workforce. This article considers the implications of this role for the professional development of early years practitioners and explores the relationship between this role and the existing role of Senior Practitioner created in 2001 (DfES 2001). For both roles, consultation and implementation have been carried out within relatively short and challenging timescales with little time for reflection. The article provides a critical review of policy developments leading to the creation of these two roles and relates this to the debate about professionalism.

Raising training and qualifications levels in the early years workforce

In England (and the whole of the United Kingdom) the range and variety of qualifications and the type and level of training required for those working with young children is confusing: the training background of staff can range from the totally unqualified to graduate and postgraduate qualifications. Overall, the early years workforce is under qualified, poorly paid and predominantly female; 40% of the workforce are not qualified to level 2 (degree level) and just 12% are qualified to level 4 or above (postgraduate level) (DfES, 2005a) within the framework for higher education qualifications (see http://www.qaa.ac.uk/academicinfrastructure/FHEQ/default.asp).

The graduate workforce in 'childcare provision' ranges from 2% of childminders (i.e. home-based carers) to 13% of workers in full day care and out of school provision (*The Providers Survey* 2005, cited in Department for Children, Schools and Families 2007). We know from research studies that the quality of provision in early years settings is linked to the quality of staff that work in them (Sylva et al. 2003). Reforming the workforce through a programme of training and qualifications is therefore seen by government as crucial in raising the quality of services.

As part of this reform process, a common core of skills, knowledge and competence has been developed for all those who work with children, young people and families, and these are required to be taken account of in developing training and qualifications (DfES 2005b). An integrated qualifications framework (IQF) for the children's workforce is under development for 2010, to promote skills acquisition, to enable career progression and to work across professional boundaries and multi-disciplinary and multi-agency contexts (http://cwdccouncil.org.uk/projects/integratedquailificationsframework.htm).

Critics of this agenda, whilst supporting a common framework of training and qualifications, also believe that this will lead to an environment that will be increasingly regulated by central government, raising questions about professional autonomy and what 'being a professional' means within this new agenda (Osgood 2006).

New professional roles

Senior practitioner

Prior to the workforce agenda outlined above, in 2001 a Senior Practitioner status was created in England. This role was developed for practitioners working directly with young children aged birth to eight years. The Senior Practitioner status was to be achieved through an early years sector-endorsed foundation degree (EYSEFD), a vocational qualification designed to integrate academic study with work-based learning. The content and delivery of EYSEFDs are described in a Statement of Requirement (DfES 2001) developed and approved by employer representatives, the early years sector and educational providers and were formally endorsed and monitored by the Department of Education and Skills (now the Department for Children, Schools and Families). Since 2006 they have become the responsibility of the Children's Workforce Development Council (CWDC) and are under review as discussed below. EYSEFDs provided a new level of professional practice and offered a progression route to graduate status/or qualified teacher status through employment-based and part-time routes. The Statement of Requirement (DfES 2001) details learning outcomes which students are required to provide evidence of having met through work-based learning and practice. However, training providers have freedom to interpret how these requirements are met, with reflective practice seen as a key focus (O'Keefe and Tait 2004; Cable, Goodliff, and Miller 2007). Early years foundation degrees represent the largest number of all foundation degrees in England, and by 2007 totalled over 360 (http://www.fdf.ac.uk/courses/index.php).

Snape, Parfrement, and Finch (2007) reported on a sample of 566 EYSEFD students across 80 institutions in England and found that, overall, students were highly satisfied with their degree experience and felt that they had benefited in terms of their work and increased knowledge and understanding. Students also reported that they saw the foundation degree as a stepping-stone to further qualifications. However, to gain increased pay, students who gained the foundation degree have generally had to move to new employment, raising issues about affordability of a more qualified workforce for employers.

Within the early years community, the introduction of the Senior Practitioner role was largely welcomed as a sign of professional recognition. However, half a decade on from its introduction many issues remain unresolved, including lack of pay and recognition for the role in the workplace, and more recently the relationship of this role to the new Early Years Professional (EYP) role described below. Government has recognised that Senior Practitioner status is problematic, with the Childcare Workforce Strategy (DfES 2005a) noting:

> However, having taken the course, many graduates have now reached Level 4 (Level 5 under the new National Qualifications Framework) only to find no improvement in pay and conditions … We recognise the need to address this issue. (32)

Practitioners themselves have expressed similar concerns. In a small-scale study of a group of practitioners in their first and second year of studying for a foundation degree in early years, O'Keefe and Tait (2004) found that recognition of the practitioners' status was a contentious issue and that although their job title and role had changed, pay and conditions had not. One student stated: 'It's drummed into you so much when you are leaving college that you are a professional … but when you get into the workplace, it's not the same – you don't get treated the same with the same recognition' (O'Keefe and Tait 2004, 33).

Critics of this approach to achieving a qualified workforce (e.g. Dahlberg and Moss 2005) have argued that underlying this model is a desire for consistency wherever training is delivered. Indeed, the stated aim of the Statement of Requirement is to set out 'exactly what is required, by employers, for recognition as a Senior Practitioner' (DfES 2001, 1).

On the other hand, providers of EYSEFDs are agreed that these degrees have opened up routes to higher qualifications and increased professionalism for many practitioners but are a strategy which has suffered from hasty development and implementation in order to meet government policy initiatives and spending targets. In 2007/8 these foundation degrees are under review and are most likely to become a progression route to EYP status (personal communication with Department for Children, Schools and Families and CWDC, 8 June 2007). More recently, CWDC have proposed a partnership with the national network of providers of EYSEFDs (personal communication CWDC, 9 November 2007) to take this review forward. Such a partnership is welcome as it promises to give providers and practitioners a stronger voice on professional routes, roles and requirements.

Early years professional status

The government's consultation on the future of the children's workforce highlighted the need for a new lead graduate professional role (DfES 2005a). In the United Kingdom teachers have typically been the lead professional in nursery schools and classes in the maintained sector (i.e. sponsored by the local authorities), working mainly with children aged three to five, despite the fact that most teacher education courses have not covered the birth-to-three-years age range. Approximately 20,000 settings in the private and voluntary sector do not typically employ a teacher. Sylva et al. (2003) recommended there should be a good proportion of trained teachers, or equivalent, holding lead positions in early years settings in order to achieve good outcomes; however, the 'equivalent' role is not defined.

The consultation around the development of the Children's Workforce Strategy document discussed two models of professional leadership: the European pedagogue; and the 'new teacher' model emerging from New Zealand and Spain. The pedagogue role, in Denmark, for example, involves a holistic approach to working with children up to age 10 and beyond, whilst the new teacher role involves working directly with children under five (Moss 2003; OECD 2006). The government response to the workforce consultation was to adopt a new 'Early Years Professional' role which is more akin to the 'new teacher' than the pedagogue model, and is proposed to have equivalence to qualified teacher status. Government intends that there will be an Early Years Professional in all multi-agency children's centres by 2010, and in every full day-care setting by 2015.

The role of the Early Years Professional (EYP) is intended to be that of a change agent who will raise standards in early years settings, and, in particular, to lead practice in the new Early Years Foundation Stage (EYFS) curriculum, covering the age range of birth to three years (DfES 2007); the EYP is also expected to support and mentor other practitioners. The prerequisite for the career route to Early Years Professional Status (EYPS) is that candidates must be graduates who are able to demonstrate that they can meet a set of national standards, achieved through a choice of four pathways (CWDC 2006). For one of these pathways, the candidate's degree can be unrelated to early childhood, and minimal prior experience of working with young children is required. This pathway is causing resentment amongst experienced practitioners who do not have the relevant qualifications to qualify for the EYPS career route, but who may be working in settings in which EYPs are gaining experience as part of their pathway to attaining the EYPS (Hevey 2007).

The introduction of the EYP role raises many issues such as the lack of parity of their status in relation to qualified teachers, and the lack of guidance on commensurate levels of pay. For example, while EYPs were initially mooted as having equivalent status to teachers, the current position seems to be that qualified teachers will lead on the Early Years Foundation Stage (EYFS) in settings maintained by local authorities (i.e. nursery schools and schools), but without birth-to-three training, whilst EYPs will be restricted to the private and voluntary sector. Additionally, levels of pay are set out and agreed for teachers, but for EYPs, they are left to market forces. Hevey (2007) has argued that this will lead to EYPs being 'ghettoised' in low pay areas (Hevey 2007). Hevey (2007) has also questioned the long-term affordability of EYPs once the initial 'transformation' funding has ended, and pointed to the emerging issue of disappointing levels of recruitment for this role, which she said is linked to an under-qualified workforce unable to meet graduate entry. More positively, Goodliff (2007) has noted that candidates report an increase in self-esteem on achieving EYPS, despite anxieties about the status and long-term future of the role.

The introduction of the Early Years Professional Status is an important initiative and crucial to the raising of standards and the establishment of a new multi-professional role. However, to ensure the success of this role, increased professional recognition will be required, preferably through a system of professional registration and linked to a pay and conditions framework. It will also be essential to determine the most enabling pathways to attaining this status to achieve the best outcomes for children and families.

Developing early years professionals within regulatory frameworks

The development of a more professional workforce through the reform process described above has been generally welcomed by those who have been working to raise the status of early years practitioners and help them achieve a sense of professional identity. However, critics of this agenda, such as Moss (2006), are sceptical that teaching and learning can be reduced to measurable technical outcomes through standards and competency frameworks. Dahlberg and Moss (2005) believe this 'technologising' of policy and practice becomes a means of governing the early years workforce, prescribing norms to which practitioners must conform. Osgood (2006, 7) has argued that regulatory frameworks can lead practitioners to 'conform to dominant constructions of professionalism' and that the 'regulatory gaze' stemming from such an agenda threatens their empowerment. She expressed concerns that the 'professionalism agenda' in England, rather than leading to a strengthened position for early years practitioners, could be a means of external control and regulation that would inhibit professional autonomy. She has argued for an alternative construction of professionalism, which acknowledges the complexity of work that early years practitioners do, to be achieved through education and training that includes going beyond technical competence, and opportunities for critical reflection and consciousness-raising.

Reflection on practice is recognised as an important component in developing professional and pedagogical knowledge and in understanding practice. According to Oberhuemer (2005), informed professional action requires a willingness to reflect on one's own taken-for-granted beliefs and an understanding that knowledge is contestable. The DfES (2001, 16) Statement of Requirement recognised the need to 'develop students as reflective practitioners', and reflection on practice has been seen as central by foundation degree providers in course development (O'Keefe & Tait 2004).

An alternative perspective on professionalism

Whilst acknowledging the constraints imposed by regulatory frameworks and externally imposed standards, there is an alternative perspective. The workforce reform agenda in England is opening up new routes to training and professionalism for a diverse and under-qualified workforce. It is possible for training providers to challenge the 'regulatory gaze' (Osgood 2006) and to interpret regulatory frameworks in creative ways. As Osgood (2006) has noted, practitioners (*and providers*) (my italics) can be active in rising to the challenge by negotiating where they are 'positioned and defined' and thus take on the role of autonomous professionals. Cable, Goodliff, and Miller (2007) have argued that students and training providers do not have to be passive recipients of workforce reform, but can be active agents with the power to enable early years practitioners to harness their own agency and thus develop a sense of professional identity.

Westcott (2004) argued that standards contribute to professional identity. Whilst acknowledging that the definition of 'profession' is ambiguous, she proposed that it might be applied to a 'community of practice' that:

- exhibits command of a specialist body of knowledge;
- sets standards for practitioners; and
- regulates its own standards of practice.

Westcott further argued that standards are an important aspect of professionalism in that they assure a common baseline of practice that can underpin professional registration, and which can then be monitored and regulated (although this formal regulation and registration of the early years workforce has yet to happen in England). Working within the Australian context, Fenech and Sumsion (2007) interviewed early childhood teachers about how regulatory requirements impacted on their professional practice. Responses were mixed, but some of these teachers offered support for regulation of their practice. For example, Sarah said 'If something goes wrong, we're protected in a way. If we're following standards and regulations then we're protected.' She added, '… it can be hard to find good staff to put in long day care centres. So I think we definitely need standards these people have to work by' (117). This perspective views regulation as enabling as well as restricting.

The view that standards and regulation can create an enabling process offers possibilities in relation to the Senior Practitioner and Early Years Professional roles. The achievement of the standards that define these roles, and the demonstration of a specialist body of knowledge and skills, can contribute to a sense of professional identity. Wenger (1998) proposed that an individual's sense of *professional* (my italics) identity within a particular community of practice is influenced by engaging in certain experiences or practices. It is possible, therefore, to make the case that such experiences and practices might be encompassed in a set of professional standards.

Exploring professionalism

So far this article has argued that the development of new qualifications and professional training routes, albeit within a regulatory and standards-based framework, has been welcomed by the early years community in England, and has provided new opportunities for professional development and recognition that previously did not exist for early years practitioners.

In the rest of the article, I use data from the English component of a six-country project on professionalism initiated within the Special Interest Group on Professionalism within the European Early Childhood Education Research Association (EECERA). As indicated in the introduction to this monograph, this group has been attempting to reach a definition of professionalism in the context of the early childhood education and care (ECEC) workforce and to explore what this means. Given the diversity of this workforce in relation to roles, qualifications, settings and the regulations that apply in different contexts, some group members agreed to work on a project entitled 'A Day in the Life of an Early Years Practitioner Project: Perspectives on Professionalism' (e.g. Dalli 2007; Miller, Cable, and Goodliff 2007; Urban 2007); key objectives of this project are to investigate how early childhood practitioners 'act as a professional' in their specific local context, and practitioners' professional *habitus* (or attitudes and dispositions). A third objective is to explore common features of practice in each context.

The project was inspired by the work of Gillen et al. (2007), who studied a day in the life of two-year-old girls across each of five countries but who recognised the impossibility of direct comparisons across cultures. Penn (1998) also has noted the impossibility of systematic comparison or straightforward matching of experiences across countries because of the parameters under which the research occurs in each country; she concluded that 'all that is possible is to listen to the separate voices and try to hear their stories' (14).

Methodology and data gathering

The project group adopted a case-study approach, for, as Bassey (1999) suggests, research into particular rather than general events is the only form of research open to people working at research part-time and with limited resources; a description which fitted the project group well. The 'Day in the Life of an Early Years Practitioner Project' is effectively a collection of single case studies.

Data for the project were gathered by the country researchers using non-participant observation of a full day (a minimum of four to six hours) in the life of an early years practitioner using video recording and an interview schedule for contextual information and other demographic details. The practitioner was recruited as a 'convenience sample' (Cohen, Manion, and Morrison 2000) and chosen as 'typical' practitioners; each researcher was required to define 'typical' for their context according to agreed criteria. Following data gathering, each project participant produced a case study of the 'day in the life' they had videoed and sought for some key themes to emerge.

Data analysis

The project is ongoing and is work in progress. Data analysis has been guided by grounded theory principles (Strauss and Corbin 1998) focusing on emerging themes from the data to illuminate the nature of the professional work of the early childhood practitioner. Preliminary data were analysed from the filming and interviews to seek out emerging themes and dispositions. In the English project (Miller, Cable, and Goodliff 2007), the themes include:

- the diversity, complexity, responsibilities and multiple demands of the practitioner's role;
- leadership, management and organisational skills (including staff training and curriculum leadership);
- acting as a conduit for information;
- knowledge of the setting, children and families;
- professional knowledge base (e.g. child development, curriculum);
- providing support and reassurance;
- being accountable for the implementation of policy and procedures;
- availability, accessibility and visibility (in relation to staff, parents and children);
- trust.

The professional dispositions identified include:

- sensitivity;
- empathy;
- awareness;
- respect for others;
- commitment to the field of early years;
- confidence.

In the following section, I present two vignettes from the case study of the English practitioner, Julie. These follow the approach of Abbott and Gillen (1999) who, challenged by 'copious amounts of data' gathered for a project investigating 'educare' for children under three, noted that 'that allowing voices to speak with immediacy, as in vignettes, was often received with particular interest by our research audience' (49). Whitehead (1999, 72) has similarly said that vignettes 'capture the essence of what goes on'. In this article I use two vignettes to provide a description of, and some insights into, Julie's professional practice and to illustrate some of the emerging themes and dispositions listed above. The vignettes are supplemented with data from the interview with Julie where she was asked to reflect on the events of the day and was asked about what 'acting professionally' meant to her within this context.

The vignettes and interview extracts therefore offer a glimpse of both Julie's internal perspective on professionalism and her perceptions of external perspectives on ECEC. The film data showed that Julie had to meet *multiple demands* in her role as manager and deal with a range of *complex tasks and responsibilities*. Her day included:

- Working in the office to deal with emails, telephone calls and correspondence;
- Joining in with children's story times and activities;
- Playing with the children in the outdoor area;
- Meeting with pre-school teacher;
- Meeting with and briefing senior staff;
- Assisting with the children's lunch;
- Meeting a parent;
- Seeing the children off on an outing in the mini bus;
- Supervising activities in the play hall;
- Meeting a member of staff to discuss 'settling in' a new child;
- Meeting with the finance director.

The vignettes and excerpts from the interview data below illustrate the range of these duties which make up her professional practice.

Julie

Julie is aged 26 and has worked in the field of early years for seven years. She works as a children's day nursery manager in a privately owned day nursery, where she undertakes extensive office-based management duties alongside some 'hands-on' work with the children. The nursery has 154 children on roll and 43 members of staff, including volunteers, whom Julie is responsible for managing. Full day care is offered alongside part time 'education' for three- to five-year-olds.

Defining a 'typical' practitioner was challenging for all project participants because of the diversity of the ECEC workforce in the home country of each researcher. In the English case study Julie was 'typical' in the sense that she was working within the private, voluntary and independent (PVI) sector, which has a high level of poorly qualified practitioners who are often poorly paid, and in a nursery that was required to meet external regulations and requirements. Julie has a National Vocational Qualification (NVQ, Level 3) (a work-based qualification) which qualifies her to undertake a managerial role in the PVI sector. She is currently undertaking an early years sector-endorsed foundation degree in early years at the Open University, a distance-learning organisation. A longer term aim is to 'top up' her foundation degree to a full honours degree and possibly achieve Early Years Professional Status. Julie is therefore working towards Senior Practitioner status but has not yet achieved this. Julie's managerial role in the nursery illustrates anomalies within the English education and care system, in that as nursery manager Julie is responsible for staff who have higher level qualifications than herself. This is illustrated in Vignette 1 where

Julie is briefing a qualified teacher, Helen, who is one of two teachers employed in the nursery on a part-time basis to work with children aged three to five years on the Foundation Stage Curriculum. In a school, or nursery school, setting maintained by the local authority, Helen would have a considerably higher 'status' than someone with Julie's qualifications.

Vignette 1: Meeting with the pre-school teacher

Julie met with the pre-school teacher, Helen, for her regular weekly meeting. Helen is a qualified teacher who works with the children aged three to five in an annexe adjacent to the main nursery. The main focus of the visit was to introduce the Early Years Foundation Stage curriculum documents (DfES 2007) which are to be mandatory from 2008 and which will replace the existing curriculum.

Julie and Helen sat either side of one of the children's low tables. Julie spread out the documents on the table between her and Helen and explained that they had arrived only the previous day. She explained that she was giving copies to key staff members who would then be part of the dissemination and training process with other staff they are responsible for (it was Julie's responsibility to ensure that this curriculum is in place and that staff are appropriately trained). Julie briefly explained the changes in the new curriculum, in particular the assessment process which she said showed 'what children should be doing by the time they are five'. She explained there would be standard assessment and reporting format across all settings.

As mentioned earlier, in a maintained school setting Helen would have seniority over Julie and as a nursery school or class teacher would be responsible for implementing the new curriculum. In the interview which took place at the end of the day, when asked about her professional practice, Julie showed that she was aware of the sensitivity of this situation:

> Acting professionally could range from how I am within meetings. For example, I had a meeting with the pre-school teacher this morning and it may have been that we disagreed on something and I could have said to her 'actually, I'm not going to take your opinion into account and what I say goes' but I don't see that as a very professional approach. I see that, the way this nursery runs in particular, everyone should be able to be included and have their say.

For Julie, being professional meant that she needed to show respect for what Helen and other staff members brought to their respective roles, as she explained:

> I need to recognise that they are professionals too and that some of them have qualifications far above what I have, and they have different experiences to me. We have to draw on that and use it to our advantage.

Julie showed sensitivity and awareness in relation to her management role. She seemed to act as a conduit for information about important events and policy documents for the nursery staff. For example, beyond discussing the new curriculum documents with the nursery teacher, she also introduced them in a senior team management meeting later in the day and discussed training plans.

In the interview, Julie commented on her role in meeting external regulations as follows:

> I think that when they [the local education authority representatives] come in from outside, it's me being able to say to them 'this is how I'm training the other staff', 'this is what I would like to do in the future' to show them that the professionalism really comes from that circle where

I'm saying 'I'm in charge and I know what's going on. If you ask me how many children are in the building, I know. If you ask me how many are going home at lunchtime, I know. If you ask me how many staff are First Aid trained, I know'.

Vignette 2: At lunch with the children

The second vignette I want to draw on illustrates another aspect of professionalism valued by Julie: involvement in the day-to-day experience of children within the nursery. In this vignette, the involvement is evident during the children's lunchtime. The children remain in their play area for lunch. The low tables are set with colourful bowls and plate and lunch is brought from the main kitchen then served by the staff who sit with the children. Julie helped to put out bowls of tuna pasta on the tables then sat with a small group of children. She chatted with the children about the colour of their mugs and plates, for example:

Julie:	What colour is this Jamie?
Jamie:	pink
Julie:	It is pink
Child 2:	I know what colour mine is – brown
Julie:	It is, you're right

Meanwhile, Julie was assisting one child sitting to her right who had difficulty feeding himself.

In the interview, Julie seemed keen to explain that her management duties did not 'distance' her from the staff and children.

I think I'm very open to all of the staff. We try to act as a team so that everybody is on the same level. For example, I'll go out and feed lunch to a baby in the same way that anybody else would. It doesn't mean just because I'm the manager, that I'm too professional to do that or that my job is to sit about in a suit in the office all day. I think it's important that the staff recognise that.

Something (else) I like to do, if I'm walking through a room, is go in and interact with the children and spend a little bit of time with them. It means that my day doesn't then become just a big, long list of meetings and it means that I can then spend time with the children and learn quite a lot from them. They see me around and the parents and staff then know that I'm quite accessible.

So I'm not someone who drifts in and then drifts out again.

Towards the end of the interview I asked Julie if she saw herself as a professional:

Yes I do. I think that my role, especially because I am the manager here, and because I'm seen as a sort of head figure within this nursery, I do see myself as a professional. I think other people see me as a professional. I think that, in the nursery set-up, what makes me a professional is the fact that I come in to do my job to the best of my abilities and I go home every day knowing that I've put in 110 per cent into that day and I've done as much as I can do. I think that the responses I get from other people make me feel that they have trust in me and they've got confidence in me.

However, she also said:

I think it (professionalism) isn't really valued as much in nursery nurses and nursery assistants – because people do see them as just carers for their children.

I think, because child raising has always been a mother's role, they (i.e. external people) get this impression that it's always just women who work in nurseries. I think that people from outside do see that being in a nursery is 'playing with children' all day and just an extension of the mother's role.

At the end of the day's filming and interview I was struck by the diversity, complexity and multiple demands of Julie's role and the energy that her relentless schedule must require. I had the sense of Julie being at the centre of all that was happening. She appeared to have excellent organisational skills and a detailed knowledge of what was happening and when. She had a clear sense of herself as a professional which seemed to stem from both her *experience* and the *knowledge* she was gaining from her studies.

In the interview Julie said that both parents and staff:

are coming to you to look for answers and they want to make sure that you've got the answers and that helps them put their trust in you.

The vignettes from the day's filming and interview illustrate the challenges faced by many practitioners, such as Julie, who take on challenging roles in early years settings which require high levels of responsibility and professionalism, whilst lacking recognition in the form of status or commensurate pay. The interview extracts suggest that Julie *is* developing a clear sense of professional identity and meeting the challenges of her role, whilst working and studying within what critics describe as a highly regulated and standards-driven environment (Dahlberg and Moss 2005; Osgood 2006). It is therefore important that practitioners such as Julie are provided with opportunities for professional development and recognition such as those described earlier in this article.

Summary and discussion

Defining professionalism in the early years workforce is the subject of much debate in England and elsewhere (Oberhuemer 2005). In this article I have argued that the diverse roles and responsibilities of early years practitioners, the variety of settings they work in, and the lack of a professional registration body and formal pay structures make it difficult to agree what constitutes an early years professional in the English context. This is particularly so when we now have a centrally defined role that carries the title of 'Early Years Professional'. This raises the question of whether those who do *not* have this title are not professionals, and the answer to this is not clear. In England qualified teachers working in early years settings have long enjoyed the sense that they *are* regarded as professionals, whereas others working with young children have not; a point made by Julie in the interview extract above, in her reference to nursery nurses and nursery assistants. Fenech and Sumsion (2007, 119), in a discussion of power relations within early childhood services, warn of the 'othering' of less qualified or non-accredited staff. Julie would appear to see herself as a 'professional' and this sense of professional identity seems to be derived from her status and position as manager in the nursery, her developing qualifications and knowledge base and the respect and confidence that she commands from others.

In developing a relatively 'new profession' in England we have a unique opportunity to influence the framing of the discourses around qualifications, training and leadership and the knowledge base that individuals (who make up any profession) need to draw on in their interactions with children and families. As the OECD (2006) report notes, the opportunity is present in England to re-think workforce roles and to identify a 'lead' early years professional who would work alongside others in multi-disciplinary teams. However, the key issues around which this initiative revolves – who that 'lead' professional will be, the supply of qualified people to fill the role, and pay and incentives commensurate with such a role – remain a challenge to be resolved.

Note

1. This article is a further development of ideas first discussed in the chapter entitled 'Developing New Professional Roles in the Early Years', in Miller and Cable (2008).

References

Abbott, L., and J. Gillen. 1999. Revelations through research partnerships. *Early Years, An International Journal of Research and Development* 20, no. 1: 43–53.

Bassey, M. 1999. *Case study research in educational settings.* Buckingham: Open University Press.

Cable, C., G. Goodliff, and L. Miller. 2007. Developing reflective early years practitioners within a regulatory framework. *Malaysian Journal of Distance Education* 9, no. 2: 1–19.

Children's Workforce Development Council (CWDC). 2006. *Early year professional prospectus.* Leeds: CWDC.

Cohen, L., L. Manion, and K. Morrison. 2000. *Research methods in education,* 5th ed. London and New York: RoutledgeFalmer.

Dahlberg, G., and P. Moss. 2005. *Ethics and politics in early childhood education.* London and New York: RoutledgeFalmer.

Dalli, C. 2007. A day in the life of an early years practitioner: The New Zealand case study. Symposium presentation at 17th EECERA Conference, August 30, in Prague, Czech Republic.

Department for Children, Schools and Families. 2007. Early years workforce strategy action plan: Discussion paper. Early Years Workforce Development Team, July 19.

Department for Education and Skills (DfES). 2001. Early years sector-endorsed foundation degree: Statement of requirement. London: HMSO.

———. 2005a. *Children's workforce strategy: A strategy to build a world-class workforce for children and young people.* Nottingham: DfES Publications.

———. 2005b. *Common core of skills and knowledge for the children's workforce.* Nottingham: DfES Publications.

———. 2006. *Children's workforce strategy: Building a world-class workforce for children, young people and families: The government's response to the consultation.* Nottingham: DfES Publications.

———. 2007. *The early years foundation stage: Setting the standards for learning, development and care.* Nottingham: DfES Publications.

Fenech, M., and J. Sumsion. 2007. Early childhood teachers and regulation: Complicating power relations using a Foucauldian lens. *Contemporary Issues in Early Childhood* 8, no. 2: 109–22.

Foundation Degree Forward. Accessed 17 December 2007 http://www.fdf.ac.uk/courses/index.php.

Gillen, J., C.A. Cameron, S. Tapanya, G. Pinto, R. Hancock, S. Young, and B. Accorti Gamannossi. 2007. "A day in the life": Advancing a methodology for the cultural study of development and learning in early childhood. *Early Child Development and Care* 177, no. 2: 207–18.

Goodliff, G. 2007. Achieving Early Years Professional (EYP) status: New EYPs evaluate the process and its impact on professional identity. Paper presented at 17th EECERA Conference, August 30, in Prague, Czech Republic.

Hevey, D. 2007. Early Years Professional Status: An initiative in search of a strategy. Paper presented at 17th EECERA Conference, August 30, in Prague, Czech Republic.

Integrated Qualifications Framework. Accessed 17 December 2007 http://www.cwdcouncil.org.uk/projects/integratedqualificationsframework.htm.

Miller, L., and C. Cable, eds. 2008. *Professionalism in the early years.* London: Hodder/Arnold.

Miller, L., C. Cable, and G. Goodliff. 2007. A day in the life of an early years practitioner: The English case study. Symposium presentation at 17th EECERA Conference, August 30, in Prague, Czech Republic.

Moss, P. 2003. Structures, understandings and discourses: Possibilities for re-envisioning the early childhood worker. *Contemporary Issues in Early Childhood* 7, no. 1: 30–41.

———. 2006. Bringing politics into the nursery: Early childhood education as a democratic practice. Paper presented at 16th EECERA Conference, September 1, at the University of Reykjavik, Iceland.

Oberhuemer, P. 2005. Conceptualising the early childhood pedagogue: Policy approaches and issues of professionalism. *European Early Childhood Education Research Journal* 13, no. 1: 5–15.

O'Keefe, J., and K. Tait. 2004. An examination of the UK Early Years Foundation degree and the evolution of senior practitioners – enhancing work-based practice by engaging in reflective and critical thinking. *International Journal of Early Years Education* 12, no. 1: 25–41.

Organisation for Economic Co-operation and Development (OECD). 2006. *Starting strong II. Early childhood education and care.* Paris: OECD.

Osgood, J. 2006. Deconstructing professionalism in early childhood education: Resisting the regulatory gaze. *Contemporary Issues in Early Childhood* 7, no. 1: 5–14.

Penn, H. 1998. Comparative research: A way forward? In *Researching early childhood education: European perspectives,* ed. T. David. London: Paul Chapman Publishing.

Qualifications and Curriculum Authority (QCA). Accessed 17 December 2007 http://www.qaa.ac.uk/academicinfrastructure/FHEQ/default.asp.

Snape, D., J. Parfrement, and S. Finch (National Centre for Social Research). 2007. *Evaluation of the early years sector endorsed foundation degree: Findings from the final student survey.* London: DfES Publications.

Strauss, A., and J. Corbin. 1998. *Basics of qualitative research: Techniques or procedures and developing grounded theory.* London: Sage.

Sylva, K., E. Melhuish, P. Sammons, I. Siraj-Blatchford, B. Taggart, and K. Elliot. 2003. *The Effective Provision of Pre-School Education (EPPE) project: Findings from the pre-school period: Summary of finding.* London: Institute of Education/Sure Start.

Urban, M. 2007. A day in the life of an early years practitioner: The German case study. Symposium presentation at 17th EECERA Conference, August 30, in Prague, Czech Republic.

Wenger, E. 1998. *Communities of practice: Learning and meaning,* Cambridge: Cambridge University Press.

Westcott, E. 2004. The early years workforce – towards professional status? An issues paper. Unpublished paper presented at the Senior Practitioner Working Group, Department for Education and Skills (DfES).

Whitehead, M. 1999. *Supporting language and literacy development in the early years.* Buckingham: Open University Press.

Discourses of professional identity in early childhood: movements in Australia

Christine Woodrow

University of Western Sydney, Australia

ABSTRACT: The provision of early childhood education and care for children and families has received unprecedented community attention in recent times. In the resulting policy flows, competing and contradictory discourses of professional identity have emerged. In part, these are also shaped by dominant political and economic discourses, and interact with existing and emerging discourses of professionalism within the early childhood sector to both constrain and expand possible professional identities. This article explores some dimensions of these policy trajectories, in particular the increasingly dominant presence of corporatised childcare, and recent strategies to regulate early childhood teachers and courses. The potential impact of these on conceptualisations of professional identity in the Australian context is discussed, and frameworks of caring, reconceptualised leadership and the concept of 'robust hope' are signposted as possible conceptual resources for building robust early childhood professional identities.

RÉSUMÉ: L'offre en matière d'éducation et d'accueil des jeunes enfants et de leurs familles a suscité ces derniers temps une attention sans précédent de la communauté. Il en résulte, sur le plan politique, une émergence de discours concurrents et contradictoires sur l'identité professionnelle. Ceux-ci sont en partie également influencés par les discours politiques et économiques dominants. Ils interagissent avec les discours existants et émergents sur le professionnalisme dans le secteur de la petite enfance qui limitent ou élargissent les identités professionnelles possibles. Cet article examine quelques dimensions de ces développements politiques et leur impact sur les conceptualisations d'identité professionnelle dans le contexte politique australien. Il inclut une analyse de l'impact potentiel de la présence grandissante du corporatisme dans l'accueil des jeunes enfants et des règlementations récentes concernant les enseignants et le préscolaire. La partie finale de cette contribution se termine par une prise en considération de cadres pour l'accueil, d'une direction reconceptualisée et du concept d'espoir puissant, comme ressources conceptuelles possibles pour la construction d'identités professionnelles solides dans le champ de la petite enfance.

ZUSAMMENFASSUNG: Angebote der Bildung und Betreuung für junge Kinder und ihre Familien haben in letzter Zeit mehr öffentliche Aufmerksamkeit erfahren als je zuvor. Aus der daraus resultierenden politischen Debatte haben sich konkurrierende und widersprüchliche Diskurse zur professionellen Identität herausgebildet. Sie sind, in Teilen, von vorherrschenden politischen und ökonomischen Diskursen beeinflusst und stehen in Wechselwirkung mit bestehenden und neu entstehenden Diskursen zur Professionalität innerhalb der Frühpädagogik. Mögliche professionelle Identitäten werden in diesen Diskursen sowohl beschränkt als auch befördert. Dieser Beitrag untersucht einige Dimensionen dieser politischen Entwicklungen und ihre Auswirkungen auf Konzeptualisierungen professioneller Identität im australischen Kontext. Diskutiert werden auch die möglichen Auswirkungen der sich zunehmend ausbreitenden kommerziellen Betreuungsangebote, sowie aktuelle Regulierungsbestrebungen für Praxis und Ausbildung. Der Artikel schließt mit einem Ausblick auf Betreuung, neu gedachte Führungsinitiative und einem Konzept starker Hoffnung als mögliche Quellen zur Herausbildung starker professioneller Identitäten in der Frühpädagogik.

RESUMEN: El suministro de educación pre-escolar para niños y familias ha recibido en el último tiempo de parte de la comunidad una atención sin precedentes. En las políticas resultantes han emergido discursos de identidad profesional concurrentes y contradictorios. En parte, esos son también formados por los discursos políticos y económicos dominantes, e interactúan con discursos de profesionalismos existentes y emergentes dentro del sector pre-escolar, para contraer y expandir posibles identidades profesionales. El artículo explora algunas dimensiones de esas trayectorias políticas, y su impacto sobre conceptualizaciones de identidad profesional, en el contexto político australiano. La discusión incluye exploración del impacto potencial que la presencia, en constante aumento, de formas corporacionales del cuidado de niños, y de estrategias recientes para regularizar cursos y profesores pre-escolares. La parte final del articulo señaliza y considera marcos de referencias del cuidado de niños, reconceptualiza el liderazgo y el concepto de esperanza robusta como posibles recursos conceptuales para formar identidades profesionales pre-escolares robustas.

Introduction

In recent times an unprecedented flourishing of community attention to early childhood provision across the Organisation for Economic Co-operation and Development (OECD) nations has given rise to some new and reinvigorated policy trajectories characterised by a range of visions: some bold and some not so bold and with varying degrees of emphasis on issues of equity, access, and quality, and uneven levels of resourcing. In the Australian context, considerable ambiguity about the beneficiaries and purposes of such provision exists (Press and Hayes 2000; Press and Woodrow 2005; Press 2007). For example, a recent communiqué from the Council of Australian Governments (COAG 2007), comprised of national and state ministers, listed early childhood provision as an item on the 'productivity' agenda, whilst other policy advocates might position early childhood services as a feminist issue, or as an issue relating to children's rights (Press 2007). In the midst of this ambiguity, the last decade also has seen the development of a National Agenda for Children (Department of Families, Community Services and Indigenous Affairs 2004); a national longitudinal study of childhood (Longitudinal Study of Australian Children – LSAC) involving 3500 children (Sanson et al. 2002); and the commitment of significant funding resources to programmes aimed at benefiting children and families through national programmes such as 'Strengthening Australian Families' (Department of Families, Community Services and Indigenous Affairs 2007) and state-based early intervention initiatives such as the 'Brighter Futures' program in New South Wales. Expansion of childcare services has been rapid and significant, with over 60% of children under five experiencing childcare in 2005 (Pocock and Hill 2007). Overlaying these developments has been the strengthening of neo-liberal discourses, a strong infusion of market ideology (Woodrow and Brennan 1999; Press and Woodrow 2005) and a proliferation of policies and practices that invariably result in increasing regulation, standardisation and accountability across the early childhood sector (Grieshaber 2000). These policy flows have created an interesting and challenging context for any concomitant 'flourishing' of professional identity within the sector and arguably contribute to both expanding and constraining possible conceptualisations of professionalism at a time that seems to be calling for new and expanded expressions of professional identity (e.g. see articles in this issue by Adams; Dalli; Karila). For example, a perceived broadening of professional identities can be discerned in the new initiatives towards integrated service provision inspired by England's children's centres, the associated leadership development programmes (National College for School Leadership 2006), and a number of other emerging initiatives in Australia (DECS 2005). In contrast, it might be argued that a narrowing professional discourse is being produced by the teacher accreditation and regulatory approaches that have recently gathered momentum in Australia (Woodrow 2007). In a context where new visions, possibilities and opportunities have emerged for early childhood, questions arise about the implications for professional discourses and identity of the changed environment: which professional identities are privileged, and which are excluded in current policy discourses? What are the implications of these? How well do the dominant expressions of early childhood professional identity fit with emerging policy trajectories? What kinds of professional identities are implicated in the emerging landscape of integrated service provision and overall expansion of early childhood provision? What resources exist to support the development of new and expanded professional identities? What is the relationship between leadership and professional identity in this expansion?

These are big and important questions and this article cannot address them all, or any, in depth. However, the questions bear citing as they do mark out some territory for further investigation as well as provide a contextual framework for the discussion in this article. In particular, this article aims to contribute to debates about current, emerging and possible constructions of early childhood professional identities by first exploring the implications for professional identity of two dominant trends in the policy landscape: (i) the increasing corporate domination in Australia of childcare provision; and (ii) the increasing regulation of teachers and teacher education. The second part of the article focuses on some implications that flow from the analysis of these trends. I argue that the current policy landscapes potentially lead to a perceived narrowing of possibilities for professional identities and the privileging of an 'entrepreneurial', self-interested professional discourse. I suggest that discussions about leadership are an important dimension to expanding the current range of professional discourses and identities so that they might respond to the challenges of contemporary contexts. Finally I consider some possible resources emerging from the work of the Robust Hope Collective in which I have been involved as a participant researcher and briefly discuss how these resources might contribute to a new activist and leadership-focused professional identity in early childhood.

Corporatising professional identity

One of the most distinctive recent changes in the early childhood landscape in Australia has been the rapid ascendancy and entrenchment of corporate provision of childcare. Childcare as a 'market commodity' is now well established on the Australian scene. Recent figures indicate that ABC Learning Ltd now owns and operates 1084 childcare centres in Australia, including some operated on behalf of the Defence Department (ABC Learning Ltd 2006, 2007). Estimates suggest that this accounts for close to 25% of childcare for Australia's children (Rush 2006). Brennan (2007) observes that this domination of childcare provision by one corporate player in the childcare 'market' now places Australia as engaged in a 'social experiment'. The speed with which one corporation has come to dominate childcare provision in Australia, its rapid expansion into international markets, and the potentially far-reaching implications in reconstructing childcare as a site of consumption (Press and

Woodrow 2005; Woodrow and Press 2007) provide considerable provocation to investigate the possible impact of corporate provision on policy trajectories, professional discourses and professional identity, particularly as the community-based sector shrinks whilst the corporate grows. Such market domination is suggestive of considerable power and influence over one important sector of early childhood policy and practice. To date, there has been little published research on the impact of this dramatic change in the character of childcare provision on staff and workforce issues.

As part of a study investigating how the dominance of corporate provision might be diminishing the space for public discussion of what society wants for its children and shaping how childcare is viewed, a number of insights emerged that are relevant to a discussion of professional identity (Press and Woodrow 2007). By tracing the relationships of the parent company ABC Learning Ltd to other entities it quickly became evident that vertical and horizontal integration of related and wholly owned companies and suppliers is a distinctive feature of the company's operations. For example, the parent company has a significant shareholding (17.99%) in the toy and equipment supplier Funtastic, which in turn enjoys an exclusive 20-year global supply agreement with ABC Learning Ltd to supply products covering 'the complete spectrum of children's development, including literacy, maths, motor skills, arts and crafts and music' (http://www.funtastic.com, 2006). Additionally, ABC Learning is entitled to a percentage of sales made to and through ABC Learning Centres. Similar relationships exist with companies supplying goods and services ranging from school photographs to staff recruitment, purchasing opportunities for 'ABC Learning Families', and an online software learning program for young children, called Broadlearn (Mediasphere). The company, through its self-designated 'Education Department', has developed its own curriculum, 'Lifesmart' (http://www.childcare.com.au). Thus, many aspects of the daily curriculum that children experience, and early childhood professionals implement, are 'authorised' and mediated through corporate relationships designed to maximise shareholder returns.

Similarly, through its wholly owned entity, the National Institute of Early Childhood Education (NIECE), ABC Learning has the capacity to provide 'in-house' training and ongoing professional development to its workforce of approximately 17,000. This enterprise enables professional habits, dispositions and competencies to be 'authorised' and authenticated by the company. It too returns profits to the parent company.

Documenting these structures and relationships led to the observation that:

> Such arrangements might be business savvy (but) they also have other ramifications, including cementing the construction of childcare as both an act, and a point of consumption ... which take(s) on wider public significance because of the very real possibility that decisions about young children's learning and well being are conflated with financial interests in returning the strongest possible dividends to share holders. (Press and Woodrow 2007, 7)

Reflecting on the implications of these findings, questions arise as to the nature of professional identities being shaped by corporate childcare. The research findings briefly outlined above provide some pointers as to how an organisation with large market share and a concomitantly large workforce builds structures and relationships which validate and promote its own brand of corporate professionalism. Indications of what this might look like can also be found in the marketing and promotional materials of the organisation where maxims such as *'our "spirit of fun" runs as deep as our "spirit of competition"'* (http://www.childcare.com.au) strongly gesture towards a professionalism imbued with commercialism and competition. Together with advertising refrains, corporate branding through uniforms, staff loyalty programs and an 'ABC Carers Share Plan', these strategies collectively embed and privilege affiliation and loyalty to the company over the profession. These practices also become normalised and spread as other organisations imitate the 'market leader', now evident in other early childhood provider organisations that have been observed to be implementing corporate uniforms and adopting other branding practices across their centres and services, with a resulting homogenisation of appearances and practices.

These trends are redolent of characterisations of enterprise culture in which the market-based provisions of goods and services and wealth as a marker of success occupy paradigmatic status and highly individualistic orientations to work and competitiveness are central (McWilliam, Hatcher, and Meadmore 1999). They are also reflective of Sachs' (2000, 2001) characterisations of the 'entrepreneurial professional' in which identity is more aligned with procedural standardisation, efficiency and accountability rather than the exercise of autonomy and knowledge-building across differentiated contexts, and where privatised concerns take precedence over community.

The values of enterprise culture are dichotomous to many of the values that traditionally have been at the heart of early childhood professional identity: notions of caring, collegiality, collectivism and community (Moyles 2001; Woodrow 2002). Whilst these discordant values have been gaining ascendancy for some time in education and more recently in early childhood discourse, the increasing domination of corporatised early childhood provision arguably contributes to their intensification and legitimation. The evidence to date suggests that the impact of this trend warrants further close investigation if some of the bolder visions about the early childhood institution as a space for privileging children's interests and promoting community building are to be achieved (Press 2007).

Professional identity and regulation of/for teacher quality

During the last 10 years, Australia's national and state governments have demanded greater accountability for teacher quality, teacher performance and teacher preparation. As a consequence, a number of strategies have been, or are in the process of being, put in place that develop uniformity of 'standards' and place teachers and teacher education under increased surveillance. These strategies include teacher registration processes and the establishment of statutory authorities such as the NSW Institute of Teachers (NSWIT) to oversee course approval processes and monitor teacher quality and accreditation. There can be little doubt that the current intensification of monitoring and regulation of teacher quality is having a significant impact on constructions of early childhood professional identity in the Australian context.

It is hard to argue in principle against strategies being put in place to assure teacher quality, given the increasing research evidence demonstrating the centrality of the teacher in the success of children's learning, and, as Elliott (2007) claims, the wide agreement on the importance of regulatory pathways to professional practice. However, almost invariably, such approaches develop and impose uniform standards and 'one-size-fits-all' regimes. In Australia, and particularly in the two states of New South Wales (NSW) and Queensland (QLD), this is resulting in the erosion of a distinctive specialist early childhood teacher identity in favour of a generic 'school-based' teacher identity. In a recent article (Woodrow 2007), I explored in some depth how teacher accrediting policies and practices in these two Australian states, together with new frameworks for teacher education course approvals in NSW (NSW Institute of Teachers 2007), have excluded or marginalised early childhood teachers and their knowledge bases. By corollary, these policies and practices privileged teacher identities derived from the compulsory school sector. I concluded that definitions of 'teacher' in these policies are increasingly becoming limited to compulsory school settings.

This is notwithstanding legislative requirements in some states for the employment of specialised early childhood teachers in 'prior-to-school' early childhood contexts. Early childhood professionals in Australia, thus, are finding themselves increasingly marginalised or excluded from debates and policy development for teacher preparation and teacher quality: as the concept of 'teacher' is a strong marker of educational discourse and pedagogical intent in Australian policy, the exclusion of early childhood teaching from this regulatory arena constitutes significant marginalisation of early childhood practice as 'teaching' and 'education'. This has strong potential for serious flow-on effects for the status, salary levels and conditions of work of early childhood teachers working in non-school contexts compared with those working in school settings or preschools set up by school authorities. In NSW, the guidelines for teacher education course approvals are so heavily weighted towards school-based curriculum content and pedagogical knowledge that there is little capacity in a standard-length teaching degree framework to include the kinds of threshold knowledges considered essential to the professional preparation of early childhood specialists. Early childhood courses in Australia typically include both a pedagogical focus on children between birth and eight years, and a sociological focus on supporting and interacting with families and community. Increasingly, these are being overtaken by overbearing and narrowly conceived discourses of schooling. Many early childhood teacher educators fear that the result will be the loss of the capacity to prepare specialist early childhood teachers for the early years of school, inevitably destroying the relationships built up over time between school and non-school settings by courses preparing early childhood teachers to work across the 0-to-8-year age range spanning the non-school and schooling sector. For universities in NSW, many are finding that they might need to make a choice between preparing early childhood teachers for non-school (prior-to-school) settings with a focus on child and community, or school settings with a focus on the school curriculum, thus replacing the previous conceptualisation of early childhood teachers as working with children across the school/prior-to-school divide.

In some ways these developments are yet another manifestation of the fragmentation that characterises the Australian early childhood policy environment and the persistent care/education dichotomy where 'early childhood is uneasily positioned between the conceptual and jurisdictional frameworks of education, health and social welfare and there is a gap between a rhetorical commitment to the inter-relationship between care and education and the practice of differentiation through policy' (Press 2007, 113). These developments also represent a lost opportunity to progress the development of distinctive and robust pedagogical constructions of early childhood teaching within mainstream discourses of teacher professionalism in regulatory bodies established by the state and national governments.

As a consequence of these policy interventions, early childhood teacher education programmes are increasingly being isolated from the arenas in which teacher knowledges are being debated and articulated. This could ultimately lead to the loss of a distinctive early childhood professional identity that spans the school and non-school sectors and which has become an established symbol of cross-sector synergies and border crossing. That such an identity should be at risk at a time when supporting children's effective transitions to school has become a strengthening discourse seems counterproductive and is hard to understand.

Reclaiming and reconstructing early childhood identities: taking stock

In the previous section of this article, I have suggested that both the dominance of corporate childcare and current approaches to teacher regulation may be shaping the production of limited and limiting professional identities. In making this suggestion I am mindful of the importance of context and the fluid nature of discourse and identity. This is not to say that a corporatised, entrepreneurial identity is the only identity that might be produced and taken up through corporate provision of childcare, nor that early childhood professionals cannot reclaim, and indeed strengthen educational discourses as part of their identity; or that early childhood professionals lack agency in taking up desired identities. In fact, interestingly, the education dimension of young children's experience in childcare is strongly emphasised in the marketing rhetoric of Australia's largest corporate childcare chain, ABC Learning Ltd (http://www.childcare.com), and current actions by the national and state governments towards teachers are contributing to a standardised, 'one-size-fits-all' teacher identity: Clearly the flows in building identity are not uni-directional and their impact is not fixed. However, my argument is that there is sufficient evidence to raise concern about which possible identities and professional discourses might be nourished, sustained and privileged in such environments and which might be at risk through these policy trajectories and interventions.

The logical question that arises from such an argument concerns the constructions of early childhood professionalism which might best serve the provisions of high quality programmes directed at the well-being of children and to sustain community-building. Internationally, there are some bold visions and claims being articulated for the role of early childhood education as not only a right and entitlement for all children, but also as a site for children's citizenship (Dahlberg, Moss, and Pence 1999; Dahlberg and Moss 2005) and the 'revitalisation' of democracy (Woodrow and Press 2007). Within this philosophical framework, and in contexts where some policy rhetoric and trajectories are indeed taking a holistic, interdisciplinary perspective on children's well-being, understandings of professionalism and professional identity that are expansive, context responsive and fluid become very important.

Within the Australian context, in earlier years, and when resources for thinking about professionalism seemed very limited, a project was undertaken to define early childhood professionalism through the codification of ethics. At the time this seemed an important strategy to support the articulation and practice of professional identity in the early childhood field. Indeed, those efforts seemed well appreciated across the sector, not the least for the position adopted on inclusiveness and for the aspirational rather than punitive character of the Code of Ethics, as well as for the opportunity to 'name' issues as ethical and professional rather than procedural (Woodrow 2002). Over time a body of research has emerged (e.g. Woodrow 2002; Hard 2004; Skattebol 2006) that clearly demonstrates how the concept and practice of professionalism is indeed a 'site of struggle' and that, as Sachs (2003) asserts, to 'seek a fixed position is futile: professionalism has always been a changing concept' (6).

A central thesis of this article, then, is that whilst particular features of the policy landscape, including corporatisation and the regulation of teachers and teacher preparation courses, might be exerting powerful influences in narrowing early childhood professional identities, there are counter-flows that suggest an imperative to develop resources to sustain multiple and robust identities responsive to elements of the changed environment. New philosophies and approaches involving holistic/integrated service delivery across traditional disciplinary boundaries (DECS 2005), and conceptions of early childhood institutions as sites for community-building, do seem to be moving in from the margins. Some literature suggests that realising the exciting potential of these shifts in community focus might require significant reconceptualisations of professional identity in which notions of professionalism are more strongly characterised by leadership (Goffin and Washington 2007), alliance building and activism (Sachs 2003), collegiality and futures orientation (Fasoli, Scrivens, and Woodrow 2007), professionals with vision and skills who can take the best of the past and run, collegially and with a clear sense of purpose, into the future. What conceptual resources would support such professional identity building?

In the next section of this article I take an exploratory journey through some ideas, concepts and frameworks that have emerged from policy research in education in Australia. In particular, I reflect on leadership as an integral part of a professional identity suited to the challenges of our times, and explore the rationale and components of a framework of 'Robust Hope' and how it might resource a new leadership. Some of these ideas are in early formative stages; others have been applied in education and early childhood contexts.

Leadership and 'Robust Hope': resources for expanding early childhood identity?

Leadership is emerging as an area requiring careful attention in discussions about the formation of early childhood identity. International and local commentators frequently draw attention to the fragmented nature of early childhood provision in Australia and the lack of clarity of vision for the field (OECD 2001; Press 2007). Similarly, leadership research in Australia consistently reveals a strong lack of identification with the concept of leadership amongst early childhood professionals (Woodrow 2002; Ebbeck and Waninganayake 2003; Hard 2004). Could there be a link between these two seemingly disparate elements? This reluctance to identify with leadership, or for early childhood professionals even to acknowledge their potential as leaders, has been variously explained through the lenses of gendered and feminist discourses (Blackmore 1999; Woodrow 2002), and developmental discourses (Grieshaber 2001). The inadequacy of the research base to inform such conceptualisations also has been noted (e.g. Muijs et al. 2004; Ebbeck and Waninganayake 2003). Could overcoming this reluctance significantly help the profession to achieve a vibrant professional community, in which understandings of professionalism are privileged, along with a view of early childhood professionals as agents of change who are willing and able to shape their own professional identities? Findings from a recent project researching early childhood leadership in the United States (Goffin and Washington 2007) concluded that 'the early care and education field's lack of clarity about its purpose, identity, and responsibility' (3) was a major issue. The researchers suggested that inadequate conceptualisations of leadership, including those focused on individuals as a 'package of characteristics' (6), dominated ideas about leadership, and there was a 'need to move beyond a reliance on individual leaders and toward a creation of a field-wide community of diverse leaders' (3). Reiterating the importance of developing not just individual leaders, but leadership capacity across the field, they stated that in order to 'affect political decision-making and exert influence during moments of opportunity, field-wide leadership is needed' (8). They continued: 'we are motivated by the need to build coherent leadership *for the field* … built from a shared foundation … networked, fieldwide leadership capable of envisioning, advancing and executing complex systemic change' (10).

This distinction between leadership as an individualised construct, and the concept of building leadership capacity within and across a field, resonates strongly with my insights through my personal involvement in early childhood research and leadership projects in Australia (Woodrow 2002; Fasoli, Scrivens, and Woodrow 2007); the distinction resonates also with concepts of participative democracy and engaged citizenship described by Sumsion (2006) as constitutive of a new activist professionalism, and the concept of 'leadership as everyday practice' as described by Blackmore (1999). The kinds of professional identities that might contribute to building such a capacity are more likely to draw on values of collegiality and community than those of self-interested individualism and it its here that the resources of the Robust Hope project (Sawyer et al. 2007) might offer different conceptual resources to those on which the field has traditionally drawn.

The Robust Hope project originated at the University of Western Sydney through a group of disparate researchers working in diverse areas of education coming together with a shared belief that a key aim of public policy should be the provision of 'hope', in particular to the socially disadvantaged. With its focus on 'reclaiming the utopian imagination for educational and social programs' (Sawyer et al. 2007, 1), the initial focus of the project has been to assemble a set of resources that 'might inform the investigation and expression of utopian possibilities in the face of the structural pressures of neo-liberalism, which in its valorising of individualism, and consequent loss of community holds out little for disadvantaged and marginalised communities, and in fact connects to a zeitgeist of hopelessness' (1). The project aims to build an open-ended conceptual framework of key ideas with which to analyse public policy and realise the possibilities of human agency in relation to those pressures.

The key elements of Robust Hope are hope itself (Williams 1989), together with a manifestation of the socio-cultural conditions which give it robustness. The resources on which the project draws include utopianism, an enhanced vision of democracy, agency, a research-based approach, caring conceived through relations of interdependency, sustainability and resilience. Thus it has both psychological and sociological dimensions. The project proposes that the psychological areas that need to be met by public policy if it is to 'pass the test' of Robust Hope are: the potential for creating resilience and happiness and for imagining a better future, thus contributing to a public good, where resilience is conceived in relation to both individuals and communities. Building resilience, within the conceptual framings of the Robust Hope project, means building both individual and community capacity, contributing to the exercise of agency through participation and activism. The appropriate sociological conditions are: a futures orientation; sustainability; and a view of democracy which emphasises notions of equality over the free rein of the market.

One of those utopian possibilities identified by researchers in the project is the realisation of the potential of the early childhood 'project' to build and transform communities (see also Moss 1999) and re-establish related democratic and participatory structures that have been eroded through the market model of early childhood provision (Woodrow and Press 2007). Here, the exploration of what might constitute democratic practice in contemporary, post-neoliberal contexts becomes a key focus for conceptual development (Giroux 2002, 2004). These two elements of the Robust Hope project, resilience and democratic possibilities, become visible as potential resources for building professional identities and have been influential in the design and implementation of three inter-related practitioner research projects funded by the University of Western Sydney that I have been involved in with my colleagues, Jen Skattebol and Leonie Arthur. The projects aim to build early childhood leadership capacity through collaborative enquiry; whilst they are still in their early stages, there are indications that expanded concepts of resilience, and explorations of democratic possibilities in early childhood, are productive avenues of enquiry and action in working towards 'reclaiming utopian possibilities', building community, and resourcing agency.

It is beyond the scope of this article to provide a full analysis of the potential contribution that the resources of the Robust Hope project might make to a reconceptualised professional identity that incorporates building leadership capacity. However, articulating the resources of resilience, and of explorations of democratic possibilities, can contribute to establishing a clarity of purpose for early childhood institutions: Goffin and Washington (2007) believe that clarity of purpose is a fundamental first step in building leadership capacity. Using the resources of Robust Hope could expand articulations of this purpose well beyond those of personal and individual 'profit' into the realm of the public good. In such a conceptualisation, new identities and new relations become imaginable and possible. As a fellow Robust Hope project colleague, and professor in education, commented at a project symposium:

> Robust hope is attentive to making connections between people to overcome the isolation, fragmentation, privatisation and individualisation of educational experiences, by making known points of contact and using pedagogies that provide reliable support systems. In forging a sense of human agency, robust hope supports the development of community-based ambitions for making social and educational changes. It is concerned to increase people's capacity to perceive and conceive future possibilities, including the possibility that human actions can make a difference. (Singh 2006)

Conclusion

In this article I have provided an analysis of some dominant features of the early childhood policy landscape in Australia, expressing some concern about their perceived influence in diminishing the range of early childhood professional identities, and their privileging of certain kinds of professional discourses and marginalising of others. As a counter to what could be a depressive paralysis response, I have invoked the resources of the Robust Hope project to reposition leadership and leadership capacity-building as a key focus for the early childhood community in its quest to privilege children's well-being and community building as fundamental purposes of the early childhood project. Accepting and acting on such a thesis will require the mobilisation of resources beyond those identified in this article: I hope, however, that the insights and resources provided through this writing effort might make a helpful contribution. Clearly much more research on professional identity formation and analysis of policy and practice is implicated.

References

ABC Learning Ltd. 2006. ABC Learning Ltd 2006 Annual Report. http://www.childcare.com.
———. 2007. ABC Learning Ltd 2007 Annual Report. http://www.childcare.com.
Blackmore, J. 1999. *Troubling women: Feminism, leadership and educational change.* Buckingham: Open University Press.
Brennan, D. 2007. The ABC of childcare politics. *Australian Journal of Social Issues* 142, no. 2: 213–25.
Council of Australian Governments (COAG). 2007. Communiqué from meeting of COAG, 20 December. http://www.coag.gov.au/meetings/201207/index.htm.
Dahlberg, G., and P. Moss. 2005. *Ethics and politics in early childhood education.* London: RoutledgeFalmer.
Dahlberg, G., P. Moss, and A. Pence. 1999. *Beyond quality in early childhood education and care: Postmodern perspectives.* London: Falmer Press.
Department of Community Services. 2006. Brighter Futures. http://www.docs.nsw.gov.au.
Department of Education and Children's Services (DECS). 2005. DECS Statement of Directions 2005–2010. Adelaide: Government of South Australia.
Department of Families, Community Services and Indigenous Affairs. 2004. The National Agenda for Early Childhood: A draft framework. Canberra: Australian Government.
———. 2007. Strengthening families. Canberra: Australian Government. http://www.facsia.gov.au.
Ebbeck, M., and M. Waninganayake. 2003. *Early childhood professionals: Leading today and tomorrow.* Sydney: Maclennan & Petty.
Elliott, A. 2007. Improving early childhood quality through standards, accreditation and registration. In *Kids count: Better early childhood education and care in Australia,* ed. E. Hill, B. Pocock, and A. Elliott. Sydney: Sydney University Press.

Fasoli, L., C. Scrivens, and C. Woodrow. 2007. Challenges for leadership in New Zealand and Australian early childhood contexts. In *Theorising early childhood practice: Emerging dialogues,* ed. L. Keesing-Styles and H. Hedges. Sydney: Pademelon Press.

Funtastic Ltd. 2006. Funtastic Ltd 2006 Annual Report. http://www.funtastic.com.

Giroux, H.A. 2002. Educated hope in an age of privatised visions. *Cultural Studies – Critical Methodologies* 2, no. 1: 93–112.

————. 2004. Neoliberalism and the demise of democracy: Resurrecting hope in dark times. http://www.dissidentvoice.org/Aug04/Giroux0807.htm.

Goffin, S., and V. Washington. 2007. *Ready or not: Leadership choices in early care and education.* New York: Teachers College Press.

Grieshaber, S. 2000. Regulating the early childhood field. *Australian Journal of Early Childhood* 25, no. 2: 1–6.

————. 2001. Advocacy and early childhood educators: Identity and cultural conflicts. In *Embracing identities in early childhood education,* ed. S. Grieshaber and G. Cannella. New York: Teachers College Press.

Hard, L. 2004. How is leadership understood in early childhood education and care? *Journal of Australian Research in Early Childhood Education* 11, no. 1: 123–31.

McWilliam, E., C. Hatcher, and D. Meadmore. 1999. Corporatising the teacher, new professional identities in education. Article presented at Australian Association for Educational Research (AARE) Annual Conference, November 30–December 2, in Melbourne, Australia.

Moss, P. 1999. Early childhood institutions as a democratic and emancipatory project. In *Early education transformed: New millennium series,* ed. L. Abbott and H. Moylett. London: Falmer Press.

Moyles, J. 2001. Passion, paradox and professionalism in early years education. *Early Years* 21, no. 2: 81–95.

Muijs, D., C. Aubrey, A. Harris, and M. Briggs. 2004. How do they manage? A review of the research on leadership in early childhood. *Journal of Early Childhood Research* 2, no. 2: 157–69.

National College for School Leadership (NCSL). 2006. *National professional qualification in integrated centre leadership England.* Nottingham: NCSL.

New South Wales Institute of Teachers. 2007. Initial teacher education programs: Supplementary documentation for program approval (mandatory areas). http://www.nswteachers.nsw.edu.au/IgnitionSuite/uploads/docs/Mandatory%20Requirements%20for%20Teacher%20Education%20Programs%20-%20May%2007.pdf.

Organisation for Economic Co-operation and Development (OECD). 2001. *Starting strong: Early childhood education and care.* Paris: OECD.

Pocock, B., and E. Hill. 2007. The childcare policy challenge in Australia. In *Kids count: Better early childhood education and care in Australia,* ed. E. Hill, B. Pocock, and A. Elliott. Sydney: Sydney University Press.

Press, F. 2007. Public investment, fragmentation and quality early education and care: Existing challenges and future options. In *Kids count: Better early childhood education and care in Australia,* ed. E. Hill, B. Pocock, and A. Elliott. Sydney: Sydney University Press.

Press, F., and A. Hayes. 2000. *OECD thematic review of early childhood education and care policy: Australian background report.* Canberra: Commonwealth of Australia.

Press, F., and C. Woodrow. 2005. Commodification, corporatisation and children's spaces. *Australian Journal of Education* 49, no. 3: 278–97.

————. 2007. The giant in the playground: Investigating the reach and implications of the corporatisation of childcare provision. Article presented at Australian Paid Care Research Network Symposium 'For Profit Providers of Paid Care', November 29–30, at the University of Sydney, Australia.

Rush, E. 2006. *Child care quality in Australia.* Canberra: The Australia Institute.

Sachs, J. 2000. The activist professional. *Journal of Educational Change* 1, no. 1: 77–95.

————. 2001. Teacher professional identity: Competing discourses, competing outcomes. *Journal of Educational Policy* 16, no. 2: 149–61.

————. 2003. *The activist professional.* Maidenhead: Open University Press.

Sanson, A., J. Nicholson, J. Ungerer, S. Zubrick, K. Wilson, J. Ainley, D. Berthelson, M. Bittman, C. Broom, L. Harrison, B. Rodgers, M. Sawyer, S. Silburn, L. Strazdins, G. Vimpani, and M. Wake.

2002. Introducing the Longitudinal Study of Australian Children. LSAC Discussion Paper No 1. Melbourne: Australian Institute of Family Studies.

Sawyer, W., M. Singh, C. Woodrow, T. Downes, C. Johnston, and D. Whitton. 2007. Robust hope and teacher education policy. *Asia-Pacific Journal of Teacher Education* 35, no. 3: 227–42.

Singh, M.G. 2006. Personal communication, 13 May.

Skattebol, J. 2006. Re/searching for shared meanings of identity: Collaborations between teacher researchers and children. PhD diss., Univ. of Western Sydney.

Sumsion, J. 2006. From Whitlam to economic rationalism and beyond: A conceptual framework for political activism in children's services. *Australian Journal of Early Childhood* 31, no. 1: 1–10.

Sylva, K., E. Melhuish, P. Sammons, I. Siraj- Blatchford, B. Taggart, and K. Elliott. 2003. *The effective provision of pre-school education (EPPE) project: Summary of findings.* London: Institute of Education, University of London.

Williams, R. 1989. *Resources of hope.* London: Verso.

Woodrow, C. 2002. Living ethics in early childhood contexts. Unpublished PhD thesis, Central Queensland Univ.

———. 2007. W(h)ither the early childhood teacher? Tensions for early childhood professional identity between the policy landscape and the politics of teacher regulation. *Contemporary Issues in Early Childhood* 8, no. 3: 233–43.

Woodrow, C., and M. Brennan. 1999. Marketised positioning of early childhood: New contexts for curriculum and professional development in Queensland, Australia. *Contemporary Issues in Early Childhood* 1, no. 1: 78–94.

Woodrow, C., and F. Press. 2007. (Re) Positioning the child in the policy/politics of early childhood. *Educational Philosophy and Theory* 39, no. 3: 312–325.

Websites

http://www.childcare.com. ABC Learning Ltd.
http://www.funtastic.com. Funtastic Ltd.

Conclusion

Towards new understandings of the early years' profession: the need for a critical ecology

Carmen Dalli[a] and Mathias Urban[b]

[a]Victoria University of Wellington, New Zealand; [b]Martin-Luther-University Halle-Wittenburg, Germany

We began our exploration of *professionalism in early childhood* from a discursive, open and deliberately *uncertain* perspective. Professionalism in this particular field, we argue, requires critical exploration, rather than premature definition. The nature of this ongoing enquiry into practices, understandings and conceptualisations of working with young children, families and communities, we further argue, is dialogic out of necessity. What characterises practices on every level of the professional system only unfolds in relationships and interactions between human beings (children and adults, professionals and lay persons). In practice, therefore, professionalism is not a possession of an individual, regardless of the level of their formal qualification; it is always the result of interaction and shared meaning-making. This is perhaps the most important conclusion that can be drawn from our investigation. Additionally, the professional system, whose complexities become visible from the different vantage points of this book, is much more than just an intellectual concept. It is real, to begin with, in its impacts: on children's lives; on practitioners' work conditions; and on shaping the institutional set-up to educate and care for young children. It touches fundamental needs of human societies. As Martin Woodhead (1996) explains: 'Through the care and education for young children, a society constructs and reconstructs community and economy, ensures continuity of tradition between generations, and makes innovation and transformation possible' (p. 12). This embeddedness in the socio-cultural, economical, historical and political context of human society makes the early childhood professional system deeply political. Its manifestations and practices are the result of individual and collective choices that reflect social dynamics, interests and power relations. Approached from this perspective, professionalism in early childhood faces a fundamental dilemma, as it is interwoven with institutions that need to be understood, as Michel Foucault (1979, 1991) analyses, as means of social control, normalisation and confinement. At the same time, early childhood professionalism is a vehicle for social transformation and hope grounded in concrete practice: 'the revelatory, gnosiological practice of education does not itself effect the transformation of the world; but it implies it' (Freire, 2004, p. 23).

As we conclude this book it is pertinent to link back to the questions that marked the starting point of our investigation:

- Do we really understand what *being professional* means in early childhood work contexts?
- How can we understand, conceptualise and theorise *profession* in these contexts?

- What can it mean to *act professionally*, at every layer of the professional system, in increasingly diverse, unequal and rapidly changing social and cultural contexts?
- Do we – can we, should we – have a common ground of understanding about these terms and their meanings?
- Are there key concepts we can agree on in order to orient practices and policies, and to direct further investigation and research?

In posing these questions we characterised professionalism as a discourse as much as a phenomenon and suggested it is fluid, contentious and constantly under re-construction. Individually, the chapters can be seen as snapshots of those constructions in different local contexts. They also serve to highlight some ongoing debates about what the future might hold for the notion of professionalism, and the early childhood profession, in different contexts.

The discussion in the special interest group on professionalism in early childhood provided some provisional answers to these questions. From an early stage, however, it became clear that the 'preliminary' nature of the shared concepts and working definitions would not settle into certainty – rather uncertainty was an inherent characteristic of professionalism in early childhood. Now, in drawing together our enquiries into diverse local practices that are influenced by, and contributing to, wider and increasingly global discourses, the phenomenon of professionalism more than ever appears to be problematic, something to be critically questioned, rather than to be presented as a universal solution. Building on some common ground we are not attempting to *solve* the problem; instead we are exploring what, for example, is problematic about early childhood professionalism when it is considered as:

- an ecological concept that is globally referenced to 'quality provision' and locally defined and determined through specific socio-historical dynamics in which people are active participants;
- a marker of individual identity, a self-identification that enables individual practitioners to take on behaviour that they identify as high quality effective practice;
- expertise that accretes from knowledge, dispositions, attitudes and experience on an ongoing basis;
- mandated by regulations and standards of practice that are externally monitored and/or imposed;
- openness to learning and to critique, and as an outgrowth of reflective practices;
- a quality embedded in practice and in relationships with children, colleagues, parents and management; and
- a marker of social status and as a distinguishing characteristic for an occupational group.

Most striking, perhaps, is the way the chapters collectively present the notion of professionalism as a site of struggle. This is exemplified not only in the unresolved question of 'what's in a name?', addressed by both Adams and McGillivray, but also in the neo-Weberian analysis of the Finnish context offered by Kinos and the sobering commentary on the Australian context provided by Woodrow. Kinos argues that the struggle is both an external one through which the early childhood occupational group tries to raise its status relative to other occupational groupings, and internal in that once achieved, professionalism requires that the occupational status is maintained and widened if it is not to become 'proletarianised' once more. Taking a different approach, Woodrow illustrates that in the Australian context early childhood professionalism is a site of struggle because of the way that the two trends of increased corporatisation of childcare provision, and increased regulation of teachers and teacher education, are acting to narrow the range of potential professional identities. She argues that the trends are privileging particular professional discourses based on entrepreneurship and a 'one-size-fits-all' mentality. These run counter to the broader purposes of community and well-being and rights inherent in early childhood work (e.g. Edwards, Gandini, & Forman, 1998; Freire, 2000b, 2004; UNCRC, 2005).

Working with different ontological perspectives the chapters in this book emphasise that it is no longer possible to treat the idea of professionalism in the early years as a unitary notion, as something that comprises a finite set of attributes that, for example, may be achieved through structural policy mechanisms like regulations or formal staff qualifications. Rather, the chapters point to the inadequacy of these structural-functionalist approaches to understanding professionalism (see Urban, chapter 2), and reveal it as something that is in constant flux, responsive to dynamics within the practitioners' immediate context, and within broader societies.

Narrow understandings of policies, and the maze of regulations, are hardly appropriate for developing the kind of dialogic and systemic professionalism outlined in the chapters of this book. Instead of encouraging democratic innovation and social transformation, policies and regulations often prevent early childhood practitioners from engaging critically with their context and its social, cultural and historical preconditions. Arguing along these lines, Jayne Osgood (2006) promotes the idea of the early childhood practitioner as an active agent who has the potential to disrupt dominant discourses of technocratic, managerial professionalism. We should and we can, she argues, create our own alternative and transformative discourse through 'naming our world', a practice originating in Paolo Freire's cultural circles of the 1960s and 70s (Freire, 2000a, 2000b) and applied in early childhood scholarship by critical authors ever since (e.g. Cochran-Smith, 2004; Derman-Sparks, 1989; Urban & Murray, 2005).

The Freireian injunction that early years practitioners should name their world and thus claim it - thereby re-creating themselves as subjects rather than objects of their world - finds three types of response in this volume. Each constitutes an attempt to reconceptualise professionalism in ways that respond to the complex realities of early childhood practice.

First response: towards a profession that speaks out and 'names' itself

Firstly, a number of chapters argue the desirability of asking early years practitioners to "name themselves" (e.g., Dalli, Dayan, Kuisma and Sandberg, Miller, McGillivray). Dayan, for example, provides a uniquely personal response by demonstrating how, in the absence of an existing model of professionalism within practicum supervision, she combined critical reflection with research to investigate what such a model might look like. In finding her answer in an evolving humanistic-democratic ideology, Dayan also discovered new questions and dilemmas, such as whose voices should be heard in articulating the nature of professionalism in practicum supervision. Dayan's conclusion was that beyond listening to the supervisors, there is much to learn from all the participants in practicum supervision: the children, the students, and the teachers with whom the students work. This quintessentially democratic notion highlights yet again the inherent tension that exists between contemporary understandings of professionalism (e.g. Ebbeck & Waniganayake, 2003; Moss, 2008;

Oberhuemer, 2005) and traditional views that foreground selection and exclusion as key distinguishing criteria.

Within the English context, both Miller and McGillivray discuss the use of the term 'early years professional' which seems to assume a given common understanding of 'the professional' - a position challenged by both authors. Miller and McGillivray both see a need for new discourses about early years professionalism, influenced by the early years' workforce itself, yet they also foreground continuing challenges about who the 'lead' professional will be; the supply of qualified people to fill the role; and how the early years' workforce can come together to create the shared vision necessary to agree on desired change to existing models of professionalism.

The chapter by Dalli (chapter 4) takes a further step towards defining professionalism from the reality of early childhood work. It offers a ground-up perspective constructed from practitioners' responses to survey questions about being professional and acting professionally. This construction provides a glimpse of an answer to the question of whether professionalism is a way of being, something that is, rather than something constructed from exclusively structural mechanisms. It shows that while structural elements such as qualifications are integral elements in New Zealand practitioners' views of professionalism, professionalism is also perceived as something that exists in collaborative relationships with others in the work environment. In this way, professionalism does not just exist as a static quality within a person but rather in the interaction of that person in particular (collaborative) ways with others.

Second response: towards a systemic (as opposed to individualistic), necessarily open, uncertain and dialogic understanding of professionalism

That professionalism exists outside of an individual practitioner constitutes the core idea within at least three chapters in this collection. Karila, Urban, and Woodrow each argue that professionalism is a multi-level phenomenon. Karila for example distinguishes between professionalism as expertise that can be analysed on the personal dimension, as domain-specific knowledge and as a phenomenon that plays out within the working environment; at the same time she sees professionalism as an outcome of societal processes that differ from context to context.

Starting from a different position, Urban (chapter 2) also argues for an understanding of professionalism that is systemic rather than individualistic and encourages openness rather than closure of knowledge and practices. Using 'hopeful examples' from three different contexts – Ireland, Germany, and New Zealand – Urban proposes that professionalism may be viewed as a construct with at least three initial cornerstones: (i) a focus on relationships within a complex ecology of the profession; (ii) space for dialogue and critical questions which value diversity; and (iii) a focus on the Freireian notion of hope, in other words that educational practice is there for a reason and that reason reaches towards change based on values and purpose.

Woodrow's conceptualisation of professionalism is likewise pinned to Freireian notions of hope. In her attempt to move beyond narrowed views of professionalism, Woodrow argues for a reconceptualised professional identity based on valuing the community, diversity, alliance-building, collegiality and an orientation to the future - which makes professional identity a public good rather than an individual construct.

Third response: towards a critical ecology of the early childhood field

This brings us to the third response we can discern in answer to the Freireian injunction to "name our (early childhood professional) world". This is a response which, true to the open ontology implied in the chapters by Urban and Woodrow, sees professionalism as part and parcel of a critical ecology of the early childhood field (Dalli, 2007; Urban, 2007).

From this perspective, professionalism and its discourses and practices would be linking the (global) macro and (local) micro systems, allowing for local and diverse practices and experiences to inform the professional body of knowledge in democratic, ground-up ways. It would be challenging and resisting predominant power relations within the professional systems that manifest in influential concepts of scientific 'evidence', policy imperatives, decontextualised effectiveness, and manageability of professional practices. Instead, a critically ecologic professionalism would actively be gathering, exploring, documenting, disseminating and theorising 'practice-based evidence' (Urban, 2009) with practitioners and local communities taking active roles in determining research and practice agendas (Dalli, 2008; also Dayan; Kinos; Urban in this publication). It would actively be addressing what Biesta (2007) calls the 'democratic deficit' of educational research and practice and contest the implicit theory/practice divide that underlies the prevailing professional epistemology by linking professional *ways of being* to professional *ways of knowing.*

Finally, within the critical ecology of the early childhood profession conceptualised in the chapters in this collection, there would also be an 'ethos of enquiry that is informed by the political and social realities' (Urban). This implies an alertness to the challenges in the settings one acts in- pedagogically, politically, industrially - as well as the 'strengths that might be brought to bear on the present to make the present better' (Dalli, 2007). In this way, being part of an early childhood field with a critical ecology would also require an ongoing awareness of the need to engage critically with the status quo - and aim to transform it.

References

Biesta, G. 2007. Why "what works" won't work: Evidence-based practice and the democratic deficit in educational research. *Educational Theory,* 57 no. 1: 1-22.

Cochran-Smith, M. 2004. *Walking the road. Race, diversity and social justice in teacher education.* New York and London: Teachers College Press.

Dalli, C. 2007. *Towards a critical ecology of the profession. Systematic approaches to policies, practices and understandings of professionalism and professionalisation in early childhood.* Paper presented at the European Early Childhood Education Research conference, Prague, Czech Republic.

—. 2008. The new teacher in New Zealand. In *Professionalism in the Early Years,* ed. L. Miller and C. Cable. London: Hodder/Arnold.

Derman-Sparks, L. 1989. *Anti-bias curriculum: Tools for empowering young children.* Washington, D.C.: National Association for the Education of Young Children.

Ebbeck, M. A., and Waniganayake, M. 2003. *Early childhood professionals: Leading today and tomorrow.* Eastgardens, N.S.W.: MacLennan & Petty.

Edwards, C., Gandini, L., and Forman, G. E. 1998. *The hundred languages of children: the Reggio Emilia approach, advanced reflections,* 2nd ed. Greenwich, Conn.; London: Ablex.

Foucault, M. 1979. *Discipline and punish: The birth of a prison.* New York: Vintage.

Foucault, M., and Rabinow, P. 1991. *The Foucault reader.* London: Penguin.

Freire, P. 2000a. *Cultural action for freedom,* 2000 ed. (United States): Harvard Educational Review.

—. 2000b. *Pedagogy of the oppressed,* 30th anniversary ed. New York: Continuum.

—. 2004. *Pedagogy of Hope. Reliving Pedagogy of the Opressed.* London: Continuum.

Moss, P. 2008. The democratic and reflective professional: rethinking and reforming the early years workforce. In *Professionalism in the early years*, ed. L. Miller and C. Cable. London: Hodder Education.

Oberhuemer, P. 2005. Conceptualising the early childhood pedagogue: Policy approaches and issuesof professionalism. *European Early Childhood Education Research Journal, 13* no. 1: 5-16.

Osgood, J. 2006. Professionalism in early childhood education: resisting the regulatory gaze. *Contemporary Issues in Early Childhood, 7* no. 1.

UNCRC 2005. *General Comment No.7*. Geneva: United Nations Committee on the Rights of the Child.

Urban, M. 2007. *Towards a critical ecology of the profession. Systematic approaches to policies, practices and understandings of professionalism and professionalisation in early childhood.* Paper presented at the European Early Childhood Education Research Conference, Prague, Czech Republic.

—. 2009. Untested feasibilities and zones of professional development: arguments for reclaiming practice-based evidence in early childhood practice and research. In J. Hayden & A. Tuna (Eds.), *Moving Forward Together: Early childhood programs as the doorway to social cohesion. An East-West Perspective.* Newcastle upon Tyne: Cambridge Scholars.

Urban, M., & Murray, C. 2005. *Changing Habit(u)s. Perspectives on change, resistance and professional development.* Paper presented at the International conference 'Honoring the child, honoring Equity 5: Reconsidering Rights and Relationship', Centre for Equity and Innovation in Early Childhood. University of Melbourne.

Woodhead, M. 1996. *In search of the rainbow. Pathways to quality in large-scale programmes for young disadvantaged children.* The Hague: Bernhard van Leer Foundation.

Index

Page numbers in *Italics* represent tables.
Page numbers in **Bold** represent figures.